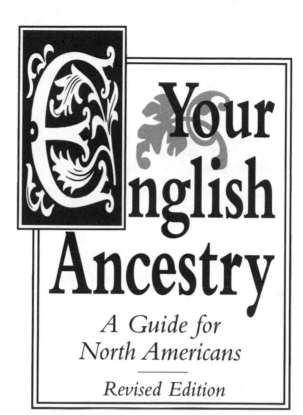

Your English Ancestry

A Guide for North Americans

Revised Edition

BY SHERRY IRVINE FSA(SCOT)

T0151326

ancestry publishing

Irvine, Sherry
    Your English Ancestry : a guide for North Americans / by Sherry
Irvine. — 2nd ed.
        p. cm.
    ISBN 10: 0-916489-84-1 (pbk.)
    ISBN 13: 978-0-916489-84-7
    1. England—Genealogy—Handbooks, manuals, etc.   2. North America—
Genealogy—Handbooks, manuals, etc.   I. Title
CS415.I78   1998
929' . 1'072042—dc21   98-17581

Some material in this publication is reprinted by permission of Corporation of the President of The Church of Jesus Christ of Latter-day Saints. In granting permission for this use of copyrighted material, the Church does not imply or express either endorsement or authorization of this publication.

Published by Ancestry Publishing, a division of
The Generations Network, Inc.
360 West 4800 North
Provo, Utah 84604
www.ancestry.com

First Printing 1998
10 9 8 7 6

Printed in the United States of America.

CONTENTS

Preface to the Second Edition v
Preface to the First Edition vii
1   Some Fundamentals 1
2   Civil Registration 26
3   The Census 47
4   Lists and Periodicals 67
5   Church Records 82
6   Wills Since 1858 103
7   Wills Before 1858 112
8   Earning a Living 130
9   Local Administration and Justice 148
10   Early English Research—
       An Introduction 165
11   Working It Out 177

APPENDICES

A   The Family History Library
       Catalog™ 184
B   The International Genealogical
       Index™ 195
C   Lord Hardwicke's Act 206
D   Addresses 211

Bibliography 220

Index 245

PREFACE TO
THE SECOND EDITION

ince I wrote the first edition of this book, genealogy has grown in popularity, the Internet has become an important tool for thousands of researchers, and significant changes have taken place in local government and in the storage of major records in England. Over these past four years my own horizons have expanded. My business and lecturing have brought me into contact with hundreds of researchers across Canada and the USA and have taken me to England several times. I couldn't help but learn from the experience. All of that is reflected in this revised edition of *Your English Ancestry: A Guide for North Americans*. I've taken the changes in England into account; there is more detail about many records; and a new chapter introduces the most accessible sources for research before 1730.

I began to think about this revision more than a year ago as a result of the wonderful experience of leading a study tour to England for the Institute of Genealogy and Historical Research, Samford University. To Joan Mitchell, director at the time, my thanks for her encouragement and for her faith in me; to the students on that trip, my appreciation for what they taught me about their origins and their perspective on English research.

For the third or fourth time, I have spent most of December and January at my desk, absorbed in writing, somewhat detached from reality. My family's forbearance is remarkable, and I know how fortunate I am.

Finally, to Lou Szucs, at Ancestry—thanks for being there.

Sherry Irvine
Victoria BC
January 1998

PREFACE TO
THE FIRST EDITION

y bookshelf holds nine different books addressing the research of English ancestry, and I have read several more besides. Can there really be need for another? I believe there is, for none of the books I have read focuses on a logical research routine for family historians based in North America. There is more than enough information on what is to be found in the records and how to interpret them. What is lacking is guidance on selecting the most efficient way to get at the records. One approach may be all very well for me, here in Victoria, British Columbia, but may not be possible for a researcher in Illinois.

Every genealogical source has several elements:
- the time period it covers
- the geographical area it covers
- how it is organized
- the information needed to access it
- availability

The genealogist who is aware of these factors, who provides the specifics for them for each new record, and who keeps that information to hand every step of the way, will have a far better chance of success. Results will also accrue to those who build a ready knowledge of alternative sources and problem-solving techniques.

Records chosen for discussion here date back to the mid-eighteenth century and can be consulted from North America without great difficulty. The arbitrary time span has been selected for several reasons. By the middle of the eighteenth century, Latin had pretty well disappeared from English documents, and handwriting was more legible. Also at this time, England adopted the Gregorian calendar, so the year began on 1 January (rather than Lady Day, 25 March) and there was no longer a ten- or eleven-day discrepancy with continental countries (see chapter 1). The other significant factor in the choice was the passage of Lord Hardwicke's Act. It became law on 25 March 1754, and from that date until civil registration began it was virtually impossible for a marriage to go unrecorded. Drawn up to put a stop to clandestine marriages, Lord Hardwicke's Act standardized the recording of marriages, laid down strict regulations regarding marriage by license, and stipulated that only three forms of marriage be legally recognized: Anglican, Jewish, and Quaker (see appendix C).

The interpretation of "without great difficulty" is, of course, mine, so the selection of records does reflect personal experience. However, I did bear some conditions in mind as I made my choice. Records included had to fall within at least one of the following categories:

- the collections of the Family History Library (FHL) in Salt Lake City
- printed records which may be in public, university or genealogical society libraries
- records which have been gathered in some central location in England
- records which have been indexed

Nine years of night school teaching and private tutoring have been the basis for the suggestions found in this book. The majority of students cannot travel to England regularly, and some may never go at all. Therefore, it is all the more important that, besides directing their research, I help my students understand how their ancestors lived. I enjoy this and encourage you to investigate and record the history of your family, the fabric of their lives, and their perspective of the times.

October 1993

1 ❦ SOME FUNDAMENTALS

very serious hobbyist of any kind eventually realizes the importance of good organization, learns the best way to go about things, and discovers the pitfalls to avoid. The genealogist is no different. Therefore, it seems a good idea to begin with a discussion of the essential elements of good genealogical research. There are twelve elements to keep in mind:

- Be organized
- Keep a record of all work done
- Work from the known to the unknown
- Develop some research skills
- Avoid duplicating the work of others
- Be familiar with local libraries and archives
- Know something of other archives and libraries
- Be familiar with the records
- Research the historical context
- Research the geographical context

- Be aware of the pitfalls
- Know how to get help

Be Organized

There are numerous methods of organization built around index cards, notebooks, three-ring binders, and computers. Many books already in existence describe different formats to help prevent paper confusion. Any system will work provided it does the following:

> *Incorporates a system of ready reference.* It must be easy to examine what you know and what you have researched so an assessment can be made and further strategy planned. (One way to do this is to keep a short summary of known facts and a log of all sources consulted for each ancestor.)

> *Contains a record of all work done.* Make a full bibliographic notation for all sources consulted, whether they revealed any helpful information or not. Note when and where the work was done and the thoroughness of the search. (A missing record may be due to your rushed efforts at the end of a day.)

> *Has room for expansion.* Whether researching one family or several, you will amass a great deal of material, so your system must expand to ensure things can stay together in logical order.

> *Is standardized.* This applies to paper size and abbreviations. Try to avoid having to recopy notes from odd pieces of paper, envelopes, etc., by carrying a stock of standard-size paper with you. (I know—you probably won't do it.) As for abbreviations, consistency ensures future understanding.

Is followed consistently. Keeping up to date is not a major chore, but having to catch up later can be a daunting task.

Keep a Record of All Work Done

Keeping a record of all work done is so important it deserves a category of its own. This record would be best kept in two ways: first, as part of a source log for each individual ancestor, and second, in an overall database (whether manual or electronic). A source originally consulted for one particular ancestor may be useful again, perhaps months or years later, for another. If the reference is only with the notes on a family, it may be missed. A database of all sources, organized on geographic and subject lines, can always be checked quickly when a new line of research is started. This is one area where a computer is the ideal tool; key-word searches will scan the list in seconds and sources can be listed by type or geographic area. Even where you find no information, it is important to note the source; nobody wants to waste time and effort doing a search a second time simply because they failed to note that the first time round was to no purpose.

Work from the Known to the Unknown

To urge you to work from the known to the unknown may appear to be stating the obvious. However, students appear in my classes from time to time set to research their descent from a (usually illustrious) forebear. Family stories of connections to noble or notorious people must have a compelling effect, but you should resist the temptation to work forward from these colorful individuals. Regardless of background, the surest way to prove any descent is by beginning with recent family and working your way back. This way the first work attempted is the easier work, the search is more focused, and it follows a chronological sequence.

Develop Some Research Skills

Research skills are fundamental to successful genealogy. The first thing to consider is note-taking, for an error early on in recording could throw off a whole line of research. Be sure the way you record information reflects the structure of the source. For example, census material is best recorded in columns similar to the original, while wills might be recorded by abstract (summarizing the key points), extract (copying exactly the relevant clauses), or photocopying. It is a good idea to note any gaps in the record, or where indecipherable writing made reading impossible. Do not be tempted to expand abbreviations in old records, for your interpretation may not be accurate; record them exactly as given. Whenever you are in doubt about what you are copying, insert a question mark in brackets. With practice you will develop your own preferences for format, but make sure that nothing will be totally obscure to other readers.

Apart from your own recording techniques, there are other things to consider. Whenever you pick up a book that might be helpful, check the index, the table of contents, and the preface or introduction, and look for a bibliography. This will reveal whether the book is worth closer examination, suggests other titles for review, or is of no use at all. Consider the degree of authority that should be ascribed to the source. Is it a primary or secondary source? Good examples of primary sources are marriage certificates, military service records, and wills, for such things are contemporary to the event. A local history describing people and events written many years after the fact is an example of a secondary source. Despite a close association in time, some contemporary sources must be regarded with skepticism. Letters and newspaper reports are two good examples of sources that may present a distorted view of events. Finally, with all these factors in mind, be sure to begin your research with a purpose, and with a questioning attitude. Plot strategic guidelines that govern the area and time frame of the search, whether the objective is one individual or everyone of a particular surname; but be sure to remain flexible in the event results prove surprising or disappointing.

Avoid Duplicating the Work of Others

One of the great delights of genealogical research is the people you meet along the way—especially those who turn out to be distant cousins willing to share their information with you. Genealogists are a gregarious bunch who never tire of talking or writing about what they are up to. Through societies, directories, and the Internet, it is possible to tell the world what you are doing, check up on the efforts of others, and locate new cousins.

Certainly, meeting or corresponding with others who share the same interests is one of the treats in store for the amateur genealogist, but there are other sources that should be consulted to ensure you do not duplicate what has already been done. One of the first places to start is with two resources found in family history centers of The Church of Jesus Christ of Latter-day Saints (LDS church). Ancestral File™, available on microfiche and as part of FamilySearch® on CD-ROM, lists the specific research interests (i.e., more detail than just the surnames, dates, and places) of thousands of individuals. Family history center patrons are encouraged to add to the database, which also indicates how to contact the contributors. The surname section of the *Family History Library Catalog* (*FHLC*) lists compiled family histories and genealogies in the LDS collections alphabetically by surname. It, too, can be consulted on microfiche or by computer (see appendix A).

Less detailed than Ancestral File, but still worthwhile, are the various genealogical directories and surname indexes. They are alphabetical lists of members' or subscribers' interests, with time period and region indicated and cross-referenced by a code number to the contributor's name and address. Most genealogical societies keep track of members' interests and regularly publish these as surname indexes. On a much larger scale is the BigR® (British Isles Genealogical Register, 2nd edition 1997), a huge register distributed on microfiche and coordinated by the Federation of Family History Societies. It is advertised in the journals of member societies, which also sell their own county sections. There is also the *Genealogical Research Directory*, published annually since 1981. It is possible to purchase all entries for 1990 to 1996 together on one CD-ROM.

The Society of Genealogists in London has a remarkable collection of material on thousands of families. This document collection is sorted alphabetically and stored in file boxes in the upper library of the society's premises in London. Be sure to have these checked. You may discover, as I did, that some avid collector of family data a hundred years ago made cryptic notes on the character of your third great-grandmother on the back of an envelope, which somehow found its way to the society collection.

The Guild of One Name Studies (GOONS) can be contacted at the same address as the Society of Genealogists. The group maintains a registry of societies and individuals researching one name only. The list has only one registration for each surname to help ensure the concentration of effort and information. A small publication, updated regularly, lists all these surnames with the name and address of the contact.

A number of published works should be considered. Not everyone expects to find their ancestry among the famous or the titled classes. Nonetheless, whenever you believe an ancestor to have been of middle-class status or better, take a moment to look up the name in the *Dictionary of National Biography*, which should be in any large reference library. A very large number of military and naval commanders appear in the *Dictionary of National Biography* along with a wide assortment of people who were neither particularly famous nor titled. You may not find your own direct ancestor, but you may come across a sibling or spouse. Most people are familiar with the standard works of peerage. Besides the narrative pedigrees of titled families, there are thousands of references to families allied by marriage, usually listed in an index. Also watch for *Dod's Peerage, Baronetage and Knightage* because it includes bishops and justices of the peace; and Burke's *History of the Commoners of Great Britain and Ireland* (ca. 1840), which lists untitled families of some social standing. There are several bibliographies listing works about English families or where to find printed pedigrees: *The Genealogist's Guide* (Marshall, 1903), *A Genealogical Guide* (Whitmore, 1953), *The Genealogist's Guide: An Index to Printed British Pedigrees and Family Histories 1950–75* (Barrow, 1977), and *A Catalogue of British Family Histories* (Thompson, 1976).

These suggestions by no means cover all of the databases and printed works about English families. There are bibliographic dictionaries of artists, musicians, architects, etc., and lists of notable people by century or period of history. New lists appear on CD-ROM all the time, and many can be accessed through the Internet and, in particular, the World Wide Web. By all means, check references wherever possible, but never forget, when reviewing family histories and pedigrees in whatever form, to look for their source citations and carry out some checks. Any connection to your family must be substantiated. Do not readily accept the unauthenticated work of others.

Know the Local Repositories

The libraries and archives in your area should become very familiar to you. The public library is worth investigating for its collections in the areas of genealogy, history, travel and topography, religion, immigration/emigration, etc. In fact, genealogy touches almost any subject, and you will discover what other areas may be useful as you learn more of such things as occupations, places of origin, and social status. Investigate how your library may be able to help through the interlibrary loan service. In some communities the local genealogical society maintains a collection in the public library. Be sure you understand how the Dewey decimal classification system works (see table 1-1) and take time to browse through the most useful areas. Bear in mind that a title might tell little or nothing about the usefulness of a book.

These same suggestions apply to any university libraries nearby. Their classification system is different (see table 1-2), as is the purpose of such a library, but these differences may act in your favor. A good history department could mean an extremely well-developed collection. University libraries also usually hold extensive newspaper collections from all over the world. These libraries must serve their academic community first, but anyone is free to visit them, and often there are ways to arrange borrowing privileges even if you are not an alumnus.

Most county towns and capital cities count archives among their public buildings. This is an added bonus. Admittedly, your past may have no connection with the place where you are now living, but the archives are worth a visit nonetheless. Check into the availability of a microfilm loan service. You may also find some standard reference books, as well as information on the holdings of other archives. Finally, there is simply the opportunity to familiarize yourself with usual archives procedure, which means less confusion for you when visiting archives on a research trip.

The most fortunate researchers will find in their community not only archives and public and university libraries, but a genealogical society library and an LDS family history center. These last two are directed solely at helping genealogists. Here you will meet other researchers who can help you, learn about local courses, and find an invaluable source of material. Visit all these repositories often and become very familiar with their collections, for you will be developing your own research strategies around them.

Libraries and Archives at a Distance

Much of your information will come from libraries and record offices that are far away. The more you know about their collections, the more precise your inquiries will be, and the more likely you will receive a helpful reply. When you are launching work in a new area be sure to write the library and inquire about collections, publications, and service fees. Visit your own libraries and archives for books which may describe the contents of those elsewhere, and in particular watch for these useful titles: *British Archives* (Foster and Sheppard, 1995) and *In and Around Record Repositories in Great Britain and Ireland* (Cole and Church, 1998).

Know the Records

There is no substitute for using the records. Steadily, your base of knowledge and experience will grow, giving you a sixth sense when deciding strategy for thorny problems. Whenever possible, do the research yourself. That way, when help is needed, precise instructions can be given to the agent; savings in time and fees should result, and you remain in control. You will have a better

TABLE 1-1

Selective Guide to the Dewey Decimal Classification System

000   GENERALITIES
      010   bibliographies and catalogs
      020   library and information sciences
      030   general encyclopedic works
100   PHILOSOPHY AND RELATED DISCIPLINES
200   RELIGION
      270   church history, geography
      280   Christian denominations and sects
300   SOCIAL SCIENCES
      325   emigration/immigration
      330   economics
      340   law
      356   army
      359   navy
      370   education
      380   commerce and trade
      390   customs and folklore
400   LANGUAGE
      420   English and Anglo-Saxon languages
500   PURE SCIENCES
600   TECHNOLOGY (APPLIED SCIENCES)
      610   medical sciences
      620   engineering
      630   agriculture
      690   buildings
700   FINE ARTS AND RECREATION
      710   civic and landscape art
      720   architecture
      740   drawing
      750   painting
      770   photography
      780   music
      792   theatre
800   LITERATURE
      820   English and Anglo-Saxon literature
900   GENERAL GEOGRAPHY AND HISTORY
      910   general geography, travel (includes atlases)
      914   geography and travel, Britain and Europe
      920   general biography and genealogy
      929   genealogy
      940   general history of Europe (includes England)

TABLE 1-2

Selective Guide to the Library of Congress Classification System

A	GENERAL WORKS
B	PHILOSOPHY—RELIGION
	BL—BX religion
C	AUXILIARY SCIENCES OF HISTORY
	CD holdings of archives and libraries
	CS genealogy, names, peerage
D	HISTORY: GENERAL AND OLD WORLD
	DA Great Britain
E—F	HISTORY OF AMERICA
G	GEOGRAPHY, ANTHROPOLOGY, FOLKLORE
H	SOCIAL SCIENCES
	HC production and economic conditions
	HD agriculture
	HE transportation and communication
	HN social history and conditions
	HS societies, clubs
J	POLITICAL SCIENCE
	JF—JQ constitutional history & public administration
	JS local government
K	LAW
L	EDUCATION
M	MUSIC
N	FINE ARTS
	NA architecture
P	LANGUAGE AND LITERATURE
Q	SCIENCE
R	MEDICINE
S	AGRICULTURE
T	TECHNOLOGY
U	MILITARY SCIENCE
V	NAVAL SCIENCE
Z	BIBLIOGRAPHY AND LIBRARY SCIENCE

chance of success researching records never used before if you have read about them first; be prepared to go back to manuals and guides for a review. For further insights look for published local and family histories, which not only make interesting reading but instruct about the records at the same time (e.g., *The Common Stream*, Parker, 1975).

Research the Historical Context

Your ancestors did not live in isolation of the events going on about them. Their actions may well have been influenced by something or someone far removed whom they knew nothing about, or by local factors. Whatever shaped their lives, there is no doubt that you, the researcher, must be aware of what was happening. One of the more interesting ways to begin a study of English history is with a dictionary of dates. These books are usually organized in columns and rows which tabulate the major events of history by year and category (such as science, politics, exploration, or the arts). There is no quicker way to bring back the details of long-past history courses. You might also locate a survey history of England either in a used bookstore (old school or university texts are just fine) or in a paperback edition. Your review of history should move from the general to the particular. Search for histories of the counties and towns of your ancestors in libraries and in bookshops that sell new and used books. The journals of local history and genealogical societies in the region will regularly list new publications. A sound knowledge of history may provide the clue necessary to pick up a cold trail.

Recreating the historical milieu is half the fun of genealogy. It is the reason I prefer to speak of family history rather than genealogy, for here is the difference between cold data and real people. What did your ancestors eat? What might be behind the front door of their cottage, tenement, house, or manor? What tensions existed in their community? What sort of a community was it?

> There they (your ancestors) lived, there they labored, there they socialized, loved, married, brewed and drank ale, sinned, went to church, paid fines, had children in and out of wedlock, borrowed and lent money, tools, and grain, quarreled and fought, and got sick and died. (Gies, Frances, and Joseph Gies. *Life in a Medieval Village*. New York: Harper & Row, 1990.)

Knowing how your ancestors lived, knowing the events that touched their lives, and gaining some insight into their personalities—these are the rewards of research, more so than a list of a thousand names and dates. It is the search for historical background which will lead you into all corners of the library because this sort of material is not confined to history books. Simple things begin to build the picture. Read about your ancestors' community in a topographical dictionary, or take time to peruse the descriptive paragraphs found at the beginning of many old directories. Most pre-World War II travel and description books create a picture of a town little changed from the days of your forebears. Among the most interesting are the volumes in *The King's England* series by Arthur Mee. Take time to look through economic histories or books on the architecture of the region. Other useful material may be found under the occupations of the ancestors—for example, books on life in the navy, coal mining, or weaving.

An interesting and sometimes helpful aspect of historical background is the origin of family names. There are several comprehensive books listed in the bibliography which provide meanings, language roots (e.g., Old English or French), and any patterns or concentrations in distribution. The most interesting is *Homes of Family Names of Great Britain* (Guppy, 1890, rep. 1996). The author has analyzed the surnames of the yeomen farmers of the country, including for each county tables of names categorized under the headings general, regional, local, and particular to the county. This information and your own plotting of name distribution in a broadly based index can offer new perspectives on a problem (reference will be made to this elsewhere in the book).

Research the Geographical Context

It really isn't possible to separate completely the historical context from the geographical. Books which link these two aspects of research more closely are historical atlases and dictionaries of place-names. In the mid-nineteenth century, Samuel Lewis produced a series of topographical dictionaries for the British Isles. The English edition for 1831 is particularly useful because it predates boundary changes by the Church of England that altered ecclesiastical jurisdictions (*Topographical Dictionary of England*, 1831, rep. 1996). Lewis's verbal snapshots provide useful and interesting geographic background. Local history in a nutshell emerges from these sorts of books, as well as a sense of how the local landscape shaped the community.

Maps are important in good genealogical research. Study modern maps, old maps, topographic maps, and specialized maps for history and genealogy. It is a very good idea to purchase a large-scale road atlas of Britain, available at any good bookstore. (Those issued by the Automobile Association, the Royal Automobile Club, and the Ordnance Survey are excellent.)

The important factors to consider are the lay of the land, lines of communication, and boundaries. Where your ancestor went to market, to register the birth of a child, or to find a ship sailing for America was likely influenced by the lay of the land and lines of communication. Old maps show roads, railways, and canals as they were. Topographic maps indicate areas with difficult terrain. The most useful maps have a scale of 1:50,000 (2 centimeters/kilometer or 1.25 inches/mile); they show tiny hamlets and sometimes large buildings. A better sense of location is given by less-detailed maps (e.g. 1:250,000), and detailed town plans are at least at a scale of six inches to the mile. Through several North American vendors and societies in England it is possible to obtain the Victorian Ordnance Survey maps (from David and Charles) and the town plans, circa 1860 to 1925 (from Alan Godfrey).

Boundaries are exceedingly important in genealogical research. They have been drawn and redrawn over the centuries, frequently with little attention to logic. Recent legislation set a timetable of changes to take effect in three stages: April 1996, April 1997, and April 1998. Some of the unpopular changes of 1974 were undone, six metropolitan counties were created, and forty-six new unitary authorities were established. These changes have meant that archival collections are on the move again; table 1-3 lists the counties and main urban authorities as they now exist, to give guidance in checking for regional and city archives. These changes emphasize the fact that modern boundaries and government reorganization affect location of records; boundaries contemporary to the period being researched influenced the collection and arrangement of the material.

Not only have boundaries been moved to reflect shifting population and matters of influence and power, but different types of divisions have been used by church and state over the centuries. Districts and sub-districts created under the new Poor Law (1834) and used for civil registration and census were changed in the 1850s. The Church of England made significant changes to parish divisions in the 1830s and has regularly closed churches and combined parishes since. Depending on where in the country and time period, you will come across such terms as *hundred, wapentake, ward, riding, rural deanery, chapelry,* and

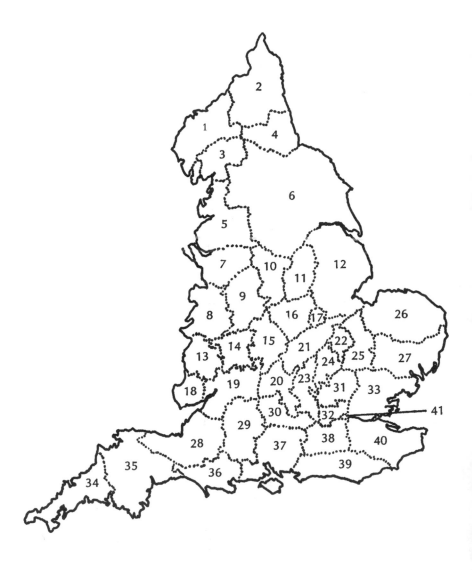

Figure 1-1 Counties of England

1. Cumberland	22. Huntingdonshire
2. Northumberland	23. Buckinghamshire
3. Westmoreland	24. Bedfordshire
4. Durham	25. Cambridgeshire
5. Lancashire	26. Norfolk
6. Yorkshire	27. Suffolk
7. Cheshire	28. Somerset
8. Shropshire	29. Wiltshire
9. Staffordshire	30. Berkshire
10. Derbyshire	31. Hertfordshire
11. Nottinghamshire	32. Middlesex
12. Lincoln shire	33. Essex
13. Herefordshire	34. Cornwall
14. Worcestershire	35. Devon
15. Warwickshire	36. Dorset
16. Leicestershire	37. Hampshire
17. Rutland	38. Surrey
18. Monmouthshire	39. Sussex
19. Gloucestershire	40. Kent
20. Oxfordshire	41. London
21. Northamptonshire	

(Bickmore, D.P., ed. *Oxford Travel Atlas of Britain*. Oxford University Press, 1953.)

———————————

peculiar—to name only some. To find out more in general on the subject refer to *Discovering Parish Boundaries* (Winchester, 1990) and *The Local Historian's Encyclopedia* (Richardson, 1993). Figure 1-2 provides some guidance on where a few of these divisions appeared.

It follows that you will refer to maps over and over again, for location and for help in selecting the correct microfilm or individual record. In the chapters ahead, explanations and advice

TABLE 1-3

The Major Civil Divisions of England in 1997

Counties	Metropolitan District Councils
Bedfordshire	Barnsley
Berkshire	Birmingham
Buckinghamshire	Bolton
Cambridgeshire	Bradford
Cheshire	Bury
Cornwall	Calderdale
Cumbria	Coventry
Derbyshire	Doncaster
Devon	Dudley
Dorset	Gateshead
Durham	Kirklees
East Sussex	Knowsley
Essex	Leeds
Gloucestershire	Liverpool
Hampshire	Manchester
Hereford and Worcester	Newcastle upon Tyne
Hertfordshire	North Tyneside
Isle of Wight	Oldham
Kent	Rochdale
Lancashire	Rotherham
Leicestershire	St. Helens
Lincolnshire	Salford
Norfolk	Sandwell
Northamptonshire	Sefton
Northumberland	Sheffield
North Yorkshire	Solihill
Nottinghamshire	South Tyneside
Oxfordshire	Stockport
Shropshire	Sunderland
Somerset	Thameside
Staffordshire	Trafford
Suffolk	Wakefield
Surrey	Walsall
Warwickshire	Wigan
West Sussex	Wirral
Wiltshire	Wolverhampton

Metropolitan Counties

Greater Manchester	Merseyside
South Yorkshire	Tyne and Wear
West Midlands	West Yorkshire

Greater London Boroughs

Barking and Dagenham	Barnet
Bexley	Brent
Bromley	Camden
City of Westminster	Croydon
Ealing	Enfield
Greenwich	Hackney
Hammersmith and Fulham	Haringey
Harrow	Havering
Hillingden	Hounslow
Islington	Kensington and Chelsea
Kingston upon Thames	Lambeth
Lewisham	Merton
Newham	Redbridge
Richmond upon Thames	Southwark
Sutton	Tower Hamlets
Waltham Forest	Wandsworth

In addition to the above, there are several dozen non-metropolitan district councils. For complete lists consult the latest edition of Whitaker's Almanac.

---

about boundaries will be included wherever necessary. Keep in mind that maps are not confined to folded sheets and pages of atlases. Books of all sorts incorporate maps that indicate many things connected with family history—for example, locations of coal mines, cotton mills, canals, battlefields, fishing ports, and historic buildings.

Be Aware of the Pitfalls

As research progresses a variety of pitfalls will arise that can impede progress or lead you astray. The most obvious one is the possible variations in names. Chances are remote that the names you are researching were spelled the same by all members of the family line over the generations. Far more likely is the use of

Figure 1-2 Some Civil Divisions of England

Section A: Counties divided into wards

Section B: A mix of subdivisions were used—wapentakes
             and hundreds; in addition, Yorkshire (ridings)
             and Lincolnshire (parts) had another level.

Section C: The hundred was the most common division,
             but others were leets (Norfolk and Suffolk),
             lathes (Kent), and rapes (Sussex).

These terms will appear in some directories and in
tax records and other early documents.

Based upon information in *Discovering Parish Boundaries* (Winchester,
1990)

---

multiple spellings by one individual in his lifetime. Try to think
of all the possible variations of the name concerned, bearing in
mind: silent first letter, whether or not a middle consonant is
doubled, silent *e* on the end, spellings that bear no relation to
pronunciation (e.g., Cholmondeley is pronounced "chum-li").
Place-names can be equally difficult. Traps for the unwary
include ancient and modern spellings; actual changes in name;
two or more places with the same name; disappearance of the
place; an inaccurate combination of town/parish/county in your
base information; and the (misleading) use of a nearby large town
by an ancestor to "avoid confusion." All these name problems can
be reduced or eliminated by being vigilant and by preliminary
reference checks with surname/place-name dictionaries and
atlases.

Some of these surname and place-name problems may be caused by indecipherable handwriting. Here are a few hints which may help. Read on in the document or register, for you may find the name written again more legibly. Failing that, look for the same letters in other names and words to try and learn something of the writer's style. A magnifying glass is helpful; be sure to have one with you whenever you are researching. As a last resort trace or copy the indecipherable words—subsequent research may provide the answer. Practice reading old handwriting and refer to books about the subject. Two are inexpensive and helpful: *Reading Old Handwriting* (McLaughlin, 1995) and *Examples of Handwriting* (Buck, 1965, rep. 1996).

Yet another aspect of the surname or place-name problem may stem from pronunciation—not how you say a name but how your ancestors said it. A student was searching for the birthplace of a third great-grandfather and read the scrawl of her grandfather's notes as Eccleton, Yorkshire. She could find no such place, but did find something close (Eccleston) in Lancashire. However, the clear statement of Yorkshire troubled her, and no appropriate birth record appeared after extensive searches in Lancashire. She studied the map of Yorkshire again and noted the village of Hickleton. Here was the answer to her problem: her grandfather had written the place-name as he pronounced it, never knowing the correct spelling.

Dates can be very confusing for the unwary. Besides the obvious problems of inaccuracies with ages or faulty memories of events, there are pitfalls for those who are unaware of the history of our present calendar. Another student of mine puzzled for a very long time over the problem of a man who apparently died seven months before his child was born, yet in advance knew the child's sex and name. There was no problem. The dates were Old Style (OS), which meant that the new year began on Lady Day, 25 March. The man, who died 10 March 1732, had lived to see his daughter, who was born in October of the same year (OS).

A brief history of the changes in the calendar makes this all easier to grasp. The Julian, or Old Style, calendar was introduced by Julius Caesar in 45 B.C. He altered the reckoning of months from a lunar to a solar basis, set the year as 365 days with a leap year every four years, retained March as the first month of the year, and renamed the fifth month (Quintillus) July in honor of himself. Later (8 B.C.), not to be outdone, Augustus altered Sextilis to August. The names of the four last months of the year remain numerical ones, based on when they fell after the old beginning, March.

A very long time passed before it was realized that the Romans hadn't quite got it right. In fact, an extra day every fourth year was eleven minutes too much per year. After fifteen hundred years this added up to a sizeable discrepancy between the solar year and the calendar. Pope Gregory decided to correct the error because of the great difficulties in calculating feast days. In 1582 it was decreed that ten days would be struck from the calendar, and 11 March was declared 21 March. The pope also decreed that the calendar year would henceforth begin on 1 January. Not everyone fell in step with the papal decree. The sixteenth century was a time of religious upheaval, and the Protestant (and Orthodox) nations were not prepared to show any acknowledgment of Catholic edicts. The English eventually adopted the Gregorian calendar in the middle of the eighteenth century. The first of January 1751 (OS) was declared to be the first day of 1752, and 2 September became 14 September.

Know How to Get Help

People love to talk about other people. Genealogists are no different; they merely talk about people who are dead. Sometimes our family and friends are not very receptive. I suspect family history societies exist as much to fill the need to talk about our ancestors as they do to provide research help. In either case, societies can be a great source of support and assistance. Swapping stories, putting queries in a newsletter, using a club library, quizzing the more experienced—in all these ways, a family history society can be of help. It is a good idea to join the society in your area, as well as at least one in England. Societies circulate current information on courses, conferences, publications and local agents, as well as the research interests of their members. If the local society does not have a telephone or a Web site, ask at the public library for the name of the contact person. Addresses of English societies can be obtained from the Federation of Family History Societies, from their Web sites, and perhaps from your local society if it belongs to the federation and receives the *Family History News and Digest*. The International Society for British Genealogy and Family History is one of several British interest groups which can help with society addresses, vendors of British genealogical materials, and advice.

Club membership is also a good way to find out about conferences and classes. Attending a conference means "genealogical immersion" for a few days. You can attend numerous lectures, talk endlessly on the subject with other enthusiasts, usually visit a display of books, charts, finding aids, etc., and often purchase tapes of the lectures you missed. Genealogy classes are regular features of community college night school programs and recreation center offerings. Facilities that offer such courses put out bulletins from time to time listing what courses are available. A course is a very good way to be introduced to genealogical research, whether as a complete novice or as a beginner in the records of a different country. You benefit from the experience of someone who knows the records well and can provide the essential information, concrete examples, and helpful tips.

At some stage, every genealogist requires the help of a professional. This is not necessarily any reflection on one's ability. Very often it is the wisest course to pay an expert in a particular area, as this can save you time and money. Just ensure that you are well informed on the records concerned so you can give specific directions, and also judge whether or not you are getting value for your money. Be sure to have a clear understanding of the professional's fees and expenses, and deal in stages, such as one hundred dollars at a time, so you can halt work easily at short notice.

The very best sort of help is self-help. If you intend to carry out extensive research over a long period of time, be sure to build a good, basic reference collection. The sorts of things you should include are:

- An atlas of England (four miles/inch or better)
- More detailed maps of areas of interest
- An outline history of England
- A county history or description/travel book for each area of interest
- At least two reference books on English research and records—several appear in the bibliography (recommended are *Tracing Your Family Tree* and a dictionary/encyclopedia type of work)
- Guides to finding aids for frequently used records

Read your books, study your maps, and be prepared to go back to them again and again (you can't remember everything). Not only that, take time to look again at the research you have already done. You'll be surprised how many times a new idea suggests itself or a missed detail seems to pop up before your eyes.

the problems created by gathering vast numbers of records (958,630 in the first twelve months) without mechanical assistance. They faced much skepticism, outright opposition, and, in many areas, very slow acceptance of the new procedures. Occasionally their own agents let them down. Registrars were paid by the entry, and a few succumbed to the temptation to create fictitious records.[1] However, despite the difficulties, the system was securely established within five years.

Keep in mind that it was not possible to achieve 100-percent coverage from day one. The marriage records are most likely to be complete because they were recorded by a church official or a registrar. In the case of nonconformists, up until 1898 a registrar had to attend the church, and it was also possible to be married in a registry office. In fact, if you fail to find a record after checking the local and central records, it is likely that the marriage never took place or that it occurred outside England and Wales. Death records have gaps, particularly for very young children, in the early years, while birth records up to 1875 present the most problems. Until that date, registration could be made without charge for up to six weeks after the birth, whereupon a fine of seven shillings and six pence was imposed—a significant sum for many families. The fine, coupled with the fact that after six months the registrar would not take the information at all, resulted in many births going unrecorded. Some parents deliberately evaded registration. With no official record of age, it was easier for children to be sent out to work at an early age, in violation of child labor laws. In a few cases, children had two birthdays—the real one and the one on the birth certificate (selected so it fell within the six-week period).

Reliability of the Records

Information found on these certificates is, needless to say, dependent upon the knowledge of the informant and the truthfulness

Registration District. *West Ham*

1895. Marriage solemnized at *All Saints Church*
in the *District* of *Woodford Wells* in the *County of Essex*

No.	When married	Name and Surname	Age	Condition	Rank or profession	Residence at the time of marriage	Father's name and surname	Rank or profession of father
148	March 11th 1895	Charles Wadsworth	25	Bachelor	Gentleman	Hotel Metropole Charing Cross London	Tom Rodney Wadsworth (Deceased)	Mill Owner
		Elizabeth Isabel Bose	24	Spinster	—	East House Woodford Green	Henry Bose	Gentleman

Married in the *Church of All Saints* according to the *Rites & Ceremonies* of the *Established Church after Banns by me*

| This marriage was solemnized between us, | Charles Wadsworth Elizabeth Isabel Bose | in the presence of us, | William Bose W.H. Bose Ethel Bose Beatrice Bose | William Bose W.H Bose E Bousfield Vicar of St Anne Sheffield |

CERTIFIED to be a true copy of an entry in the certified copy of a Register of Marriages in the District above mentioned.

Given at the GENERAL REGISTER OFFICE, LONDON, under the Seal of the said Office, the   5th   day of   June   1974

MB 056270

Form A513 (S.34421) Dd.151833 40M 9/73 Hw.

Figure 2-2 Certified copy of an entry of marriage

The design of the certificate is Crown copyright and is reproduced with the permission of The Office for National Statistics.

of his or her statements. Birth and marriage certificates are likely to be more reliable because the information was given directly by the people concerned to the registrar, or passed on by a church official. View the age and occupation columns on the death certificate with circumspection, for that information is second hand (perhaps coming from servants or persons with failing memories).

Contents of Death Certificates

The death certificate indicates the following: date, place, and cause of death; occupation and age of the deceased; and the identity and address of the informant. After 1969, the date and place of birth replace the age at death. Take careful note of the informant, as this person may prove to be a previously unknown family connection. The lack of any parental information makes the death certificate the least valuable, although the address and age information may lead to other records. It is possible to research several generations without death certificates, and some genealogists do this to save money. A death certificate is very important, however, when the cause of death was unusual to the extent that a newspaper report and/or inquest resulted. Always follow up in such cases.

Contents of Marriage Certificates

The marriage certificate contains the most information of the three. As a bonus, there is an opportunity here to verify your selection—check the index entries for both the bride and the groom; the details should match exactly. The certificate reveals the date and place of the marriage; the names, ages, addresses, and occupations of the bride and groom; their status (i.e., bachelor, spinster); the names and occupations of their fathers; and the

CERTIFIED COPY OF AN ENTRY OF DEATH

Given at the GENERAL REGISTER OFFICE, LONDON.

Application Number 4987B

REGISTRATION DISTRICT Bury Saint Edmunds

1879 DEATH in the Sub-district of Bury Saint Edmunds in the County of Suffolk

No.	When and where died	Name and surname	Sex	Age	Occupation	Cause of death	Signature, description, and residence of informant	When registered	Signature of registrar
443	Sixth of February 1879 at No 27 Butter Market	Nancy Caley	Female	86 years	Spinster	Old Age	George Richardson occupier No 27 Butter Market	Eleventh of February 1879	John Priest Registrar

CERTIFIED to be a true copy of an entry in the certified copy of a Register of Deaths in the District above mentioned.

Given at the GENERAL REGISTER OFFICE, LONDON, under the Seal of the said Office, the 31st day of May 1951

DA 765743

This certificate is issued in pursuance of the Births and Deaths Registration Act 1953. Section 34 provides that any certified copy of an entry purporting to be sealed or stamped with the seal of the General Register Office shall be received as evidence of the birth or death to which it relates without any further or other proof of the entry, and no certified copy purporting to have been given in the said Office shall be of any force or effect unless it is sealed or stamped as aforesaid.

CAUTION:—Any person who (1) falsifies any of the particulars on this certificate, or (2) uses a falsified certificate as true, knowing it to be false, is liable to prosecution.

Form A504 Dd. 8264295 20m 10/81 Mfr(2160)

Figure 2-3 Certified copy of an entry of death

The design of the certificate is Crown copyright and is reproduced with the permission of The Office for National Statistics.

names of the witnesses. These statements are not always complete or fully accurate. Before 1870 the age column is likely to show merely the words "of full age." The status column should indicate a previous marriage but does not always do so. Addresses can be particularly frustrating. Where the same address is shown for bride and groom, it is probable that they were avoiding the necessity of having the banns read in two parishes. Such addresses, more often than not, fail to produce a result when the appropriate census return is consulted. Nonetheless, it would be unwise to make such an assumption. Doubts may also arise over the information on the fathers of the couple. The marriage certificate was supposed to indicate whether either father had died. If so, the word "deceased" would be entered under the name. However, where this does not appear you cannot be sure that he was still alive at the time. If the father's name has been omitted altogether, it may be that he was unknown and you have come up against an illegitimacy.

Contents of Birth Certificates

The birth certificate leads you back another generation on both the father's and the mother's sides. There is the usual date and place of the event, the sex and full name of the child, name and occupation of the father, name and maiden name of the mother, and the identity and address of the informant. Where the certificate shows the child having the same last name as the mother, it was probably an illegitimate birth. In some such cases the certificate will list the father's name, but after 1875 he had to be present and give consent for his name to appear. There was a reason for the change. Before this date, the mother of an illegitimate child could name whomever she pleased without verification. Adoption is a more difficult matter. In the modern, legal sense of the word, adoption did not exist before 1 January 1927. Anyone

Figure 2-4 Certified copy of an entry of birth

The design of the certificate is Crown copyright and is reproduced with the permission of The Office for National Statistics.

"adopted" before that date was really fostered. To trace the natural parents of a fostered child it is first necessary to know that the child was fostered, but it is preferable to know more, including some sense of where and when the birth occurred so that research can continue in vital and, perhaps, poor records. Illegitimate children were often brought up as children of their grandparents; in some cases a master fostered an orphan apprentice. The Legitimacy Act of 1926 did make it possible for a child born out of wedlock to be legitimized by the subsequent marriage of the parents, but they had to re-register the child and this was not always done. In 1975 the Children's Act laid down conditions under which an adopted person can seek the original birth record. For further information see *Tracing Missing Persons* (Rogers, 1986) and *Tracing Your Family Tree* (Cole and Titford, 1997).

Obtaining Certificates

There are several ways to go about obtaining certificates from a North American base. Microfilm and microfiche copies of the national indexes are becoming more readily available throughout England and Wales and in North America. The Family History Library (FHL) in Salt Lake City has a virtually complete series up to 1980. These indexes, up to the early twentieth century, can also be viewed at any of the LDS family history centers; in fact, many of them have extensive collections on permanent loan, rendering ordering unnecessary for some searches. More recent years are available in Salt Lake City only. Despite the improvement in access, a search through many years of indexes may require a large order of fiche or film. Up until 1865 for births, marriages, and deaths there is a different film for each quarter of the year, and this division can be increased again by different films for two to four sections of the alphabet. The marriage indexes are fortunately confined to one per year from 1867 onwards, but birth and death indexes revert to at least four films per year early in the twentieth century. Even with the modest handling fee, a protracted search could be costly, making the hiring of an agent in Salt Lake City or London a reasonable alternative. You may be able to alleviate this problem at a nearby family history center by ordering indexes, if they will be converted to indefinite loan and held on site.

Assuming you do not have precise-enough information to write directly to the correct local registrar, what would be the logical steps to obtain a certificate of birth, marriage, or death? To begin with, think carefully about the years which should be searched for the event. Be generous in your estimates of earliest and latest possible years for a birth, marriage, or death to have occurred. Then check the collection of civil registration indexes at an LDS family history center. What can be consulted immediately on film or fiche? How large an order would be required to cover the remaining period of the planned search? Also ask yourself how sure you are of the facts. Is the possibly large order something of a fishing trip, a gamble? Decide in the circumstance what is the best search method considering budget and objectives. If you decide to employ a record agent, be sure to have a full understanding of search fees, certificate charges, and method of payment. Also be aware of possible spelling variations for the name in question—close together in the alphabet makes for a shorter search.

For anyone doing this search at the FHL, an order for certificates can conveniently be placed at the counter on the British floor. The price is essentially the exchange rate for the cost of picking one up in person at the Family Records Centre. A researcher would also be able to place such an order on your behalf. A second option is to prevail upon an understanding friend or relative visiting London to do the legwork for you.

Family history societies provide a third alternative. Many of the English societies offer certificate schemes. For a moderate fee over and above the current charge, someone will visit the Family Records Centre (perhaps even do a short search) and forward the certificate.

Whenever you are confident that the base information is correct and complete, a direct application can be made to the local superintendent registrar. Addresses for local offices can be found in English telephone books (often available in large public libraries, or consult phone directories on the World Wide Web) under the heading "Registration of Births, Deaths, and Marriages." Please remember that these offices are very busy registering the events of today. Make the inquiry brief and to the point, and include the correct postage in British stamps or two International Reply Coupons (sold by the post office). If the request can be filled, you will receive a form to complete and a further request for payment, including postage, in pounds sterling. The charge is similar to that levied at the Family Records Centre for a personal application.

You may have noticed that nothing has been said about writing directly to the Office for National Statistics. At the time of writing the cost of a certificate applied for by post without the correct reference number is more than twice what it costs to apply in person or to write to a district office. Nonetheless, the address is supplied in appendix D for those who really can see no alternative.

Family Records Centre

Many of you will have the opportunity to travel to London. If you go be sure to arrange to search for some vital records at the new Family Records Centre. It is about a ten-minute walk from the Angel tube station, and there is much closer access by bus (a number 19 or 38 from the West End; get off one stop before the Sadlers Wells Ballet on Rosebery Avenue). For anyone who visited St. Catherine's House, it is easy to appreciate the marked contrast in facilities. The building is modern and the ground floor area for the ONS is spacious. There are comfortable chairs where one can take a rest or check notes. Labeling of sections is clear, although some of the overseas records are a bit difficult to find. The process of queuing for payment has improved. Coats are left in a room on the lower level fitted with lockers (you need a one-pound coin, which is returned), and coat lock facilities. Also downstairs are washrooms, vending machines, and an eating area.

Staff at the information desk will answer questions, and they have a list which identifies the registration district for every parish. It may be possible to figure this out for yourself from the maps showing district boundaries on the walls, or because you know the place names of the area. Addresses for all local registrars can be obtained at the desk.

Volumes of indexes are grouped by type and in date order. Between the shelves are lectern-style tables long enough for several people to work side by side. Do not be greedy about space; take only one volume off the shelf at a time and be sure to return it to its proper spot. Have a notebook handy, or several application forms, on which to record the details. At certain times of day and in certain sections (especially marriages) the aisles will be crowded, but nearly everyone is polite and considerate. If you want to avoid crowds go early in the day. When placing an order, decide whether to return to collect the certificates or to request that they be sent by post (mailed three days later) to your home or to an English address. Before making the trip read *Basic Facts About Using the Family Records Centre* (Collins, 1997) or *Never Been Here Before?* (Cox and Colwell, 1997).

In addition to the standard indexes to births, marriages, and deaths from 1 July 1937, there are finding aids for a number of twentieth-century records (adoptions, air births and deaths, Service Department returns, Indian Service, Army and Navy deaths in two world wars, Royal Air Force deaths in World War II, events abroad since 1966). Indexes beginning in earlier times are:

- Regimental Registers of Birth 1761–1924

- Chaplains' Returns of Births, Marriages, and Deaths 1796–1880

- Ionian Islands, Births, Marriages, and Deaths 1818–1964

- Marine Births and Deaths 1837–1965

- Consular Births Marriages and Deaths 1849–1965

- Army Returns from 1881 of Births (to 1945), Marriages (to 1965), and Deaths (to 1950)

- Natal and South Africa Deaths 1899–1902

Some of these have been released recently on microfiche and may be held by libraries and archives elsewhere in Britain. At the time of writing they are not in the FHL in Salt Lake City.

Reading the Indexes

Now for a few words of advice and caution, whether you or anyone else is reading the indexes on microfilm or in person at the Family Records Centre. As has been mentioned, the indexes are arranged by event and year, the majority with separate volumes for each quarter. Where there are four volumes per year, they are labeled *March, June, September,* and *December,* and contain the events registered in that particular quarter. Bear in mind that the quarter of the year in which registration took place is not necessarily the same as the quarter for the actual event. For example, some February and March births could well show up in the June volume if they were not registered until early in April.

TABLE 2-1

Registration District Codes 1837–1851

I	London, Middlesex
II	London, Middlesex
III	London, Middlesex
IV	London, Surrey
V	Kent
VI	Bedfordshire,Berkshire,Buckinghamshire, Hertfordshire
VII	Hampshire, Sussex
VIII	Dorset, Hampshire, Wiltshire
IX	Cornwall, Devon
X	Devon, Somerset
XI	Gloucestershire, Somerset, Warwickshire
XII	Essex, Suffolk
XIII	Norfolk, Suffolk
XIV	Cambridgeshire, Huntingdonshire, Lincolnshire
XV	Leicestershire, Northamptonshire, Nottinghamshire, Rutland
XVI	Oxfordshire, Staffordshire, Warwickshire
XVII	Staffordshire
XVIII	Gloucestershire, Shropshire, Staffordshire, Warwickshire
XIX	Cheshire, Derbyshire, part of Wales
XX	Lancashire
XXI	Lancashire and Yorkshire
XXII	Yorkshire
XXIII	Yorkshire
XXIV	Durham, Yorkshire
XXV	Cumberland, Lancashire, Northumberland, Westmorland
XXVI	Herefordshire, Monmouthshire, part of Wales
XXVII	part of Wales

TABLE 2-2

Registration District Codes 1852–1946

1a	London, Middlesex
1b	London, Middlesex
1c	London, Middlesex
1d	London, Kent, Surrey
2a	Kent, Surrey
2b	Hampshire, Sussex
2c	Berkshire, Hampshire
3a	Berkshire, Buckingham, Hertfordshire, Middlesex, Oxfordshire
3b	Bedfordshire, Cambridgeshire, Huntingdonshire, Nottinghamshire, Suffolk
4a	Essex, Suffolk
4b	Norfolk
5a	Dorset, Wiltshire
5b	Devon
5c	Cornwall, Somerset
6a	Gloucestershire, Herefordshire, Shropshire
6b	Staffordshire, Warwickshire, Worcestershire
6c	Warwickshire, Worcestershire
6d	Warwickshire
7a	Leicestershire, Lincolnshire, Rutland
7b	Derbyshire, Nottinghamshire
8a	Cheshire
8b	Lancashire
8c	Lancashire
8d	Lancashire
8e	Lancashire
9a	Yorkshire
9b	Yorkshire
9c	Yorkshire
9d	Yorkshire
10a	Durham
10b	Cumberland, Northumberland, Westmorland
11a/b	Wales

Try to maintain both flexibility and skepticism while searching for appropriate entries. Do not assume that the first likely entry is the correct one. Are you sure it is the only possible one? Just how certain are you of the name and the possibility of alternate spellings, or of the place and the possibility of registration in another area? Each index entry shows a name, place, and code number—for example,

Nuttall, Martha   Bury   21 183

As of the second quarter of 1866, the death indexes add a bonus: the age at death. From the third quarter of 1911, birth indexes add the mother's maiden name, and in the second quarter of 1912, the spouse's name appears in the marriage index volumes.

The name of the registration district may not be enough geographic information. There were about six hundred of these in the nineteenth century. Part of the numeric code does identify the region where the event took place, and a list of these is provided in tables 2-1 and 2-2. At the Family Records Centre, a detailed list of places and codes is at the information desk. If you are reading films, a good atlas might help because district names have a geographic basis. You may also wish to know the names of the registration districts and subdistricts in a given area before beginning a search. These can be found in *St. Catherine's House Districts* (Wiggins, 1988).

Solving Problems

There is no doubt that sometimes you must be prepared to gamble on a certificate. However, if you have done your map work thoroughly, you can reduce the odds. The search for the certificate of Mary Ann Moorhouse provides a good example. I had found her in four different census returns. She wasn't always consistent about her age, but I felt confident that she was born in either 1847 or 1848. The problem was her birthplace. She had given the census takers, over the years, three different answers: Bury, Newchurch, and Haslingden. Bury was a town and a large parish. There were two places called Newchurch in Lancashire, and Haslingden was a town and the name of a registration district. The birth indexes revealed sixteen different Mary Ann Moorhouse entries spread over this geographical area in 1847 and 1848. Careful map work told me that one Newchurch fell within Bury Parish and the Haslingden registration district. I gambled on the index entry for Haslingden. When the certificate came it proved to be the correct one, but it revealed a fourth, and the most accurate, answer for Mary Ann's birthplace—Whitewell Bottom. All four answers are in some sense correct. Mary Ann Moorhouse was born at Whitewell Bottom, which fell within the jurisdiction of the chapelry (see chapter 5) at Newchurch in Rossendale (where she was baptized) and the parish of Bury. There were registration offices at Bury, Haslingden, and Bacup, but a map reveals that Mr. Moorhouse would have found the going shorter and easier between Whitewell Bottom and Haslingden.

It may not be possible to make an intelligent guess from a list of names—Moorhouse was so common that several listings appear within the same quarter and the same area. In such cases you can apply for a check. At the Family Records Centre, simply turn the application form over and specify the detail which must match; most often the name of one or both parents. Half the standard fee is returned where no certificate can be supplied; if your application is for the correct record the standard certificate rate is due. It is possible to request that several entries be checked, but you must indicate if the process stops at the first correct match or goes through your entire list. Take some care with how the check is worded; avoid a situation that is too limiting. If using an age for a pre–1866 death record, provide a range. If using a father's name for a birth certificate, such as John James Stevens, write "John and or James Stevens."

If an obviously correct entry cannot be found, consider the possible reasons and how to adjust your parameters to be sure all possibilities can be caught in the search. Have you been generous enough in time frames for the years when a birth, marriage, or death occurred? Have you studied maps, checked names of neighboring parishes and districts, and allowed for the fact that people moved about? Have you considered all spelling variations or ways that a name could have been misconstrued? A name such as James Russell might be mistakenly indexed as Russell James. Some individuals have been indexed under a middle name. These central indexes are based on the reports sent in by district registers. In the days when the copies were made by hand there was plenty of room for errors in copying or for an entry to be missed. If the area of an event is known, make application directly to the local registrar's office. This advice applies to all searches made in London or in the indexes at the FHL in Salt Lake City.

Some other points are interesting to note. If a time of birth is given, it probably indicates a multiple birth. Where no name has been given for a child, the parents may not have chosen one, or the infant may have died. Sometimes parents changed their minds and the names on the certificate and the baptismal register differ. It was not uncommon for children to be given the same name as an older brother or sister who had died, or even who was very frail, so it is possible to come across a family with two children bearing the same name.

Marriage certificates were supposed to indicate whether a woman had been previously married; the term *formerly* will precede her maiden name. This was dependent on the woman telling the registrar that she was widowed. (Divorce was rare, requiring an act of Parliament.) If you cannot find a marriage, and age makes it possible for the bride to have been married before, consider this alternative: search only by the groom's name, using the bride's forename as a check detail. Another tactic for finding an elusive marriage is to carry out a broadly based search in the birth indexes for children, then work from what that suggests.

Choosing the Best Research Method

Where problems such as those just described complicate a search, they may influence the method selected. Efficiency, and savings in time and money, might be achieved by enlisting the services of an agent in Salt Lake City or London; or a combination search might work out for the best.

There are hundreds of William Nuttalls in Lancashire. In a search for one who died in the 1840s, some indexes were searched in the local family history center and some were searched by an agent, producing a list spanning three years that gave nine possibilities, all in the same parish. Rather than order nine checks—a costly option—a letter, with return postage, was sent to the local registrar giving a likely address gleaned from the 1841 census and an age range. The reply came back that the certificate could be supplied upon completion of the application and payment. The local office staff had taken a moment to compare details.

Take time to study the details on a certificate. Look for new place names on a map; look up the meanings and origins of new surnames; compare to the facts you have found elsewhere; note witnesses and informants; consider what the certificate does not reveal (such as whether a father is deceased); if unfamiliar, find out what the occupation was. Then consider where these details can take the next stages of the search; whether to a census, or to directories, or to parish records, or poor records, to name a few. Also be sensible enough to review tactics and ideas. Some good sources for that are *Tracing Your Family Tree* (Cole and Titford, 1997), *First Steps in Family History* (McLaughlin, 1998), and *The Family Tree Detective* (Rogers,1997).

Note

1. Park, *Genealogist's Magazine*, 1996.

Obtaining a Certificate of Birth, Marriage, or Death

1. Set parameters of time span, geographical area, and spelling variations, or decide if a survey should be done and a list of possibilities drawn up.

2. Check maps and gazetteers to be sure names of neighboring districts are known.

3. Calculate the number of volumes or films involved and the degree of difficulty (e.g., looking through variations like Oyles and Hoyle would be more time consuming than Clark and Clarke).

4. Visit the nearest LDS family history center and check if any appropriate films are in on loan.

5. Select from these options the most efficient research method: doing all the index work yourself and ordering from the local registrar; hiring an agent for the entire process or just to collect the certificate; collecting a list of possibilities and having a check done in London; joining an English society which has a certificate program for members.

6. If the search seems too big a task, or if the first attempt has been fruitless, consider alternate sources or tactics: voter lists, directories, census, siblings, or other family members.

3 &s; THE CENSUS

ensus returns are a key element of historical inquiry for the nineteenth century, not only for genealogists but for historians interested in many facets of the past. Their value stems, of course, from the fact that they form a very nearly complete record, compiled in a uniform manner, with central organization and storage. A few people did manage to evade the enumerators, some gave misleading answers through fear, embarrassment, or mere vanity, and some gaps occur; but on the whole the nineteenth-century census returns are a reliable source.

Contents of Census Records

The family historian usually consults a census record for information on ages, birthplaces, and relationships. These details are of first importance. Table 3-1 gives the dates for each of the nominal census returns presently available for public search. For the returns from 1851 through 1891, the information requested by the enumerator was name, age, sex, marital status, relationship to the head of the household, occupation, and birthplace. Other details sometimes appeared, such as whether blind, deaf, dumb, or lunatic, or the number of people employed by a farmer or business owner. Generally, the farther away someone was from his birthplace, the less specific the notation. For those born in the county of enumeration the parish is shown; for those born in another county it may be only the name of the county; for those born farther afield, the country. Addresses are given, as well as the name of the census district and sub-district. Each enumerated section is carefully described so that it can be found on a detailed map.

The earliest available census, for 1841, is not nearly so informative. The names of everyone at an address are listed, together with columns indicating age, sex, occupation, and birthplace. Unfortunately, the age and birthplace information is extremely vague and may actually be misleading. For anyone age fifteen or under, the age should be given exactly, but for those older, ages were to have been rounded down to the nearest five years (e.g., thirty-four would appear as thirty). Some enumerators rounded up by mistake, while inaccurate replies could be significantly exaggerated (e.g., someone aged forty-one but reporting thirty-nine would be listed as thirty-five). In 1841, birthplaces were recorded merely by a letter code: Y, N, I, S, F (or FP). These cryptic entries meant yes, no, Ireland, Scotland, or foreign parts (in reply to the question "Were you born in the county?"). An affirmative reply could mean anything from the same house to the other side of the county, while "no" could be equally confusing—a few miles away across a nearby county boundary, or at the other end of the country. Finally, this census gives no information about relationships, which sometimes means as many new questions arise as are answered. You may have to spend some time determining whether the people residing together were all one family, connections and in-laws, or some haphazard group of lodgers.

Important as this information is, the potential value of census returns goes far beyond a collection of facts on specific individuals and families. If your ancestors lived in a small town or rural parish (in 1851 slightly over half the population lived in urban areas), the returns for all of it can be read in a couple of hours. An urban area will take longer and will be easier to follow if a street plan is handy. Take time to look over the whole parish or the neighborhood, noting families of the same name— it is often possible to identify relations. Quite a bit of information about the area will emerge. Is there a concentration of people of the same occupation, social status, or birthplace? Who else is in the house? Servants can be relations or apprentices; elderly lodgers can be in-laws. Is it a pleasant residential area with servants in most homes, or a crowded street near a factory or mill? It is possible to tell how many families are in one household by the single (new family) and double (new household) slash marks at the edge of the "names" column.

Availability of Census Records

A one-hundred-year rule applies to the release of census information; thus, in 2002 the 1901 census will be made available. To consult it now requires a very specific request as to the address and the name you expect to find, the reason for the application, a statement that the individual concerned is dead, and payment of a steep fee (forty pounds in 1997). A separate address for this is noted in appendix D, or you can complete an application at the ONS information desk on the ground floor of the Family Records Centre. The 1911 census cannot be accessed in this manner, partly because of confidentiality rules and partly because it is, physically, more of a problem.

RAY contd				REED contd				REYNOLDS contd		
Sarah	66	001	125	Hannah	63	139	145	Herbert	9	683	54
Thomas	60	039	80	Hannah	2m	001	34	James	26	043	185
William	20	001	31	Henry	62	260	194	Jane Emily	5m	201	184
RAYMOND				Henry	5	001	48	Lettice	62	071	99
Elizabeth	33	626	132	James	2m	001	48	Louisa	27	254	185
Elizabeth	2	001	132	Jane	28	001	34	Mary Ann	22	137	184
Emma	8	001	66	Jane	25	999	143	Rebecca	33	287	54
Henry	3	001	66	John	43	248	84	Richard	62	149	163
Isaac	14	073	66	John	28	259	34	Robert	17	001	177
John	46	008	66	Joseph	2	001	84	Samuel	43	999	177
John	44	601	132	Mary	61	948	129	Samuel	15	001	177
John	20	008	66	Mary	24	001	145	Susan A.	8	001	54
Louisa	42	047	66	Mary Ann	49	137	48	Thomas	25	043	184
Rhoda	6	001	66	Mary A.	20m	001	59	William	31	071	54
Richard	1m	001	66	Robert	27	667	129	William	19	001	177
William	16	073	66	Robert	25	227	42	RICH			
RAYMONT				R. R.	18	325	20	Charles	5	001	40
George	10	001	67	Sarah	25	063	59	Eliza	32	001	40
RAYNER				Sarah	16	260	48	Elizabeth	57	001	61
Elixer (f)	37	001	77	Sarah	2	001	48	Elizabeth	7	001	40
Emma	16	001	55	Stephen	22	197	35	Emma	5	001	29
Johnathan	89	203	201	Susan	39	226	84	George	32	001	29
Samuell	26	001	77	Susan	23	260	48	George	11	001	40
Sarah	58	287	55	Susan	11	001	84	George	1	001	29
William	61	287	55	Thomas	18	259	35	Harriet	3	001	29
READ				William	55	260	48	Harriot	10	001	40
Augustus	50	153	198	William	40	999	143	Henry	25	001	61
John Henry	27	777	190	William	40	999	145	James	3	001	40
Mary	49	516	76	William	3	001	48	John	58	001	61
Peter	51	515	76	REEVE				John	35	001	40
READD				John Edward	7	027	145	John	14	001	40
Eliza	8	001	177	Joseph	48	173	145	Sarah	8	001	40
Frances	34	237	177	Julia	6	027	145	Sarah	7	001	29
Hannah	12	001	177	Mary Ann	40	132	145	Sophia	30	001	29
Henry	34	001	177	Mary Louisa	16	121	145	William	18	337	100
Henry	10	001	177	REEVES				RICHARDS			
James	2	001	177	Fanny	13	164	97	Elizabeth	33	318	38
Mary Ann	4	001	177	REVES				Emma	8	318	38
Sarah	14	001	177	Emma	23	074	114	James	34	318	38
Susan	6	001	177	REYLAND				James	4	001	38
REED				John	70	001	194	Mary Ann	9m	001	38
Caroline	3	001	59	REYNOLDS				Robert	6	318	38
Edwin	2m	001	34	Ann	68	249	163	Sarah A.	10	079	38
Eliza	27	013	34	Ann	6	001	166	RICHARDSON			
Eliza	16	005	25	Denham (m)	13	001	177	Elizabeth	29	658	156
Eliza	9	001	84	Elazabeth	32	260	166	Elizabeth Ann	4	654	156
Elleaner	23	968	44	Elazabath	1	001	166	Mary	25	211	76
Emma	13	001	190	Eliza	4	137	166	Robert	37	651	154
George	29	667	34	Emily J.	4	001	54	William	35	654	156
George	27	601	19	Emma	1w	001	166	William	2	654	156
George	24	001	145	George	30	154	166	RIDGWELL			
George	11	001	48	George	3	001	166	Thomas	68	095	200
Georgiana	1	001	34	George C.	36	071	54				
				George R.	2	001	54				

Figure 3-1 Sample page from The East of London Family History Society 1851 Census Index Series. The first column indicates age, the second indicates code for parish of birth, and the third indicates folio number. (Baker, J., ed. Vol. 1, pt. 2. Essex: Havering and Romford, 1984.) Reprinted by permission from the society.

on CD-ROM (1990–1996), and some probate and nonconformist church records—all in the same building.

County Record Offices and libraries with local studies collections also hold copies of the nominal census returns (usually
only those for their immediate areas). It may at some point be
worthwhile to plan a search, an expanded search, or a repeat
search right on location where there is ready access to records
which cross-reference to the census (for example, directories and
electoral rolls). Staff members at these archives and libraries may
do simple searches (a fee may be charged) if you provide specific
details as to the census year, the location, and names. Assistance
with such requests or with finding a research agent may be
offered by the area family history society.

Indexes

A researcher in North America can check for census indexes in
several ways. Visit the nearest family history center and inquire
about the finding aids. The FHL acquires copies of all nominal
indexes, but they will not necessarily be found in individual family history centers. Regular patrons may have donated some
booklet indexes which match your needs, and you should find
copies of the street indexes for the larger towns (usually of forty
thousand or more inhabitants). If you plan much census work,
purchase a copy of *Marriage and Census Indexes for Family
Historians* (Gibson and Hampson, 1998), which lists all nominal
lists and describes how to obtain details from them. Use the
Internet to access information on the county in question; you
may find a World Wide Web site containing a census finding aid
(see appendix D). Being a member of the county family history
society is the best way to ensure that you are informed of all cur-
rently available indexes. For 1851, fully searchable data from

Devon, Norfolk and Warwick, is available on CD-ROM, and many other places have book or fiche indexes.[1]

Most significant is the 1881 census index project, which has been accessible in its entirety since 1996, when the largest single section (Lancashire) was finished. Innumerable volunteers worked over many years to generate this vast and indispensable tool; every researcher owes these people a debt of gratitude. The 1881 index is arranged on a county basis with each of these sections composed of four sorts.

> *Surname*: alphabetical by surname, given name, then by age; use for the initial selection of entries.
>
> *Birthplace*: alphabetical by surname, then by birthplace, given name, age; can identify those of the same surname born in the same location.
>
> *Census place*: alphabetical by surname, then by census place, given name, age; can identify those of the same surname living in the same area.
>
> *Census as enumerated*: by census place, address, surname, given name; shows who was at the same address.

Additional information, such as occupation and the identity of the head of the household, appears in the various sections. The inclusion of several descriptive details helps with the identification of individuals with common names, and with the reconstruction of one or more families in one area. This index covers all of England, Wales, and Scotland, so if an ancestor has "disappeared" it is possible to search across borders. Considerable time is saved by the complete coverage: large cities can be searched quickly, and a methodical troll through several counties becomes a practical strategy. Another value is the fact that the latter part of the nineteenth century is outside the years indexed for those parish registers included in the IGI. The 1881 census index is widely available in all family history centers, and in the FHL, as well as in many places in England. From May, 1999, the 1881 census and index is available for purchase as a set of 24 CD-ROMs.

Local and regional indexes prepared by family history societies vary in format. Some provide surnames, Christian names, ages, and folio numbers, generally arranged alphabetically within each registration district (see figure 3-1). This is particularly helpful in differentiating between the many records for families and individuals with common surnames. More commonly all you see are lists of surnames with folio numbers, although there may also be a list relating these folio numbers to enumeration and ecclesiastical districts.

The printed census finding aids are produced in England and therefore refer the user to the record class and identification numbers used by the PRO.[2] Some explanation will help you understand local indexes and plan a search. When the 1841 census was taken the country was divided into the same districts and sub-districts that had been adopted four years earlier for civil registration. Apart from adjustments to ensure that no districts straddled county boundaries, this arrangement continued through the other enumerations. Once the statistical work was done, returns were kept together according to their districts and stored in boxes. The boxes were referred to as bundles. When the PRO took control of the material to make it available for public search it assigned each year a record class code (see table 3-1) and each bundle a number.

Census indexes, whether booklets or fiche, relate to part of a single record group, and perhaps only part of one bundle. The volume containing the page reproduced in Fig. 3-1 contains only HO 107, part of bundle 1772. The term *folio* is sometimes further clarified by the letter *r* or *v,* standing for *recto* or *verso* (signifying the front or the back of a page). This is explained by the fact that a folio number refers to a sheet of the enumerator's book (both sides), so they appear printed in the upper right hand corner of what, to the reader, is every other page. If an index gives only the folio number, be sure to examine both sides.

Record group and bundle numbers do not appear on the FHL place name finding aid to census films. You will find some PRO references in the *FHLC* for the 1841 and 1881 censuses. Once you begin to read a census film you will spot the folio numbers; with a little care and a good map at hand you can relate nominal index references to the FHL films. Problems sometimes arise when researching large cities, such as London or Manchester— usually where a road or street is long and runs through more than one district.

TABLE 3-1

Dates of Census Returns and Census Record Group Codes

1841	6 June	HO 107
1851	30/31 March	HO 107
1861	7/8 April	RG 9
1871	2/3 April	RG 10
1881	3/4 April	RG 11
1891	5/6 April	RG12

HO refers to Home Office and RG to Registrar General.

Choosing the Best Research Approach

Before anything else, select the census year or years which need to be consulted, and the region. Decide what you are looking for. It may be a specific individual or family in an identified place, their names and approximate ages already known. Or it may be that you seek all individuals of a particular name over a fairly wide area. Tenacious, patient genealogists are sometimes prepared to spend the time trolling through a large urban area for one person.

With objectives set, the next steps are to review the region on a map, check for finding aids, and note the number of films to which the search might extend. Nineteenth-century maps of rural areas (at one inch to the mile, published by David and Charles) and towns or cities (at fifteen inches to the mile, published by Alan Godfrey) are readily available. Finding aids can be identified by consulting *Marriage and Census Indexes for Family Historians* (Gibson and Hampson, 1998), by checking the *FHLC,* by visiting a nearby genealogy library, or by writing to the county family history society and requesting a list of census indexes for consultation or sale.

Finally, you are ready to order the selected films at the nearest LDS family history center. For most people it takes about two hours to read a full reel of film, depending on the handwriting and how the enumerator handled family groups. Lists with a surname on every line take longer to read than those which include the surname just once for each family (beside the name of the head of the household).

If the opportunity arises, the best thing to do is put yourself in the midst of the full collection of finding aids and census returns. It is easy to change tactics and parameters, and larger areas can be covered in less time. This can be done in at the FHL and at the Family Records Centre in London. At the Family Records Centre you can also purchase a reel of census film (five pounds in 1997) and take it home for more study. The PRO Reprographic Department will, in addition, sell segments of the 1891 census on microfiche.

Potential Pitfalls

To better understand the problems associated with the interpretation of census information, it is useful to know something of the way the data was collected and the attitudes of people at the time. Opposition was widespread. The census was attacked as an infringement on liberty, as likely to lead to new taxes, and as the first step towards the imposition of conscription. Some believed a census would reveal weaknesses, such as the inability to mobilize military forces. However, by the end of the eighteenth century the controversy surrounding population growth and the ability of the nation to feed itself was raging (Thomas Malthus's *Essay on the Principle of Population* was published anonymously in 1798), and the bill "for taking an Account of the Population of Great Britain and of the Increase or Diminution thereof" passed in the House of Commons without opposition on 31 December 1800.[3]

The census returns of 1801 through 1831, inclusive, had very similar objectives: to discover the number of persons, families, and houses; and to gain broad information about the types of occupations people were engaged in. It was the responsibility of the local overseer of the poor to collect this data. Questions were also asked of the clergy regarding numbers of births and marriages over the years to determine whether the population was increasing or declining. In 1840 the Population Act established a new system for the census. The emphasis switched from the family to the individual, and the full returns, rather than a local summary, were then sent to London for analysis. The system adopted in 1841 has remained essentially the same to the present day, apart from developments in data processing.[4] In 1841 it was quite a feat to arrange that the census be taken everywhere at the same time and that it take only one day, or at most, two.

All this efficiency, which included a form delivered to and collected from every door, did not completely dispel people's suspicions about the census. The poor were most likely to be skeptical. The laws of settlement were still being enacted after the introduction of the New Poor Law of 1834 (see p. 153). With the local overseer of the poor collecting census information until 1831 it is no surprise that many people remained reluctant to state truthfully their place of birth. Also, misleading information could be recorded in the birthplace column because of lack of knowledge or slight inaccuracies. For example, some gave the place of registration or baptism instead of the actual place of birth. Those not legally married, afraid of public censure, would probably tell the enumerator they were man and wife. Some parents would lie about the ages of children who might have been working at an early age in violation of child labor laws. In some areas the mixture of fear, suspicion, and hostility was sufficiently strong that the enumerator did the entire report himself from memory. Needless to say, errors crept in. As with any record, the information is only as reliable as the informant, and there is no way of judging reliability without some cross-checking.

One way to get some idea of the reliability of an ancestor's replies to the enumerator is to look them up in as many returns as possible. Unless the person told the truth all the way through, inconsistencies appear. Chances are someone who stretched the facts in 1851 did not recall exactly what they had said when responding again ten, twenty, or thirty years later. The inconsistencies may mean extra work for you, but it is much better to verify possibilities than to take one census search as factual and be led completely astray.

Problems with Location

Probably the most recurring problem with census returns is that of location. Those whose ancestors tidily resided in one small village for generations are fortunate indeed. Frequent moves within urban neighborhoods or between parishes, or even counties, can sometimes stymie the most persistent researcher. The key is to have an address for the time of the census (not always easy when your prey had the temerity to change lodgings within days of enumeration!). Addresses can be found through civil registration certificates, trade directories, poll books and electoral rolls, and rate books. Details on accessing these sources are found elsewhere in this book. School admission records, often in county record offices, can provide addresses of pupils and parents, and special occupational lists may help; see *Tracing Your English Ancestors* (Rogers, 1997) for more ideas.

Do not neglect your ancestor's relations. The birth certificates of brothers and sisters can reveal a family's movements. Marriage certificates, unfortunately, tend to lead researchers to disappointment. Addresses recorded on them were often only temporary, used to establish the residency requirement. A different problem arises in large cities, where you can be fooled by the fact that several streets had the same name or a single street was split between two districts. In addition, street names sometimes changed, or a street did not exist at the time of a census, one or two years before the address was recorded elsewhere. For all these circumstances, maps are a help; and further insights on location problems are contained in *Making Use of the Census* (Lumas, 1997).

Some assistance with a location problem can sometimes come from a search in the IGI (see appendix B). Using the CD-ROM format, it is possible to search for a baptism or a marriage throughout the British Isles or in selected counties. For the earlier returns, 1841, '51 and '61, where locally published indexes do not exist, consider this an option unless the county concerned is poorly represented. A church event close to an enumeration date would provide the location information on which to base a search. This technique works well for names which are not common, or where the forename allied to a common surname is unusual.

For the latter part of the nineteenth century, the 1881 census index is available to help, and once it becomes accessible on CD-ROM it too will permit wide-ranging searches. Presently, using the fiche, you must work methodically through a chosen group of county index sections. When collecting likely entries, both of these indexes lend themselves to use as distribution surveys. You may want to search the 1871 or 1891 returns, but no indexes can be found or location information is nil or vague. Provided the name is neither common nor broadly distributed across England, the areas of concentration can be selected as places to begin a search. Besides the 1881 census index, the IGI, some probate indexes, and a reference in *Homes of Family Names of Great Britain* (Guppy, 1890 rep. 1996) are good starting points for developing a plan based on distribution.

Do not ignore family legend in this search for an elusive address. Be sure you have explored any suggestion, no matter how fantastic it seems, that has appeared in interviews, old letters, etc. Bear in mind, too, that some strange things could have happened to the spelling of the surname, or that names can be transposed accidentally when recorded.

Anyone in an institution or not on solid ground on census night, adds a challenge to the search. Such places as barracks, workhouses, and hospitals accommodating at least two hundred people were listed at the end of the district. Families on canal barges were enumerated wherever they were. No census of the crews of ships at sea or in foreign ports was done before 1861. After that time they appear in special shipping schedules. For 1861 the FHL has an index to those on board ship (about 120,000), and the 1881 index has a separate shipping segment. For ships in British ports, they are listed at the end of the enumeration for the town—this is straightforward, provided the ship was in its home port (names of these are listed). If the vessel was away from home, the search is more difficult, involving some research or deduction as to where it went. *Lloyd's Register of Shipping* may help (see chapter 8).

Additional Tips

Sometimes you may have difficulty selecting the correct film. The local place names used in censuses are actually civil parishes. It is possible that the ecclesiastical parish of the same name is in a neighboring civil parish, or that the parish name you are look-ing for does not appear in the census finding aid or the *FHLC* at all. There are aids to help you in Salt Lake City and at the Family Records Centre. If researching elsewhere, you may solve the problem with a good map or gazetteer, or with one of the finding aids which cross-references ecclesiastical parishes with census districts. There is a series of booklets, *Registration Districts in 1836* (Murrells, 1992–96), and several finding aids for the London area (see the Bibliography).

Sometimes there is simply no alternative to a protracted search through many rolls of film. This may seem futile or too big a task to contemplate. However, don't come to this conclu-sion or give up before you are sure that all possible finding aids have been searched and that everything has been done to narrow the geographic area.

The census record, once obtained, offers much useful infor-mation and perhaps some unexpected bonuses. There are the basic facts for each member of the household. In the case of older family members, particularly in the 1851 census, the birth-place information can lead back to parish records created long before the beginning of civil registration. Pay careful attention to everyone in the house on census night; information on visiting

CENSUS RECORD SHEET – ENGLAND/WALES/SCOTLAND

date of census **1851**   Ref.No. **HO107/1792**   District No. _____   Page No. **241**

County **SUFFOLK**   Ecclesiastical Dist./Parish **BURY ST. EDMUNDS**

Town or Village **BURY ST. EDMUNDS**   Road/Street/etc. **27 BUTTER MARKET**

Date of Search **24 Jan/85**   Scope **READ ENTIRE FILM**   Condition of Record **GOOD**

Name and Surname of Each Person	Rela-tionship	Status	Age of M	Age of F	Rank, Profession or Occupation	Place of Birth
BONFELLOW, EDMUND	Head	Marr.	31		Draper employing 6 men	Norfolk, Gillingham
SARAH ANN	Wife	"		26		Essex, Ingrave
EDMUND	Son	—	1			Suffolk, Bury St. Edmunds
ROBERT WALES	Son	—	2mo.			Suffolk, Bury St Edmunds
RICHARDSON, ELIZABETH	Sister	Widow		63	Housekeeper	Essex, Upminster
WADSWORTH, ELIZABETH	Niece	Unm.		17		Canada West
MILES, SARAH ANN	Mother-in-law	Widow		62	Fundholder	Essex, Ingrave
KITCHEN, HENRY J.	Apprentice	Unm.	18		Draper	London

Figure 3-2 This very interesting return was extremely valuable to my research. Finding all these relations in the same house was a real bonus. There are some potential problems for the unwary. There is a mistake in the infant's name (it should say *Robert Miles*). The sister is actually a half-sister, and the niece is the daughter of a half-brother. Remain alert to the fact that relationships were often described differently.

relations could provide new data as to family origins. Note the occupants' relationships to the head of the household, but remember that our ancestors did not use such terms as cousin, niece, or sister-in-law in the same strictly defined ways that we do today. Where a person's origins are proving elusive, all these connections, regardless of definition, should be investigated. A very young child born several years after the others might actually be the illegitimate offspring of an eldest daughter, even though not identified as such. Remember, too, that the servants in an urban household could come from a place with family connections. Be sure to read through the entire district where you find your ancestors in case other family members live nearby. Also note the neighbors, and the enumerator's description of the subdistrict. All of this can help provide a better picture of the surroundings.

Simple bad luck could block your search for a census record. A missing entry could be the result of damage to the records or human error. Occasionally pages have been torn from the census books and even complete volumes lost. Occasionally an enumerator, slightly confused perhaps, missed an entire street. When you do not find your own direct line ancestors, be especially alert for other families of the same name and note them. The information in these entries could parallel that of the missing entry, or could lead you to other records. With common names, jotting down possibilities becomes too large a task; narrow the list by selecting the known Christian names that appear in the family, and/or by limiting your notes to those of similar occupation or place of origin.

Census returns, better than any other single type of record, help to create a picture of your ancestors. To track a family through several censuses builds a history of that family, where they came from, where they lived, their fortunes and misfortunes, their neighbors, and their neighborhood. But don't leave it there. Refer to some secondary sources, such as good local histories or old newspapers, which can supplement the work you have done on your own family. These add descriptive details and help you interpret the material found in the census returns. Make a point of checking the appropriate volume of *The Victoria History of the Counties of England*. In addition, some idea of the uses of census data can be obtained from *Family History and Local History in England* (Hey 1987). If you require more information on researching census returns prior to a visit to London, *Making Use of the Census* (Lumas, 1997) and *Never Been Here Before?* (Cox and Colwell, 1997) are very helpful.

Notes

1. *1851 British Census (Devon, Norfolk, and Warwick only)*. Salt Lake City: The Church of Jesus Christ of Latter-day Saints, 1997. The data is fully indexed and gives names, ages, relationships, occupations, and birthplaces.

2. *1881 British Census and National Index: England, Scotland, Wales, Channel Islands, Isle of Man, and Royal Navy*. Salt Lake City: The Church of Jesus Christ of Latter-day Saints, 1999.

3. *Guide to Census Reports, Great Britain, 1801–1966*, 1977.

4. Nissel, 1987.

Obtaining Census Records

1. Determine the name, place, and census year of interest.

2. Consult *Marriage and Census Indexes for Family Historians* to see whether nominal indexes or street indexes exist.

3. Consult the fiche guide to census returns or the *FHLC* at an LDS family history center, noting the number of films to cover the desired region. (With towns and cities check for a street index when you are working from a definite address.)

4. Compare this information to what you found in step 2. (The lack of a precise address and a search of three or more films would make a nominal index a valuable shortcut.)

5. Where an LDS family history center is not accessible but nominal indexes do exist, write the local library and inquire about search services; or consult the index by purchasing it or writing to the custodian, and with that information hire a researcher in England or in Salt Lake City to consult the films.

6. Where information is scarce or where an initial search has had no result, consider a survey search in the IGI or the 1881 census index. Further options include checking directories and electoral rolls, verifying that all nominal indexes have been identified and consulted, and searching for related family events in the indexes to civil registration.

4 &s; LISTS AND PERIODICALS

ivil registration and census returns are excellent starting points for English genealogical research. These records can take you back several generations, are remarkably complete and well organized, have been brought together in central locations, and are reasonably accessible. It is possible, too, to go back and forth between the census and the records of civil registration, building an extended family of direct and collateral ancestors. However, common names, frequent moves, human error, and missing records are among the problems which can block this process. As you move into the first half of the nineteenth century it will be necessary to consult other records which are neither as complete nor as well organized and indexed. If you have followed the tenets of good genealogical research explained in chapter 1, you will enjoy the new challenges. Knowledge of the records, how they are organized, and where they are deposited will now be very important, as will an ability to develop a strategy for finding the sources.

Important to that strategy will be the sources presented in this chapter. They straddle the centuries, link sources in a logical sequence, and add information about the lives and times of your ancestors. These tools provide facts which support searches in the basic records and can lead to new sources. Finding directories, poll books and electoral rolls, rate books, newspapers, and periodicals will sometimes be challenging and the search itself may be tedious, but the effort will be worthwhile.

Directories

The publication of directories was a commercial enterprise, so the object was to attract listings and to introduce buyers to sellers. Directories often included sections on local history and statistics, and sometimes area maps. The genealogist's most common reason for consulting directories is to obtain an address to assist in the search for a census. Useful though this can be, directories can and should be used for many other reasons. Supplementary information could include a description of the town or region, complete with lists of officials, major property owners, industries, schools, churches, cemeteries, transportation schedules, and topography. In towns, where listings are often by street as well as by trade or by name, you can usually construct a diagram of your ancestor's neighborhood. Directories are also particularly well suited to survey searches, in which you look over a wide geographic area and a span of years for a particular individual or the distribution of a surname.

The first list of the inhabitants of London appeared in the seventeenth century, and by the middle of the eighteenth century most cities had trade directories. In the nineteenth century county directories made their appearance, and the scope of the books broadened. Three publications give some idea of the directories available for the different counties of England. The first (not so easy to find) is the *Guide to the National and Provincial*

Directories of England and Wales Excluding London Published Before 1856 (Norton 1950). The second, published more recently, continues the survey and is entitled *British Directories: a Bibliography and Guide to Directories Published in England and Wales (1850–1950) and Scotland (1773–1950)* (Shaw & Tipper 1989). The third title may be more accessible: *Directories and Poll Books, including Almanacs and Electoral Rolls in the Library of the Society of Genealogists* (1995). Even if you never actually search through directories at the Society of Genealogists, this inexpensive listing of their holdings is a useful tool for planning a directory search because it presents an excellent range of what is available. Do not neglect to check the locality section of the *Family History Library Catalog (FHLC)*; look under the heading "Directories" for both the county and the specific place-name.

In recent years numerous old directories have been reproduced as books and on microfiche (an economical format which allows large books to be separated into county sections). The Society of Genealogists sells Pigot's 1830 directory in county segments of one to six fiche per county. From Australia comes the British Directories Project, which breaks up hundreds of directories, mainly 1820 to 1900, into county sections sold separately on microfiche (see appendix D for both of these addresses).

A logical directory search would follow these steps. Visit any local libraries that have good English history collections. English directories turn up in university and public libraries and in genealogy society libraries. In the 1970s a number of the White's county directories of the 1820–50 period were reprinted by the English firm of David and Charles. These seem to be the most commonly available. Scan any books of local history for your area of interest as well, as they often include excerpts from county directories. Next, visit a family history center of the LDS church, which will have not only the *FHLC* but probably some directories on microfilm among the indefinite loan holdings, or among those items ordered in by another researcher. If neither of these options is open to you, write to the appropriate library in England and ask about their directory holdings for the time and place of interest, and for their scale of charges for copying and/or the search. It is also wise to inquire of the family history society in that area as to its publications and whether assistance is available for simple list work such as this.

Directories appear on microfilm in many libraries. The Metropolitan Toronto Library, for example, has an extensive collection of London volumes in this form. Knowing the location of wide-ranging collections can facilitate research. In London you can locate a large array at the Guildhall Library, the London Metropolitan Archives, and the Society of Genealogists; and you could probably supplement this with more in the large LDS family history center on Exhibition Road. Whether in London, Salt Lake City, or some other place, employing an agent with access to many directories may be an efficient way to consult them.

When embarking on a directory search, there are several points of caution to keep in mind. In the first place, directories were usually six to eighteen months out of date because of the time lag between data collection and publication. Secondly, always read the title page carefully so you know the scope of the listings. Check the geographical area covered and the types of people listed, for it was late in the nineteenth century before directories began to appear with full lists of inhabitants. In most editions, the subjects were people engaged in trades or professions, the gentry, nobility, and more prosperous farmers. Usually only the names of business proprietors or heads of households were listed. Sometimes the names were limited to those who had paid the subscription price. If a name just isn't there, expand the search to other years and other locations: your ancestor may have moved or been overlooked. As you search, watch for and note others of the same surname, particularly those engaged in a similar occupation. These could be relations.

Poll Books and Electoral Rolls

There is a distinct difference between poll books and electoral rolls. Poll books record the open vote in contested parliamentary constituencies up until the adoption of the secret ballot in 1872. Perhaps 5 percent of the adult male population was eligible to vote before the First Reform Bill of 1832. Electoral rolls begin with the First Reform Bill, listing all those entitled to vote in parliamentary elections. They continue to the present day. With the Third Reform Bill of 1884, which extended the vote to agricultural laborers, about two-thirds of the adult male population became enfranchised.

Poll books survive from the early eighteenth century. Not only do they indicate the names of the voters, they also show how they voted. The surviving records may be the original work of the polling clerk or may be copies or transcripts. In the towns or boroughs, those who could vote were determined by local custom, but it was generally the freemen or liverymen. In the counties, only those who held freehold property to the value of forty shillings per year (i.e., that could be rented for that amount) were granted the vote. From 1780 to 1832 the records of land tax assessment also served as the electoral rolls, since payment of this tax qualified someone to vote. As a result, these very useful lists became part of the records of the clerk of the peace and have survived in large numbers (see chapter 9).

Lists of electors are very useful because they indicate the qualifications which made each person eligible to vote. Arranged alphabetically within each polling district, they show addresses, including current residence, properties owned, and tenancies held in the district. In the county constituencies the overseer of

115

SURVEYORS.

Morris, T. (land) Stow-hill
Barber, E. S. (land) Com.-st
Davies, J. (house) Llanarth-st
Langdon, J (& architect) Stow-hill
Maule, J. (road) Cemetery-road
Morris, J. (timber) Stow-hill
Pritchard, E. (land) Com.-st
Prujean, J. (land, &c.)
Salter, J. (town) Clarence-place
Webb, N. (licnsd. valuer) Llnrth-st.
Young, A. (timber) Skinner-st

STONE MASONS.

Biggs, Wm. Marshes-road
Christophers, R. Bane's-well
Davies, J. Canal-side, nr. Dock
Davies, T. King-st
Haddon, C. Great Dock-st
James, E. Commercial-st
Jenkins, C. Ebenezer-terrace
Lewis, D. Pillgwenlly
Leyson, T. nr. Mill-st. bridge
Rees, W. Melon's-bank
Richards, T. Caroline-st
Thomas, Thomas, Hill street
Watkins, H. Com.-st. (freestone)
Watkins, T. Commercial-st
Williams, J. Stow-hill

SOLICITORS.

Birch and Davis, offices, High st.
Dawson, —   „ Stow-hill
Hall and Jenkins, „ Com.-st.
Harwood, T.,   „ ditto
Llewellin, T. M., „ Llanarth st.
Owen, J.,   „ High st.
Phelps, W. T. H. „ ditto
Prothero, Towgood, & Fox
Phillpotts, J.   „ Com.-st.
Woollett, T.   „ Council Hs.

STRAW BONNET MAKERS.

Bothemly, J, Commercial street
Francis, M,   ditto
Davies, F, Commercial road
Gale, Misses, Commercial st.
Grant, Misses, Commercial st.
Gwyther, Misses,   ditto
Harper, H, Corn street
Haynes, Mrs, George street
Holmes, Misses, High street
Loder, M, High street
Michael, M, Commercial street
Moss, M, High street
Williams, J, Commercial street

SURGEONS.

Brewer, W. & W. H., High st.

SURGEONS CONTINUED.

Brewer, Jehoiada, Commercial st.
Fry, Henry,
Harrhy, J, High street
Hawkins, J, High street
James, W, Commercial road
Jefferies, — Pillgwenlly
Jones, J. W., Commercial street
Morgan, W. W., Commercial st.
O'Reilly, C, Pillgwenlly
Thomas, J, Commercial street
Woollett, R, Dock street
Young, Dr, Victoria Place

TAILORS.

Bryan, J, Commercial street
Bryant, W. H., High street
Davies, T, High street
Edwards, L, Commercial street
Grant, J, Skinner street
Gwyther, J, Commercial road
James, T, Stow-hill
Lewis, T, Commercial street
Lewis, W. Stow-hill
Morgan, E, High street
Morgan and Son, Commercial st.
Polak, S, Commercial [street
Shelley, F. Cross street
Watkins, J, Ship and Pilot
Weaver, J, Commercial street
Williams, H, Queen street
Williams, J, Canal side

TALLOW CHANDLERS.

Compton, W, High street
Morgan, J,   ditto
Lewis, J. & D., Skinner street

TANNER.

Davies, David, High street

TIMBER & SLATE MERCHTS.

Batchelor, Tom B., Canal side
Cook and Nicholas, ditto
Newport Timber & Slate Co.
Powell, T., (timber)
Young, John, (timber)
Young, Adam, (timber)

TEACHERS OF MUSIC.

Evans, D. High-st
Groves, J. H. Commercial-street
  (organist, St. Paul's)
Pollock, W. G. Stow-hill
Pittman, B.
Price, T. R. Commercial-street
  (organist, St. Woollos)
Tilley, J. Maindee Common

Figure 4-1   Page from the directory of *History of Newport* (Scott, J.M. Newport: 1847).

Note the differences between the directories represented in figures 4-1 and 4-2. The Newport directory is organized by occupation, then alphabetically by name. At the time of its printing, the majority of people listing themselves in the directory were tradesmen seeking to be hired. In the more recent directory shown in figure 4-2, people are listed first by place of residence, then by name. Occupation and exact address are listed as well.

436 **SOUTHGATE.**

Southgate—continued.

Parish Louisa (Mrs.), dressmaker, 10 Hawthorn terrace, Chase road
Pasmore Albert T. White Hart P.H. Chase rd
Pickard Wm. Crown P.H. Chase side
Pigram John, shopkeeper, Enfield road
Piper & Co. drapers, Chase side & stationers, High street
Plater Alfred, boot maker, 1 High street
Prentice Frederick, tailor, High street
Reading Rooms (George James, sec.; Franklin Young, librarian), Chase side
Ridenton James, plumber, The Green
Roberts & Vivian, surgeons, High street
Roberts Edward Coldridge M.R.C.S.Eng. surgeon & medical officer & public vaccinator, Southgate district, Edmonton union & medical officer of health to local board, High street
Russell Henry, butcher, Chase side
Satchell William, lath render, Chase side
Saundercock James Henry, beer retailer, High street
Seaman James T. butcher, Chase road
Shambrook Matilda (Mrs.), confectioner, Chase side
Sharp Geo. Fredk. beer retlr. Chase side
Shepherd Francis, tailor, 5 Ivy cottages, Travers road
Simmonds Henry, boot maker, High st
Simmons Wm. fishmonger, 1 Travers rd
Smith David, florist, Nursery cottage, Nursery road
Snow Albert, draper, The Green
Spearen Reuben, greengrocer, Chase sde
Stracey Edward Hewett, baker, High st
Taylor Robert, watch & clock maker, High street
Temple Frank, grocer & provision dealer, Market place, Chase side
Thomas William, farmer, Enfield road
Tomlin William, inspector of weights & measures, 2 Fern lodge, Chase side
Tullet Frederick, dairyman, High st
Village Hall (James Jiggins, keeper), High street
Vivian Richard Thomas L.R.C.P. Edin. surgeon, see Roberts & Vivian
Wadkins Samuel T. greengro. Chase side
Wadkins Wm. hair dresser, Chase side
Walter Jn. Stephen, saddler, The Green
Ward James, nursery, Chase side
Watkin William & Sons, wheelwrights & ironmongers, Market pl. Chase side

SOUTHGATE LOCAL BOARD.

Clerk, Wm. Mnsfld. Ellenor, Locl. Bd. offs
Treasurer, John Woodrow Cross, London & Provincial Bank
Medical Officer of Health, Edward Coldridge Roberts, High street
Surveyor & Engineer, Charles Griffin Lawson, Local Board offices
Sanitary Inspector, J. W. H. Brown, Local Board offices
Collector, William Sanders, Fairfield road, Upper Edmonton N
Metropolitan Police Station(Y division), Chase side; Soloman Dingle, stn. srgt.; 2 sergeants, 16 constables & 2 patrols
Fire Brigade Station, The Green, 1 steam fire engine; Charles G. Lawson, capt.; W. F. Broadberry, lieut. & 11 men

SCHOOLS :—

National, Chase road (boys); George James, master
National, Green (girls & infants) ; Miss Elizabeth E. Beresford, mistress ; Miss Mary Buckmaster, infants' mistress
Mixed, Tile Kiln lane, Palmer's green ; Miss Elizabeth Shirley, mistress
The Chase (infants); Miss Alice Thurgate, mistress

Palmer's Green, N.

PRIVATE RESIDENTS.

Algar Samuel John, Stonard road
Andre Carl, Hazlewood
Argenti George, The Lodge
Ashley Edwd. F. 16 Palmer's Green vils
Baines Thomas, Fern cottage
Bamlet Fredk. John, 8 Broomfield villas
Bamlet Robert, 10 Broomfield villas, Bowes road
Barrett Frdk. Geo. 15 Palmer's Green vils
Bates Walker Henry, Park villa
Beckingham Chas. A. 9 Palmer's Grn. vils
Braines Thomas, 1 Palmerston crescent
Cathie Alex. 4 Broomfield vils. Bowes rd
Casey Thos. Cambridge lodge, Bowes rd
Chandler Fredk. Firtree cottage, Fox la
Clear Mrs. Stonard road
Coakill William Alfred, 5 Broomfield vils
Collingwood William, Moffat road
Colliver Frederick, Truro house
Dart William, Fairleigh, Bowes road
Davis Charles, Bourne hill
Devin Paul, 3 Palmer's Green villas
Dew George, 1 Eaton ter. Stonard rd

the poor drew up the list, while the town clerks performed this task in urban areas. The time lag between the first draft and the final list probably created a built-in element of error. However, these lists were made on a yearly basis, so they are a very good way of tracing an ancestor's movements. Sometimes you need to confirm how long someone lived in a particular district before the first census or between census returns. Electoral rolls and poll books (especially after 1780) are probably the best way of doing this. Coverage is likely better than for directories, and it may fill gaps where directories are not available.

These records are usually held in CROs and local libraries, though there are a few examples in the Family History Library (FHL) collection. As a matter of routine, where you have access to the *FHLC,* check the locality section under COUNTY— DIRECTORIES or COUNTY, TOWN—DIRECTORIES. The best way to ascertain which electoral rolls survive for any given area is to consult *Electoral Registers Since 1832 and Burgess Rolls* (Gibson and Rogers, 1990). With this information, you can write to the repository, hire a researcher, or utilize help offered through fellow members of the area family history society. Assistance from someone "on location" will also ensure there is a match between the area to be searched and the parliamentary constituency (the basis or organization for these lists). The survival and location of poll books is listed in *Poll Books c. 1696–1872: A Directory of Holdings in Great Britain* (Gibson and Rogers, 1994). In most instances you will have to write the local record office about services and fees and/or hire a researcher. Remember to check the holdings of the Library of the Society of Genealogists, as one agent may be able to check many locations in one visit there.

Rate Books

Rate books comprise another type of record which can be consulted to find an address for the census, to obtain information about family moves, or even to help prepare some sort of name survey. They go back a long way, predating directories by at least a hundred years. In some areas and periods they may be more comprehensive than directories or voters' lists, but they can be more difficult to use, especially in densely populated areas. This is because there was usually no pattern to the lists; they simply follow the ramblings of the rate collector. Possessing good contemporary maps of the parish or district will reduce the search to manageable proportions.

Rates (taxes collected for local purposes) were assessed to support such services as sewers, schools, and poor relief. In fact, collection of rates grew out of the system of parish-based poor relief imposed in Elizabethan times. For example, to raise the money necessary for the support of the poor in his district, the overseer of the poor set a rate to be charged every property owner and tenant. Lists were made of everyone "rateable" and also, in many cases, of those excused for reasons of poverty. Sometimes the lists identified the land or house. Sub-tenants and lodgers were not included.

Many rate books are held in local history collections, but some are still with local authorities. Sadly, many of these records were sacrificed to aid wartime paper shortages, and others were simply shredded to get them out of the way.[1] Fortunately, some family history societies have turned their attention to rate books. For example, the North Middlesex Family History Society has been engaged in indexing Islington Rate Books. Direct your inquiries to the appropriate County Record Office or family history society.

Newspapers

Newspapers may have escaped your consideration simply because of the apparent problems of accessibility. However, these

Freeholder's Name.	Where Freeholder lives.	Where Freehold is situate	The Nature of Freehold.	Occupier's Name.	Mainwaring	Byng	Burdett	Pages of Cheque Bk.	Pages of original Poll.
Adams, Wm Godfrey	New road	Whitechapel	house	John Cotton				272	
Alexander, Robert	Goolman's fields	Petticoat lane	do	Thomas Poind				338	
Atkinson, Joseph	Bishopsgate without	Rosemary lane	do	John Usborne				331	
Appleton, John	Orchard lane, Tottenham	Houndsditch	do	Thomas Compton				371	
Allison, Ambrose	Aylesbury street	Whitechapel	do	William Maddull				92	
Baldock, Thomas	Prescot st. Goodman's Fields	Mill yard, Whitechapel	houses	Barter and others				243	
Bristow, Isaac	Doctors commons	Whitechapel	house	Elizabeth Wright				245	
Bullock, Henry	Whitechapel	do	do	Mary and Fanny Dow				263	
Brown, Alexander	Leather lane	do	do	Wm Cross				291	
Brett, Job	Whitechapel	do	do	Charles Duddings				293	
Bridge, William	Goodman's fields.	Mill yard, Whitechapel	do	J. Halbort				300	
Brockholes, Robert	Whitechapel road	Whitechapel	house	Arthur O'Leary				301	
Brown, George	Oxford	do	house	Mrs Brown				305	
Baxter, Thomas	60, Stretton ground, Westminster								
Brody, Joshua	Gun street, Spitalfields	Whitechapel road	do	Henry Bullock				328	
Brabrook, James	Charlotte street	Whitechapel	do	Mrs. Fillingham				330	
Brown, Richard	Hitchin, Herts	Rosemary lane	do	Wm Gain				351	
Bates, William	Gloucester terrace, New road		do	unknown				347	
Bowyer, Daniel	Shadwell	Rosemary lane	do	Mr. Daniel				50	
		Swallow gardens, Rosemary lane	do	William Nanfun				50	
Burt, Andrew	Booth st. Spital fields	Wellclose square	messuage	John Dixon				192	
Coates, James	Whitechapel road								
Carter, John	Epping forest	Black lion road, Whitechapel	do	Mr. Brown and others				250	
Creed, John	Mile end	Leman street, Goodman's fields	do	Wm Roe				231	
Cuff, Joseph	Whitechapel	Prescot street	do	George Maling				261	
Casey, James	Essex st. Whitechapel	Whitechapel	do	Joseph Cuff				276	
Clark, Mark Beauchamp	Totham	Essex street	houses	James Casey				290	
Cawthorne, Wm	Idol lane, Tower street	Whitechapel	do	Mr Heyward				323	
Clun, Peter	Prescot street	Rosemary lane	do	Levy and others				357	
Cockland, Stephen	Petticoat lane	Prescot street	house	Peter Clun				359	
Conner, James	Goodman's fields	Whitechapel	do	S. Cockland				367	
Coastable, John	Colchester st, Whitechap.	Colchester street	do	John Warren				367	
			do	self				370	

Sworn.

Figure 4-3 Middlesex Poll Book.

1913

1406 SOUTHGATE (NORTH-EAST) PARLIAMENTARY POLLING DIST. (DIST. T)—con.

PARISH OF SOUTHGATE (part of)—SOUTHGATE NORTH ELECTORAL DIVISION (part of)—NORTH EAST WARD OF THE URBAN DISTRICT OF SOUTHGATE—continued.

OCCUPATION Electors.	DIVISION ONE.	Parliamentary Electors, County Electors and Parochial Electors.

ARLOW ROAD, WINCHMORE HILL, N.—Continued.

T	80 Sadler, Harry George	...	Dwelling house ...	1, Arlow-mansions.
T	81 Watts, Thomas Alexander	...	Dwelling house ...	2, Arlow-mansions.

ARUNDEL GARDENS, WINCHMORE HILL, N.

T	82 Allensby, Charles Reed ...	...	Dwelling house ...	3, Arundel-gardens.
T	83 Martin, William ...	...	Dwelling house (successive)	71, Devonshire-road and 9, Arundel-gardens.
T	84 Webb, Alfred ...	...	Dwelling house (successive)	35, Park-avenue and 35, Arundel-gardens.

AVONDALE ROAD, PALMERS GREEN, N.

T	85 Webb, Arthur ...	...	Dwelling house ...	3, Avondale-road.
T	86 Wollard, Charles ...	...	Dwelling house ...	5, Avondale-road.
T	87 Budd, Archibald William...	...	Dwelling house ...	9, Avondale-road.

Figure 4-4 1913 Voters' List (Society of Genealogists).

are not insurmountable and you may have some lucky breaks. Newspapers are not only a source for notices of birth, marriage, and death, but they often provide a broad range of personal information and local color. Not until the middle of the nineteenth century did newspapers begin to resemble our modern daily. Factors in the change were increased literacy, the railways, and improvements in illustrations. As the appeal of newspapers spread, so the scope of what was reported increased. By the 1880s local papers included articles on ordinary people and everyday events. Sports, festivals, agricultural fairs, concerts, and the names of those involved all received attention. Advertisements placed by local businesses increased too. More material on the history and content of old English newspapers can be found in *An Introduction to Using Newspapers and Periodicals* (Chapman, 1993).

Collections of English newspapers are difficult to find in North America. However, most university libraries of any size have *The Times* of London on microfilm. *The Times* first appeared as the *Daily Universal Register* on 1 January 1785, changing to its familiar name three years later. It is an invaluable source for contemporary news; birth, marriage, and death records; and lengthy obituaries. Where you find *The Times* on microfilm you will probably also find *Palmer's Index* (released on CD-ROM in 1997), which covers the period from 1790 to 1941. Unfortunately, notices of births, marriages, and deaths were omitted, although the editorial-style obituaries were indexed.

The first steps to obtaining newspaper information are to decide which paper would be appropriate and whether or not copies survive for the period of interest. Once again, a finding aid has been prepared: *Local Newspapers 1750–1920: A Select Location List* (Gibson, 1987) includes all those for which there is a run of four years or more. Another way to check is to look in *Willing's Press Guide,* which should be available in any good public library. Although this is an annual list of current newspapers, it does show in what year each newspaper began publication. There is an eight-volume catalog to the newspaper collection of the British Library at Colindale in north London *(Catalogue of the Newspaper Library, Colindale)*; it may be available in a few locations. The Newspaper Library will also provide photocopies of specific pages of a newspaper at a reasonable rate. Finally, an inquiry to a local library will elicit information regarding newspaper holdings, search policy, and fees.

Where you cannot be specific about the date and place of an event, a newspaper search may become more difficult and more expensive. It is unlikely that library staff will undertake the search. If you have determined that a local paper did exist for the time and place of interest, a local agent can be engaged. Be sure to set limits as to issues searched, perhaps by requesting that the agent work for a set period of time and report. Try to select an event for which you know the date to within a week or two, whether it be personal or some important local happening. Where you are short of specific dates, consider asking library staff whether vertical files (or clipping files) are available. Local figures of repute will probably be represented in such a collection. In this case, it may help to give a little more than just a name; the person's occupation or place of residence, for example, may be the keyword for the filing system. Gibson's guide, referred to earlier in this section, gives some information on newspaper indexes. It would also be worthwhile checking with the library and the area family history society for any other local unpublished indexes which may relate to your search.

Periodicals

Three very informative periodicals appear in bound volumes in North American libraries with some regularity; if there is a large library near you, be sure to investigate. These are the *Gentleman's Magazine*, the *Illustrated London News*, and the *Annual Register*. They all contain listings of births, marriages, and deaths (though usually of the higher classes), and informative accounts of current events. The FHL has indexes to the *Gentleman's Magazine* on microfilm and microfiche. For any significant figure in your family tree, or where an ancestor took part in important events, and even when you simply want additional information about a particular point in time, all three of these can be invaluable. The *Annual Register* includes dispatches from theaters of war, a section on significant court cases, and another called "The Chronicle." The latter is fascinating. It is a random selection of interesting news items from all over the country, one for almost every day of the year. Find any one of these publications and you are likely to wander, quite happily, off topic. *The Gentleman's Magazine* and the *Annual Register* both began publication before the middle of the eighteenth century, while the *Illustrated London News* first appeared in 1842.

It is possible to search a vast range of periodicals, published since 1845, for articles (more than 1 million) of general historic or genealogical information. The *Periodical Source Index* (*PERSI*) for many years has been an ongoing project of the Allen County Public Library in Fort Wayne, Indiana. First available in printed form and on microfiche, it is now accessible on the Internet (http://www.ancestry.com) and can be purchased on CD-ROM from Ancestry (searching is easier in these forms). The microfiche format can usually be found in LDS family history centers. Articles in journals of history and genealogy will touch on more specific topics—perhaps a place or family of importance to your research—and provide new insights on the use of records.

Note
1. Harvey, 1992.

Locating Lists
(poll books, electoral rolls, rate books, directories)

1. Identify the dates and area of the search.

2. Select the most relevant of these sources.

3. Check the holdings of local libraries and the nearest family history center, including the *FHLC* for anything that can be brought in on loan.

4. Check the appropriate finding aids about survival and location of collections in England; and, for directories, consider the option of purchasing printed or microfiche reprints.

5. When required, ask the County Record Office or library about fees and services.

Newspapers and Periodicals

1. Using finding aids, determine which newspapers existed in the time period and area of interest.

2. How and where can these be accessed?

3. Do local repositories have clipping files?

4. Consult *PERSI* for articles about families, places, and/or resources.

Designed to support the English woolen industry, acts of Parliament in 1666 and 1678 decreed that all bodies, except of those dying of the plague, had to be wrapped in a shroud made of wool. The requirement remained in place, though over time it was increasingly ignored, until repealed in 1814. Registers, or accounts, may record the sworn affidavit confirming use of a woolen shroud, or fees paid for non-compliance.

In 1783 a tax of three pence was charged against each entry made in a parish register. This may have reduced the number of events recorded because there was no penalty if nothing was written. There was another way to avoid payment: paupers receiving parish relief did not have to comply, and people in some parishes took advantage of this potential loophole. In other words, your noted pauper ancestor of the 1780s may not have been on relief at all. The tax remained in force until 1794. Look for adult baptism or multiple baptisms in a family after that date.

Two pieces of eighteenth-century legislation had a direct impact on parish registers. At that point two things affected church registers. The first was the adoption of the Gregorian calendar, which meant that England fell into step with most of Europe. To do this, 1 January 1752 was declared the start of the year (before that time it had been 25 March), and 2 September of the same year was followed by 14 September. The other change resulted from the passage of Lord Hardwicke's Act in 1753. This legislation, which took effect 25 March 1754, was primarily designed to put an end to hasty and clandestine marriages (see appendix C for a detailed explanation). The act introduced the first standard forms for recording vital statistics. Each parish was required to record marriages in a particular type of register with a set layout. The marriage had to be by banns or license, and the obtaining of a license was made more difficult. Only three forms of marriage were recognized as legal: Anglican, Quaker, and Jewish. There was some incentive to comply with the new law: any child born to a couple not married by one of the recognized forms was regarded as illegitimate, and the assets of any illegitimate person who died without issue reverted to the Crown.

An example of one of these early standardized marriage registers came to light during a search of the records for the London parish of St. Botolph Without Bishopsgate.

> Banns of Marriage Between Matthew Wadsworth and Elizabeth Caley were published on Sunday July 19, 26 and August 2, 1767. The said Matthew Wadsworth of the Parish of St. Botolph Aldgate, London, Bachelor, and Elizabeth Caley of this Parish, Spinster, were Married in this Church by Banns this Ninth Day of August in the Year One Thousand Seven Hundred and sixty seven by me Thomas Dunmor. (*St. Botolph without Bishopsgate Parish Register*, vol. 1.)

The bride, groom, and two witnesses were all able to sign their names. For marriages before Lord Hardwicke's Act there had been no requirement to sign (or "mark") anything.

When researching the hundred years or so before civil registration, keep in mind that England was experiencing dramatic change resulting from industrialization and rapid growth in population. The Church of England did not create new parishes whenever and wherever they were needed. In many cases chapelries served the needs of new clusters of population. These were not always licensed to perform marriages, so your ancestors may have been required to travel a fair distance to get married at the parish church. In other cases the records of a chapelry may have been incorporated into the parish register. In the countryside the total number of parishes remained remarkably stable from the late thirteenth century to the 1830s. From time to time, a small parish became a chapel of ease of a larger neighbor, or a section of a large parish became a parish in its own right. In the towns, particularly once industrialization began, there was considerably more change. A large number of churches were constructed in the first half of the nineteenth century. When beginning research in a parish check the date of earliest entry in the registers, noting whether the church was always a parish church and the abutting parishes, especially if linked at any time as a parent parish or dependent chapel.

Rose's Act came into force in 1813. It standardized baptismal and burial registers. From this point on you can be fairly certain that all registers will reveal standard information. Separate volumes now had to be maintained for baptism and burial. Baptism entries were required to indicate date of baptism, name of the child, names of both parents, their address, and the father's occupation. Burial entries included the date of burial and the name, age, and address of the deceased. However, for all the record keeping that was improved by this measure, there was a downside. The printed books tended to curtail the longer entries of some ministers (mainly those who had treated their registers more like a parish diary).

With the introduction of civil registration in 1837, the restrictive terms regarding legal marriages set down in 1754 no longer applied. Marriage in the Church of England by banns continued, but people could marry in any church and in a registry office, upon the purchase of a license from the local registrar. Marriages in nonconforming chapels and churches retained one additional requirement until 1898: the local registrar had to be in attendance.

This short outline of church history is centered around factors affecting the registers of baptism, marriage, and burial. The parish was also a unit of local government, and church officers in a sense served double duty as civil officials for social welfare and many aspects of administration. The parish became the basic unit of local welfare in the sixteenth century. It recorded much on local affairs and reported annually to the bishop on these matters (more on this in chapters 9 and 10).

The point here is the value in building an understanding of church organization and the relationship with local courts and other civil authorities. The Church of England was organized hierarchically. England and Wales were divided into two provinces, York and Canterbury, with an archbishop at the head of each (see figure 7-1). The Province of Canterbury and its archbishop took precedence over York. At the next level were the dioceses, each headed by a bishop, then archdeaconries, rural deaneries, and parishes (some of which were extra-parochial, outside the local authority—the *peculiars* already referred to). Locating different types of parish records and some probate records will be assisted by your understanding and knowledge of jurisdictions and authorities.

Research Strategy

To ensure success in any search for church records, be sure you include these preliminary elements: background reading about the records so you know something of history, organization, and content; map and gazetteer work so you are aware of parish and diocesan boundaries; and thorough research into the location, availability, and completeness of the records. There is no doubt that considerable success in a parish register search can frequently be achieved without all this work, but sooner or later you will reach an impasse. If you haven't already done this review, you will have to do it then. Never give up without being absolutely sure there is nothing more to be done.

Further Insights

Those of an inquiring disposition will want to know more. Among books already cited, useful details about organization and the registers in general can be found in *Discovering Parish*

Boundaries (Winchester, 1990) and *Tracing Your Family Tree* (Cole and Titford, 1997). *A Companion to the English Parish Church* (Friar, 1996) is a reference work which provides definitions and essays on officials, architecture, traditions, legislation, etc. Parish registers reflect the character of the incumbent minister. Some contain brief, hardly helpful entries (e.g., some baptismal records do not name the child), while others go on at length about the weather, local celebrations of great naval victories, and the foundling left on the church doorstep. Wonderful examples of the wide range of styles exhibited by local vicars are recorded in *The Parish Registers of England* by Charles Cox (rep. 1974). Remember that the pages of family history society journals and local and parish histories can also be sources of interesting and practical information.

Maps and Gazetteers

As soon as a new place-name emerges (perhaps from a census or a will), look for it on maps and in a gazetteer. Use contemporary and modern maps—what was the area like more than a hundred years ago, and is the place, and its church, there today? Note the lay of the land, railways, roads, and canals, and any boundaries, For the latter it is best to consult the *Atlas and Index of Parish Registers* (Humphery-Smith, 1995) because the maps show parish, archdeaconry, and diocesan boundaries within each county. Gazetteers will give locations, a little history, and descriptions, including churches and burial grounds. *A Topographical Dictionary of England* (Lewis 1831, rep. 1996) is readily available. More compact and equally useful is *A Genealogical Gazetteer of England* (Smith, 1968, rep. 1995), which extracts all place-names from *Lewis' Dictionary* and provides population and ecclesiastical jurisdiction just before major changes by the Church of England. Any of these resources will help you determine whether you have the correct parish name. Also take time to list abutting parishes even if they are across a county line. A series of booklets, *Contiguous Parishes* (Allen and Thompson, 1997-) makes this task unnecessary for most of the counties of England and Wales (see Bibliography).

Availability of Records

To be sure you know what registers survive for any given parish and where they are located, several resources must be checked. Where access to a family history center of the LDS church is possible, check there first. It will probably be impossible to resist the temptation to look at the International Genealogical Index (IGI) right away. However, do be sure at some point to check the *Family History Library Catalog* (*FHLC*) locality section, under ENGLAND, COUNTY, PARISH NAME—CHURCH RECORDS, and take a look at the Parish and Vital Records List. The catalog lists all parish registers and/or bishops' transcripts held in the Family History Library (FHL) and indicates, by an *X* off to the right, which of these have been incorporated into the IGI. The Parish and Vital Records List is a set of fiche which accompanies the IGI. It lists parish and other vital records that have been extracted, or are in the process of being extracted, for inclusion in the IGI. So from either source you can determine whether a parish is in the IGI and whether the baptisms and marriages were taken from actual registers or bishops' transcripts. In addition, you learn what part has been indexed and about any significant gaps in the records.

The LDS resources are only part of the picture. What has been filmed and/or included in the IGI may not be all parish registers of baptism, marriage, and burial that can be consulted. You require a complete picture of surviving registers and bishops' transcripts, along with format, location, and access. By now you will have looked at the maps in the *Atlas and Index of Parish Registers* (Humphery-Smith, 1995). The second part of the book can help you determine the range of surviving resources for individual parishes. It lists all the parishes of England within each county in alphabetical order. There are columns to indicate whether the registers have been deposited with the County Record Office; the parish is in the IGI; copies are in the Society of Genealogists collection; there is some coverage in *Boyd's Marriage Index* (discussed later in this chapter) or the Phillimore collection of marriages; the parish can be found in Pallot's Index; and whether there are nonconformist records at the Public Record Office (PRO). For each of these items, only the extreme outside years appear; for example, if there is one baptism in 1587 and no more entries until 1625, the start date will show as 1587.

To focus more closely on surviving records, take the following steps.

1. Contact the COUNTY RECORD OFFICE—most publish at least a list of parishes in the collection, usually with outside dates for records of each type of event for every parish.

2. Look up the parish in *Parish Register Copies in the Library of the Society of Genealogists* (1995) for more precise details of baptisms, marriages, and burials. It is sometimes possible to find a copy was deposited here, based upon a transcription made prior to a register being destroyed by fire.

3. Look up the parish in the appropriate volume of the *National Index of Parish Registers* (Steel and others, 1976ff), a continuing project listing registers and their locations.

4. Check the county resources listed on the Internet and the home page of the COUNTY RECORD OFFICE for recently released finding aids and details of collections.

5. Check for surviving bishops' transcripts in *Bishops' Transcripts, Marriage Licenses, Bonds and Allegations: A Guide to Their Location and Indexes* (Gibson, 1997).

Some Church of England registers remain in the care of the incumbent minister of the local church. The Parochial Registers and Records Measure, which came into effect 1 January 1979, directed that all records be deposited with the diocesan record office (usually the County Record Office) unless certain standards of storage were met. A few local parishes chose to keep their records. Where you must write to the incumbent minister, his address can be found in the current edition of *Crockford's Clerical Directory*, which should be available in any large public library. The Church of England stipulates the fees which ministers should charge for a search in the registers. When writing, be sure to include return postage and to inquire as to the current charges.

The International Genealogical Index

A complete description of the arrangement and content of the IGI appears in appendix B. This discussion centers around strategies for using it effectively.

How you use this tool and to what effect will depend in part on the information you start with. How common is the name? What county or counties are involved in the search? Is it known how long the family was in the area? What is the overall extent of the registers or bishops' transcripts available?

The IGI on CD-ROM allows searches of the entire country for one name. The search will, in fact, cover all the British Isles unless you instruct the computer to filter out Scotland, Ireland, and Wales. Where information is specific, this is not necessary as the search is quick. (Filtering can take several minutes, but it is worth waiting for when seeking a common name.) The pertinent entries can be marked, placed in a holding file and, at the completion of your session, printed out or downloaded onto a disk.

When you find the marriage of a probable ancestor, you can instruct the computer to locate and display all children born to a couple with the indicated names. This "parent search" saves an immense amount of time, can indicate children born in a neighboring county and thus far unknown to you—and can lead you astray. The search cannot differentiate between more than one couple of the same names having children at about the same time. Take a careful look at the list. Consult the film of the original parish register and be absolutely certain that you have identified your ancestors and their own children. On the other hand, remember that if the name of a parent is different in one entry from that used in your instructions, it will not be found. This search will also work when you locate the baptism of a probable ancestor. All the possible siblings of this individual will be displayed as the children of his parents, or couples with the same names. Once again, sort them out, and consider if something may have been missed.

Reference has been made to filtering, or specifying the geographic area from which listings should be displayed. It is also possible to filter dates, to specify an exact spelling, or, for example, to instruct the computer to find only those Thomas Baxters who married someone whose first name was Sarah.

The computer asks you to search for a baptism or a marriage. It does not show listings of these two events together, but it is an easy matter to click a couple of commands and switch from one type of search to the other.

The IGI continues to be available on microfiche, and there is no reason to abandon this format in favor of the CD-ROM—sometimes all the computer terminals in the family history center will be busy, and sometimes you may want to concentrate on the listing for one county only, with baptisms and marriages mixed in together. In certain circumstances it can prove faster to work with these mixed and county-sorted listings, and there may be an advantage to making copies of the frames or pages and taking them away to study. If the surname is extremely common in the county, the fiche search loses its attraction and it is better to use the filter commands and the computer holding file to create a limited list.

Your research in the IGI in whatever form may produce what seems to be the exact entry, or several possibilities, or nothing at all. For every instance, verify that the IGI incorporates the time period and the region that define the search. Bear in mind that no linkages are made—you must find proof that baptism and marriage entries for the same name more that sixteen years apart indeed relate to the same individual. Then begin to plan your next move. Where an entry has appeared, order the microfilm of the register. If there are several choices, are they all in one parish? If so, order the film or films. If not, and even if they are, consider what other records might help you select the correct individual. It may be that you need to go to a census, or something which reveals occupation, or follow more than one of these people forward in time to see what became of them. Where you have nothing to show for your IGI work, investigate the extent of gaps in what has been indexed. Some part of the records may have been filmed for the FHL but not indexed; some may not have been filmed at all. If the records for the relevant time and place have been included in the IGI, consider adjusting your parameters, trying alternate records, or building the search around a sibling.

The Registers

Parish registers become the prime source for research before 1837, once it becomes impossible to use the records of civil registration and census returns. The content of printed register books, marriages from 1754 and baptisms and burials from 1813, has already been discussed (see pages 85–86). Before those dates there was no set form for what went into register entries. The requirement for parchment, made in 1598, was a significant cost to poorer parishes. They might have made do with small books of poor quality. Many parishes put all the listings together in one volume—the baptisms at the front, marriages somewhere in the middle, and burials toward the back. If space ran out for one section, more would be listed further on. Sometimes all entries of whatever type appear mixed together in date order. Take time to scan the film of a register to be sure you do not miss a section.

What the local minister or parish clerk entered in his blank book was entirely up to him. For baptisms you will usually find the name of the child, the names of his parents—but not the maiden name of the mother—and the date. There might occasionally be additional information, such as the father's occupation. For marriages you will find the full names of bride and groom, whether or not of the parish, if by banns or license, and the date. The statement that both were "of the parish" does not necessarily indicate any more than three weeks' residency (bride and groom's residing in the same parish saved having banns read in two places and hence two fees). (The term *sojourner* will apply to someone in the parish for this residency requirement.) In burial entries there was a range from the essential details of name, age, and date to comments about the cause of death or the character of the deceased. Notes almost always appear for vagrants and for epidemics (such as the plague).

Some of you researching in the north of England will come across the wonderful additional details found in Dade registers (named after the designer, Rev. William Dade). These appeared in Yorkshire and some neighboring areas between 1770 and 1812. Baptism listings included the father's occupation, place of abode, and the descent (i.e., parents) of the father and mother. In burial registers, similar extra details about occupation, dwelling place, and parentage were also included. The marriage records were left as established by Hardwicke's Act of 1754.

Other Resources

Sooner or later you will come up against an entire parish or a period of years for a parish which is not included in the IGI. In this case, all that work to determine what survives, and where, will pay off. You will know immediately where else to look for the registers or whether to seek alternate sources because the records are missing. If it is a matter of a different repository, you can then make a choice as to whether to hire someone to search the registers or to do some work yourself initially using resource aids. There are many possibilities should you choose the latter course.

Additional Indexes. If you belong to the local family history society in England you will know from their journals whether or not they operate a marriage index. The majority of these indexes cover the period between 1800 and the beginning of civil registration in 1837. There is usually a small fee for the search. A positive result here can save much work. There is, once again, a Gibson publication, *Marriage, Census and Other Indexes for Family Historians* (1996), which will guide you to marriage indexes for every county.

Marriage Licenses, Bonds, and Allegations. There is another alternative when a marriage record proves elusive. There may be existing records of marriage licenses, bonds, and allegations. When a couple was to be married by license rather than by the reading of banns, bonds and allegations were drawn up. Application for the license would be made to the bishop of the diocese in which both parties lived. However, if two dioceses were involved, the couple went to the vicar-general of the archbishop of either York or Canterbury, and if two provinces were involved, to the Faculty Office of the Archbishop of Canterbury. Usually the groom and his supporter signed a statement to the effect that there were no legal impediments to the marriage. The bond obligated them to pay a significant sum should any statements in the allegation prove to be false. These records contain such details as name, age, residence, occupation, and condition (e.g., bachelor, widow), and the location of the marriage. The FHL has a good selection on microfilm. These will be found listed in the *FHLC* locality section under ENGLAND—CHURCH RECORDS or ENGLAND, COUNTY NAME—CHURCH RECORDS. There is a finding aid, *Bishops' Transcripts and Marriage Licenses, Bonds and Allegations: A Guide to Their Location and Indexes* (Gibson, 1997).

Boyd's Marriage Index. Yet another important aid to locating marriages is *Boyd's Marriage Index*, compiled over a number of years by Percival Boyd and his assistants. The original is held by the Society of Genealogists, but there is a copy in the FHL, and it may turn up, in whole or in part, in family history centers on microfiche. Only English parishes are included, between 1538 and 1837. The index has approximately 7 million entries from over four thousand parishes; however, no county is completely covered. The Society of Genealogists has printed a county-by-county list of the represented parishes, with dates, entitled *A List of Parishes in Boyd's Marriage Index* (1987).

Additional Publications. Other possible shortcuts in a parish register search are Pallot's Index, the Phillimore transcripts, and the publications of various societies. The first is held by the Institute of Heraldic and Genealogical Studies. It is mainly an index to marriages in London parishes, 1780 to 1837. The parishes in this index appear in one of the columns in the *Atlas and Index of Parish Registers* (Humphery-Smith, 1995). You can purchase a list from the institute as well; there is a search fee. Phillimore, the local history publishers, printed marriage registers for many counties earlier in the twentieth century. Societies and dedicated local historians have completed similar projects of indexing or transcription. Many of them have been acquired and filmed for the FHL; others remain in English libraries and record offices. Careful study of the *FHLC* listings, county bibliographies, and inquiries to societies and archives in England will inform you of alternatives to filmed original registers. Bear in mind that transcripts may contain less than complete information from the registers, and that the act of copying was another step which might have introduced an error.

Burial Records. Records of burials also appear in transcripts of monumental inscriptions. What was inscribed on the stone may differ from the register entry, and may include references to other family members, buried elsewhere. The FHL has some lists; others are in printed local or parish histories. Many county societies have recorded the essential details of inscriptions from all burial grounds. Check with the appropriate society or the Federation of Family History Societies. A large collection is in the library of the Society of Genealogists; check the two-part guide, *Monumental Inscriptions in the Library of the Society of Genealogists* (1987).

As the nineteenth century advanced, churchyards in crowded cities closed down and municipal cemeteries opened in the suburbs. Some registers have been transferred to record offices and libraries, but many remain at the cemetery office or with the local authority. Directories and gazetteers will indicate when these burial grounds were established. For Greater London there is a guide which includes information on location, years of operation, and access to the records: *Greater London Cemeteries and Crematoria* (Wolfston and Webb, 1997).

Dissenting Churches

There is a long history of congregations of differing faiths existing either secretly or openly. In the early days of the Reformation they fell generally within the category of Protestant, but many more denominations came and went under a variety of names. You will see a number of words used to describe those outside the Established Church of England—dissenters, nonconformists, and recusants being the most common. A recusant was anyone who refused to attend the services of the Church of England, but it came to apply mostly to Roman Catholics.

Religious nonconformity was regarded as a serious matter; at times in history anyone who worshiped in a different way was seen as a potential traitor. Elizabeth I passed an Act of Uniformity in 1559 which provided for fines every time a person failed to attend Sunday service. Despite persecution and the emigration of many Puritans and other dissenters to the Continent and America, adherents to nonconformity grew in number, eventually achieving supremacy under Oliver Cromwell from 1653 to 1660.

The restoration of Charles II was soon followed by legislation against dissent. Another Act of Uniformity in 1662 required all ministers to conform. Further legislation of the 1660s made it an offense to attend a service held by any nonconforming minister and forbade such a minister to come within five miles of a town (The Five Mile Act). Only those who took the sacrament of the Established Church could hold office. (It was easier for those holding different beliefs to avoid attention in a town or city.) If you come across an adult baptism it may be that someone who had fallen on hard times was forced to conform in order to receive parish relief.

Toleration arrived initially with William III and Mary (1689). Dissenting meeting houses could be licensed, burial grounds could be established, and, from 1791, Catholics could worship openly. The last barriers to a seat in Parliament and other public offices were removed in 1829. The start of civil registration in 1837 was a response in part to concerns that church registers had ceased to be a reliable basis for estimating the population, and to pressure from nonconformists for freedom to marry in their own way.

In the seventeenth century the Protestant nonconformists fell mostly into three groups: Independents, Baptists, and Presbyterians. They were all opposed to the rule of the church by bishops, but differed from one another on such matters as infant or adult baptism. The Independents later came to be known as Congregationalists. Registers from these denominations begin in the seventeenth century. Methodism was begun by John and Charles Wesley as a reform movement within the Church of England. It eventually split into several groups such as the Wesleyan Methodists and Bible Christians. Methodist registers survive from about 1780.

Location of Records

Most nonconformist registers up to the commencement of civil registration in 1837 were transferred to the Registrar General for safekeeping. These are now in the possession of the PRO. Microfilmed copies are available at the Family Records Centre and through LDS family history centers. The baptism and marriage entries from those registers which were authenticated by the PRO in the 1830s to 1850s are in class Registrar General (RG) 4. They have been indexed and included in the IGI. There are three ways to check what can be readily accessed. Look in the locality section of the *FHLC* under the appropriate parish name, or in the Parish and Vital Records List. The *Atlas and Index of Parish Registers* (Humphery-Smith, 1995) shows which parishes have nonconformist registers in the PRO.

A number of these records are in the PRO but are not indexed, and some are not in the PRO. The unindexed records include more than 300 volumes in RG8 and more than 1,600 volumes of Quaker records. The library at Friends' House in London holds copies of the latter, and the List and Index Society has produced a catalog. Registers not in the PRO have emerged (some ministers kept registers in their private papers) and have been deposited in local libraries and record offices. If a check of reference books reveals a dissenting chapel but no collection of registers in the PRO, write to the local repository. For many small, short-lived congregations, no registers survive (but it is better to check first before coming to this conclusion).

Beginning in 1742, Presbyterians, Independents, and Baptists cooperated in the launch of a register of births, with entries signed by witnesses. Not many chose to use this registry in the early years (a fee was charged), but between 1770 and 1843 nearly fifth thousand births were recorded. This is Dr. William's Registry; it includes mainly the better off and a large number of Londoners. The register was handed over to the PRO and included in RG4, so it is part of the indexed material.

Records of Roman Catholic churches tend to be retained in local custody. Because of persecution, few Catholic registers are available from before the Catholic relief acts of the late eighteenth century. The Catholic Record Society has published many records, including parish registers and the very useful *Returns of Papists, 1767* (Worrall 1980 and 1989) in two volumes. Roman Catholics were regarded as a possible threat to the security of the country, and on several occasions between 1660 and 1791 something like a national census of Catholics was attempted. That of 1767 is particularly detailed. Vol. 3 of *The National Index of Parish Registers* (Steel, 1984) discusses Roman Catholic and Jewish records in detail.

New Resources

In 1999 it became possible to access the IGI via the World Wide Web, and to purchase a set of five CDs entitled *British Vital Records Index.*[1] Searching for birth and marriage records now has some added options—and you can work at home at any itme of the day or night. Whether using the on-line version of the IGI (see web sites, page 219) or the computer or fiche format in a family history center, the same principles and cautions apply, as described in this chapter and in Appendix B. The set of CDs contains about five million records from a variety of sources, and from other parts of the British Isles, as well as England. As with the IGI, it is an index. Be sure to follow any likely entries through to the original records.

Conclusion

The parish registers of the Church of England and the records of nonconformist churches are the primary resource for research from the sixteenth to the nineteenth centuries. The amount of material is vast, their existence is inconsistent, location and access anywhere from easy to difficult. Make no assumptions about the thoroughness of your research and its results without knowing all about the records. Be prepared for surprises, disappointments, and roadblocks: people in the wrong county; strange spellings of a surname; discovering a Congregational family; illegitimacy; no copies of registers in the FHL; gaps in the records. It is all easier to deal with if you have done your homework.

Notes

1. *Vital Records Index British Isles.* Salt Lake City: The Church of Jesus Christ of Latter-day Saints, 1998. The information in this CD is taken from a partial collection of records dating from 1538 to 1888. It is not possible to access a list of the sources on which it is based. Details given for each event are some or all of: surname, given name, mother, father, spouse, event type, place.

Researching
Church of England Registers
and Nonconformist Records

1. Select the name(s), place or region, date or time span to be searched; note how common the name is and possible spelling variations.

2. Identify the parish or parishes to be searched; note continuous parishes within and without the county; note the archdeaconry and diocese; read about the area to learn of any dissenting congregations.

3. Assess the extent of the collection of the FHL using the locality section of the *FHLC* and the Parish and Vital Records List.

4. Compare this to information on all surviving registers, transcripts, and extracts taken from the *Atlas and Index of Parish Registers*, County Record Office guides, PRO publications, and other reference books.

5. Check for all finding aids, such as Boyd's and Pallot's indexes, and any others generated in the locality; consult *Marriage and Census Indexes for Family Historians*.

6. If access is not possible through LDS family history centers, ensure you have all possible information to direct the research of an agent.

6 ❦ WILLS SINCE 1858

ills are generally recognized as a valuable genealogical source, but they are all too often ignored by researchers. To some, accessibility seems an insurmountable problem, while others hold no hope that their ancestors ever made wills. As with most things, the truth lies somewhere in between. There is no doubt that only a small percentage of the population left wills, but that number grew steadily over the nineteenth century, and no hard and fast rules can be applied to define who prepared wills. It is always worthwhile to check.

Contents of Wills

The potential genealogical value of wills is significant. In fact, the information they can provide ranges from "nothing new" to something akin to winning a lottery. Wills frequently refer to numerous family members, giving relationships. They also can provide interesting descriptions of real estate and personal property, current addresses of beneficiaries, information on collateral branches of a family, and fascinating insight into personality. There was considerable upward and downward social mobility in England, and wills can reveal the rising and falling fortunes of one's ancestors and their relations. Sometimes, too, wills uncover the existence of previously unknown branches and provide the locations of family members who emigrated.

Drawing Up a Will

The customary procedure was for the testator to write out the will or to have it drawn up by a solicitor. The will would name the executor(s) to carry out the instructions contained in it. This responsibility was usually given to close relatives, and often the principal beneficiary. A beneficiary could not witness a will; this was customarily done by servants, neighbors, or the solicitor and his clerk. Occasionally the testator made an amendment to the will, called a *codicil*, which also had to be witnessed. Codicils are always part of the document. After the testator's death an executor took the will to the district probate registry or to Somerset House. Up until 1926 each district office held jurisdiction over a defined area, but after that date an executor could take a will to any one of the offices. The office would issue a grant of probate. The date probate was granted, together with the date of death, would be noted on the will. Each will had three copies: one for the district office, one for Somerset House, and one for the executors.

Letters of administration (*admons*) were granted when named executors had died or refused to act, or where there was no will but there was reason for a legal record (e.g., because the estate was of some value or because property was involved). The nearest relative made application to a probate registry. Strict rules laid down how the property of someone who died intestate should be allocated. These rules changed from time to time, but in general terms the order of consideration was spouse, children, parents, siblings, nephews and nieces, grandparents, uncles and aunts, and first cousins. Where no next of kin could be located the estate reverted to the Crown. For more specific information on the formula, consult *Whitaker's Almanac* for the appropriate year. Information given in the letters of administration was full name of deceased, address, occupation (or marital status for women), date and place of death, name/address/occupation of administrator with his/her relationship to the deceased, the gross value of the estate, and the value after death duties.

The year 1858 is significant because at that time responsibility for the granting of probate passed from the Church of England to a central civil authority. When the jurisdictional switch was made, more than three hundred ecclesiastical courts gave up their probate function to the Principal Probate Registry in London or to one of the district probate registries throughout England and Wales. Somerset House was for many years the home of the Principal Probate Registry of the Family Division. In June of 1998 it is moving to First Avenue House, 42–48 High Holborn.

Research Strategy

Gathering Preliminary Information

Before going ahead with the search for a will you must gather some basic information. To gauge the probability of finding a record, list the facts about the family and consider them in the context of what is known about probate in general. Members of the laboring classes (perhaps 95 percent of the population) did not generally leave wills. Prior to the Married Women's Property

than hiring an agent). Another is to save the work for a trip to the FHL or to hire an agent there. The search can also be done in London at The Principal Registry of the Family Division, First Avenue House, or, alternatively, using microfiche at the Library of the Society of Genealogists.

Obtaining the Will

Two microfilm collections of probate at the FHL are listed consecutively in the microfiche version of the locality section of the *Family History Library Catalog* (*FHLC*) under ENGLAND—PROBATE RECORDS. The first is the copies of wills from 1858 to 1925. The preamble will tell you, and the list of films will indicate, that the records are arranged by year and then by month. Men's wills generally precede women's, and both are partially sorted by the first letter of the last name. Having found a listing first in the calendars, you will know the year and month and be able to select the correct film.

The other collection is that of copies of wills from the District Probate Registries, 1858 to 1899. Any will probated at a district office in the first forty years will be included. These records are sorted by year, then by month, and then by court. The names associated with each particular court are grouped by first letter of the last name. Once again, the calendars will provide the details needed to select the correct film.

The alternatives to doing a microfilm search in a family history center are to get the help of an agent in Salt Lake City or London, or to make a direct postal application to the office in York (the address is in appendix D). For this it is necessary to provide the details or to specify a three-year period for the search. There are fees for copies or to examine the wills at the London office.

Death Duty Registers

After 1796 a legacy duty was payable. The amount varied from time to time, but certainly after 1815 a significant proportion of legacies were affected. In 1853 the Succession Duty was expanded even further to include the inheritance of land. The Death Duty Registers exist from the introduction of the legacy tax until 1903. The registers give the name of the deceased, the date of death, the date of the will, the place and date of probate, the name and address of the executors, and the beneficiaries and their relationship to the testator (this influenced the amount of duty payable). This information may not only supplement what is in the probate index and the will, but may reveal some differences between what the testator wished and what actually resulted. If the testator died intestate, the Death Duty Registers will certainly provide more information than the grant of administration.

The Death Duty Registers are held by the Public Record Office (PRO) in class numbers Inland Revenue (IR) 26 and IR 27. For the years from 1858 to 1903 they are not available at the FHL. The PRO has split the collection. Indexes can be consulted at the Family Records Centre in London or at the PRO, Kew. Copies of the Registers for 1796 to 1857 are available at the Family Records Centre (more about them in chapter 7) and for the later period at Kew, but you must give five days' notice as the Registers are stored off-site. These more modern registers are less accessible because there are national probate records for the same years. They may be more difficult to get at but are worth considering because of the potentially interesting and sometimes different information. A detailed description of how to search for a Death Duty Register at the Family Records Centre is in *Never Been Here Before?* (Cox and Colwell, 1997).

Further Suggestions

When researching wills, think in terms of a broad landscape. Not only are the probate records of the direct line valuable, those of collateral relations and even unrelated people can add to your knowledge. The wills of unmarried sisters, or married sisters with no children of their own, are a prime source of detail about a family—they were inclined to keep track of the strands of a family and remember them at death. An ancestor of yours may have witnessed a probate, or been owed a debt and thereby gained mention in a will where neither blood nor marital relationship existed.

A testator seldom mentions parents because a will is about the next generation. This fact renders the will an essential document for anyone seeking living relatives—in fact, for any twentieth-century research. The reasons are clear: probate records are always public; there are no post-1900 census returns open for scrutiny; and many more people are making wills. Cross-checking the results of a vital records search with probate records is an essential strategy for recent research.

For research after 1858, probate records should be part of any research strategy. When you locate a death, search for the probate record. If a death is proving elusive, consider the probate indexes as a quicker means to searching more years. Expand the search to collateral relations to build a more complete picture of the family and how they interacted with one another. With an unusual name, collecting wills even for those you do not consider to be family is a sound tactic; surprising results do emerge. For further information on using wills in your research consult *Wills, Probate and Death Duty Registers* (Cox, 1993).

Obtaining a Will: 1858 to the Present

1. Gather all helpful particulars—name, date of death, place, occupation; where the name is common and other details vague or unknown, consider other sources first which may provide additional facts.

2. If a general survey search is planned, set parameters of name (with spelling variations), years, and geographic area.

3. At a family history center, consult the Locality section of the FHLC under ENGLAND—PROBATE RECORDS—INDEXES; from the list of probate calendars 1858 to 1957, note the films which match your name and dates. Decide whether to order these films (make sure they have not come into the center already) or to get assistance.

4. If you are quite certain, to within three years, that a probate was granted, and you know the name and place, you can apply directly to England to the York Sub-Registry. A fee applies.

5. Once the details from the calendar entry have been found, and if the date is prior to 1925, you can make an application for a film of the probate. Look under ENGLAND—PROBATE RECORDS.

6. If the search has not been successful, consider possible sources of error and search for other family members; if certain a record should exist, obtain the death record and then try applying to the local registry office (get the address from the Principal Probate Registry in London). Human errors happen, and the central registry may not have received its copy.

7 ⚜ WILLS BEFORE 1858

efore 1858, jurisdiction over matters of probate rested with the ecclesiastical courts. The preamble to those early wills serves to reflect the significant place of religion in the lives of our ancestors.

In the name of God Amen I Martha Bayley widow of Brook Street in the Parish of South Weald in the County of Essex being in perfect mind and memory thanks be to God do make and ordain this my last Will and Testament in manner and form following that is to say first I give my Soul into the hands of Almighty God and I commend my Body to the earth to be decently buried in Christian Burial at the discretion of my hereafter named Executors not doubting but through the Merits of Jesus Christ to enjoy a happy resurrection…(The will of Martha Bayley proved 9 February 1778. Public Record Office, Probate 11/1039.)

It was clearly a matter of duty to God to respect someone's last wishes, so wills came within the purview of the church courts.

Unfortunately for genealogists, this ecclesiastical system was complicated, involving more than three hundred courts. To do research, you must determine boundaries for these and identify the appropriate authority. At the first or lowest level of authority, a will was to be proved in the court of the archdeaconry in which the testator resided. If the testator held property in two or more archdeaconries to the value of five pounds or more, the will had to be proved in the bishop's (diocesan or consistory) court. In a large diocese the powers of the consistory court may have been delegated to commissary courts acting in different archdeaconries. If the testator held property in two or more dioceses, jurisdiction passed to the prerogative courts of either York

TABLE 7-1

Guidelines for Selection of Appropriate Ecclesiastical Court

Property in one archdeaconry	Archdeacon's court
Property in more than one archdeaconry but one diocese	Bishop's court
Property in more than one diocese but one province	Archbishop's court (Prerogative Court of Canterbury or York)
Property in more than one province	Prerogative Court of Canterbury

or Canterbury. For those holding property in both provinces, or in Ireland or abroad, and for those who died abroad or at sea, the Prerogative Court of Canterbury (PCC) took precedence. Table 7-1 outlines these divisions in property. There is no need to guess which courts applied to the area of your search; the sources described on page 121 include information about all the courts which functioned in a county.

Searching for a will would not be so difficult if everyone had followed these guidelines. However, people failed to follow them for a variety of reasons. Pretension, a desire for privacy, or the executor's residing elsewhere were three common explanations. Another reason was bishop's visitations. Usually a bishop did the rounds of the archdeaconries in his diocese every three years. During a visitation, the lower court was inhibited from acting for three to six months. During that time the work of the lower court would be transferred to the bishop's court. Complications also arise where a parish was exempt from the jurisdiction of the archdeacon or the bishop. Attention has already been drawn to these peculiar parishes in chapter 5. The authority over one or more peculiar parishes may have been granted to the dean of the diocese, another ecclesiastical authority, a college, a manor, etc. This can mean that the probate records are deposited with an archives some distance away. Once again, the various guides to probate records will provide the necessary information.

Process of Granting Probate

The steps involved in the granting of probate before 1858 were much the same as those outlined in the previous chapter. They are summarized in Figure 7-2. A will could be made by a male over the age of fourteen and a female over the age of twelve, subject to the restrictions of 1540, which prevented married women from owning property in their own right. In 1837 the age limit was raised to twenty-one for all. Verbal (nuncupative) wills were acceptable. Three witnesses were required and the testator had to have resided at the place of death for ten days or more (unless this was the last wishes of a military man on active service). If the testator wrote the entire document himself it is called a holographic will. If the normal preamble is missing, the deceased may have been a nonconformist.

The process of probate was extended in some cases by a dispute. If this happened the proceedings can be in one of several locations. The County Record Office, as the diocesan repository, may have the church court records. If you are fortunate, some sort of master name index exists. Some "testamentary causes" were heard at the Court of the Arches in London (associated with PCC wills), and others were heard in the Court of Chancery or other equity courts. For additional information read *Prerogative Court of Canterbury Wills and Other Probate Records* (Scott, 1997), *Church Court Records* (Tarver, 1995), and, for an amusing account of the London courts, *Hatred Pursued Beyond the Grave* (Cox, 1993).

National Probate Collections

Our middle- and upper-class forebears were more likely to prepare wills. Hence, they were more likely to find their way into the listings of two national probate collections which fall within this pre-1858 period: wills proved at the PCC and the Death Duty Registers. A third source, the Bank of England Will Extracts, though more limited in scope, may also prove helpful.

Prerogative Court Of Canterbury

As was pointed out, the PCC was the senior ecclesiastical court. More of the grants of probate through this court were from the southern part of the country and from the more prosperous segments of the population. As time went on, due to gradual inflation, increased wealth, and more people making wills, there was an increase in the use of this court. Also, as the nineteenth century advanced some of the lower courts ceased to function. PCC wills are deposited with the Public Record Office (PRO) and can be viewed on microfilm at the Family Records Centre in London or through the library facilities of the LDS church. These wills extend from 1383 to 1857 and they have yearly indexes. Some are printed, copies of some are at the Family History Library (FHL), and there are a number of useful consolidated finding aids.

Death Duty Registers

The Death Duty Registers provide an even better opportunity for finding the will of an ancestor where date and location information is vague or unreliable. These registers were mentioned in chapter 6 because they cover such a long period—from 1796 to 1903. They can be very helpful before 1858, when the only central indexes available cover a small portion of those making wills. For someone who died intestate the Death Duty Registers are particularly helpful because they list all the members of the family of the deceased concerned in the distribution of the estate. Key pieces of information given in these records are the court where the grant was made, the names and addresses of all concerned, and their relationship to the deceased. The complete run of Death Duty Registers and their indexes (in several sections; see page 125) are held by the PRO. The pre-1858 Death Duty Registers are on microfilm at the Family Records Centre; for the years 1812 to 1857 they are on film in the FHL. The indexes can be consulted through LDS family history centers, at the Family

Records Centre, or at Kew. The indexes alone are sufficient to determine the location of the probate court involved.

The death duty was a tax on legacies. It was not always applied in the same way, so the number of wills affected varies. Up to about 1805, the registers cover only about 25 percent of the grants of probate and administration. This percentage rises to significant proportions after 1815 and improves again in 1853, when the tax was expanded to all sorts of succession, including the inheritance of land. The guiding figure for the value of a bequest up to 1853 was twenty pounds, but this was interpreted in different ways, revolving around such factors as whether the bequest went to other than immediate family members, or whether real estate was sold to raise money. After the Succession Duty Act of 1853, duty was payable on the personal and real estate of those estates valued at more than one hundred pounds (a bequest to a spouse remained exempt). What the precise terms were is not particularly important; having some idea as to how many were caught in the net is.

Bank of England Will Extracts

The Bank of England assumed management of the government's funded debt in 1717, and it immediately began keeping records of investments held by individuals in annuities, bonds, and stocks. From 1807 to 1845, the bank maintained an office where clerks copied into registers those passages of wills making reference to Bank of England investments. All wills involving such investments were required to be proved at the PCC after 1812. In 1845 the recording of bequests of stock ceased.

The Bank of England presented its collection of investment registers to the Society of Genealogists in 1985. The society has indexed the registers of will extracts for the years 1807 through 1845: thirty-one thousand entries from all parts of the country and all walks of life. The index is readily available on microfiche, sold by the society for a reasonable cost. There are clear explanatory notes, and the references can be used to determine the correct FHL film number or to find the correct volume in the Library of the Society of Genealogists. The actual extract is made up of passages of the original wills that mention bonds, stocks, or what were termed *consols*—consolidated annuities—a number of government securities brought together in 1751 and generating a steady 3 percent. The extract also contains information about the address of the testator, the name of the executor, and the court where probate was granted. There are sometimes additional details noted in the margin. The extracts from 1717 to 1807 generally have partially sorted indexes in the front of each volume; those for 1726 to 1788 can be found in the LDS collection.

Research Strategy

When planning your search, take time to consider why you have decided to locate the grant of probate. Is the will to be part of a logical progression that has already produced results, or is the search yet another cast for evidence about an elusive family? How you go about the search will be influenced by your objective and the specifics you have in hand. If you know quite a lot about your subject—such as full name, date and place of death, social standing, and occupation—you will be able to discern with some precision which court records apply. Your tactics will be different if you are searching methodically through national or regional records for a particular person, or even all references to a particular surname. In that case the logical approach is to start with the PCC indexes or the Death Duty Registers because of their scope and centralization.

If the facts are vague or nonexistent, you must apply some parameters to the probate search. Select a most likely time period and geographic area. These may have to be adjusted, and they may not fit neatly with the arrangement of indexes or the boundaries for probate (see figure 7-1). Start with the PCC and work your way down through all the courts. The same cautions apply here as for a post-1858 search. Always keep in mind that many factors influenced where and when probate or administration was granted, and that you may have to alter your initial guidelines or look beyond your own direct line. The executors may have taken the will to a higher court to ensure privacy or because they lived some distance from the home of the deceased. Nonconformists were inclined to use the PCC because it was a more secular court and because they could avoid going before the local Church of England clergy. Wills were not always proved soon after death; in fact, probate could be delayed many years. A three-year search beyond the date of death is always advisable. It may also happen that you will be disappointed when the will turns up because your particular family member is not mentioned. This may have occurred because some sort of arrangement had been made before the testator died, or because there was not enough to divide among all the children and those less in need were not left a portion. Whether for this reason or because you simply cannot locate a will for the particular person, remember to search for the will of another family member (particularly an unmarried sister).

These suggestions apply to the ideal situation where the records survive and are accessible. When planning your search, take into account the availability of the records because this may influence the order in which you research the various courts. These pre-1858 probate records are scattered, but much effort has gone into improving their accessibility. There are now finding aids, printed indexes, and an extensive collection in the FHL.

Figure 7-1 The provinces and dioceses of the Church of England, sixteenth to nineteenth centuries.

1. Durham
2. Carlisle
3. Chester
4. York
5. Lincoln (and 16)
6. Lichfield
7. St. Asaph
8. Bangor (3 pts)
9. St. David's
10. Llaudaff
11. Hereford
12. Worcester
13. Gloucester
14. Oxford

15. Peterborough
16. part of Lincoln
17. Ely
18. Norwich
19. London
20. Salisbury
21. Bath & Wells
22. Exeter
23. Bristol (2 pts)
24. Winchester
25. Chichester
26. Rochester
27. Canterbury

It may take a little extra effort, but it is not difficult to determine what survives for a given time, place, and court. Getting at the records is a different problem, influenced by the usual factors of time, films or volumes involved, and who must do the work.

After deciding on the scope of your search, the next task is to discover the courts where the probate could have been presented. Begin by looking for copies of *Probate Jurisdictions: Where to Look for Wills* (Gibson, 1994) and *The Atlas and Index of Parish Registers* (Humphery-Smith, 1995). If neither of these is available refer to the *Genealogical Gazetteer of England* (Smith, 1987), which indicates the archdeaconry and/or diocese for every parish. All these reference works also point out which parishes are extra-parochial (i.e., in a peculiar). Identifying the Church of England jurisdictions generates a list of the courts which operated in the area; you are then ready to check for the availability of surviving records.

Make an effort to check the listings in *Probate Jurisdictions: Where to Look for Wills* (Gibson, 1994). Have the details with you when looking for the probate records listed in the locality section of the *Family History Catalog (FHLC.)* Look under ENGLAND, COUNTY—PROBATE RECORDS. You now know what exists and what can be seen through a family history center. If there is a large reference library nearby, investigate its collection as well.

Let us assume for the moment that you do have fairly specific information about your ancestor and can select a diocesan or archdeaconry court. The FHL in Salt Lake City holds an extensive selection of records on microfilm for these courts in many counties. The collection also includes probate act books. Probate act books can be described as the diaries of the courts, in which the key details of grants of probate or administration were recorded. They can be sufficiently detailed to substitute adequately for the actual will. Whatever the type of probate record, the catalog will reveal the number of films required to cover the years that interest you. Be sure to note any gaps.

The records of the Prerogative Court of York are at the Borthwick Institute, York University. Most archdeaconry and diocesan wills are located at County Record Offices. There are a variety of finding aids and indexes. You will discover this through checking Gibson's guide; otherwise write directly to the County Record Office. Where good indexes exist on location, a search there by an agent could prove to be more efficient. Trial and error will sort this out for you.

If you live some distance away from a family history center you must choose access according to circumstances—such things as the exchange rate for English currency; whether or not you visit Salt Lake City regularly or have an agent there; whether your primary interest is the PCC or the lower courts. The complete collection of PCC indexes is at the Family Records Centre in London; the FHL also has an extensive portion. Both locations have available on microfilm the probate records of the PCC. In fact, London and Salt Lake City offer such extensive pre-1858 probate collections that reference to guides to sources is worthwhile: *Prerogative Court of Canterbury Wills and Other Probate Records* (Scott, 1997); *Will Indexes and Other Probate Records in the Library of the Society of Genealogists* (Newington-Irving, 1996); and *Researching British Probates 1354–1858, Vol. 1, Northern England* (Pratt, 1992).

Helpful Indexes

There are many probate indexes and calendars which are invaluable, particularly for overseas researchers. Some find their way into North American university libraries, and some are in the FHL. It is important that you scout around once the probate courts have been identified. For the most part, the finding aids are arranged by the names of the testators; however, some societies and record offices have initiated projects to bring other names in wills into the light. For example, the Essex Family History Society has created a Wills Beneficiaries Index of those receiving legacies where the surname is different from the testator's. This section discusses several indexes—broadly-based and easily found.

Yearly PCC Indexes. You may fail to find an ancestor among the probate records of the lower courts, or you may come to a search of the PCC wills directly. Indexes to PCC wills up to 1700 have been issued in printed volumes by the British Record Society; these are at the FHL on film or microfiche. Indexes to administrations up to 1664 are at the Family Records Centre, and the remaining thirty-five years, to 1700, are in progress. In the Family History Library on film and fiche you will find volumes for 1581 to 1660. It is useful to remember that during the Commonwealth, 1653 to 1660, there was only the one probate court in London. In other words, for a short time the PCC indexes are complete national indexes. Unfortunately, this had the effect of reducing the number of wills—London was just too far away.

Use of these indexes is not always simple. The early ones refer to names of registrars rather than years (the Family Records Centre has conversion tables). One can also be found in *Prerogative Court of Canterbury Wills and Other Probate Records* (Scott, 1997). The names of these registrar appear in the *FHLC*.

The yearly indexes must be used to search administrations from 1750 to 1800 (or you can apply to the Society of Genealogists; see below) and to search wills and admons, 1801 to 1852. These are not in the FHL. The indexes are only partially alphabetical, grouped by the first letter of the last name.

Consolidated Will Index 1750–1800. The Society of Genealogists has published a consolidated index to PCC wills covering the last half of the eighteenth century. It was originally published in book form, but as individual volumes have gone out of print the format has been changed to microfiche; the price is reasonable. This index indicates name, year, county, and folio number. A great deal of time can be saved by searching through fifty years of wills at once. Note that this is for wills only; to check for administrations of anyone dying intestate you must revert to the annual indexes. (An index is in progress, and names will be checked for a fee.) A copy of the wills index is in the FHL, and you may find that a genealogical society library or other reference library nearby has accumulated the entire set.

Index to PCC Wills and Admons 1701–1749. This finding aid includes wills and administrations and is the result of the efforts of a group of volunteers called the Friends of the PRO. The binders containing the fully alphabetical listing can be consulted at Kew and at the Family Records Centre.

Printed Index to Wills 1853–1858. This is another fully alphabetical consolidation of probate indexes. See chapter 8 for information on special lists of soldiers and sailors.

Death Duty Registers Index. The other central index to help you locate an elusive probate record is that of the Death Duty Registers, which can also be found in London at the PRO Chancery Lane, and in Salt Lake City at the FHL. The indexes for the more important pre-1858 period are divided into several sections. Before 1812 they are separated three ways: a PCC will index, a PCC administrations index, and a county courts index. From 1812 to 1857 there is a will index for all wills, irrespective of court, and an administrations index separated into PCC and country courts. The indexes are arranged yearly by the first letter of the last name, an arrangement that will slow your research. Remember that death duties were applicable in a majority of cases after 1815, so the Death Duty Registers Index is a more comprehensive tool than the records of the senior court. The LDS collection includes indexes for the period 1812 through 1857 and the registers themselves. It is worth repeating that, where an ancestor died intestate, the Death Duty Register of the administration is probably more informative than the court record, and that where a will exists the Death Duty Register reports the actual distribution of the estate.

Index to the Bank of England Will Extracts 1807–1845. This has been mentioned earlier in the chapter, but because it is readily available and captures a cross-section of people it warrants a mention in this list. It does provide a single index to some of the PCC probates for much of the period when consolidation is lacking (1801 to 1852).

This discussion highlights the impressive array of finding aids for the probate records of the PCC, including the index consolidations that simplify a search. Study the guides mentioned and the *FHLC*. A thorough search of these probate sources can be undertaken, much of it without the necessity of taking a trip or hiring an agent.

Inventories

Many inventories were destroyed during the Civil War and Commonwealth, 1642 to 1660. An inventory was required but the practice of making them fell into disuse; most that survive are from the late seventeenth or early eighteenth centuries. Whether a national or local collection, these documents are generally stored separately from wills and finding aids are less easy to come by—the PRO keeps PCC inventories at Kew. Once you have found a will, check for an inventory because it will be rich in details of the life of your ancestor. Historians have been able to show that the estimations of value could be wildly inaccurate, but this is not so important when the list of contents and description of the house can conjure up a vivid picture of how an ancestor lived (see *Village Records*, West, 1997).

Common Problems

To bring this discussion to a close it may be useful to summarize some of the common problems which stand in the way of locating a will. The executors may have attended a court at another level or at a location different from the one your research suggests; human error in indexing can hide a probate record as can variations in spelling; the will may have been proved considerably later than expected; the will may have been lost. Whatever the problem, if you feel reasonably certain there was a will or a grant of administration, be sure to check all possible sources and try all possible strategies outlined in this chapter. It has been acknowledged that the number of people in England making wills was limited, but that fact alone should not discourage you from searching for one. Locating wills may take more effort than usual, but they are such important sources of information that you should not hastily omit them from your search plan.

TABLE 7-2

Process of Probate

1. Testator made will.

2. After death the will was dispatched to the court.

3. Probate was granted and recorded in the Act Book (diary of the daily actions of the court). The record included the name, residence, and occupation of the deceased; names of executors with notations of any relationship to deceased; and the date of the will, death, and probate.

4. Date of death and value of personality (personal property other than land) was noted on the original will, which was preserved among court records.

5 A copy of the will was returned to the executors.

6. Where there was no will, a grant of administration was made.

7. The executors or administrators took out a bond (usually to two times the value of the estate) stating that they would fulfill their duties.

8. There could be special bonds governing the care of young children which would be filed with the wills and copied into the act books.

9. A list of goods and chattels, or inventory, was attached. (These are most likely to be found from 1680 to 1750.)

Obtaining a Will: To 1858

1.   Determine the objective of the search: either to locate the will of a particular individual, or to survey all wills for a surname in a given area.

2.   Select the geographic area for the search and look up jurisdictions for each level of ecclesiastical court.

3.   Consult *Probate Jurisdictions: Where to Look for Wills* (Gibson, 1994) for details of surviving probate records and their locations in England, and check this against FHL holdings; look under ENGLAND— PROBATE RECORDS and ENGLAND, COUNTY—PRO- BATE RECORDS.

4.   From these sources note any indexes and finding aids.

5.   Decide whether a check of central indexes (PCC, Death Duty Registers, Bank of England Will Extracts) should be part of the search.

6.   Itemize records and locations to be consulted, then prepare a research plan (i.e., the order in which the records of the different courts should be checked) based on known facts about the subject, accessibility of the various probate records, and estimated costs.

7.   Stay current with projects of family history and record societies; for example, the Wiltshire Record Society plans to issue a series of volumes containing the name, date and place details in Wiltshire wills.

8 ⚜ EARNING A LIVING

erhaps the most revealing information to be discovered about an ancestor is occupation. When this is known you can begin to picture and research home, dress, daily round, and education or training. This is family history. The records may not always reveal specific genealogical facts, such as place and date of birth or parentage, but the indirect gains can include valuable clues along with the slice of social history.

Records of education and occupation vary almost as much as the number of schools and jobs. They can reveal little or nothing, or provide considerable detail on career and family. This chapter presents each topic separately with brief background, steps to assist in the location of records, and sources for further information.

Education

Compulsory state education is a relatively modern phenomenon, present in England since 1880. Before that date there were a variety of schools catering to different classes and denominations, fee-paying and charitable. There were the public schools (such as Eton and Harrow), grammar schools (many established by an ancient endowment), charity schools, dame schools, ragged schools, factory schools, schools run by churches and chapels, and schools in union workhouses. Remember that in England a "public school" is really what in North America is called a private school—an independent institution for fee-paying students. The age at which a student could leave school rose very gradually. In 1880 it was set at ten; it was raised to eleven in 1893; and it was raised to twelve in 1899, where it remained until 1947, when it jumped to fifteen. Oxford and Cambridge were the only universities prior to the nineteenth century.

For those of us researching from a distance, school records are not readily available, so you might well ask why they should be considered. These records may supply parents' names and, in some cases, birth information. From 1876 to the Second World War, the local education authority could request birth records from the registrar to assist in planning. In some cases these duplicates of vital records are available for researchers. School records can also supply addresses for cross-referencing with the census, and they can provide considerable background information on entire families. The latter depends on the survival of the school log book which records everything from misdemeanors, to prize givings, to special holidays.

Deciding which school to research and locating its records can be a challenge. If you are fortunate the name of the school is close at hand. Among the old books in your home may be a prize awarded to an ancestor. If the inscription does not identify the school, perhaps there is a school crest which can be identified. If your ancestor went on to higher education, he would have supplied details of his schooling to the university. There may be a family tradition to check on, or you may have to do a little research into which schools were in your ancestors' area. The location of the record is likely to be with the County Record Office, a local library, or the education authority. Some schools maintain all of their records, but more and more older records are being transferred to archives and libraries. An inquiry to the county archivist is a good place to begin your search.

Many registers of the public schools and grammar schools have been published. These sometimes appear in large libraries, and there is a selection of registers and other documents among the collections of the Family History Library (FHL). Large numbers of these printed lists have been brought together in the library of the Society of Genealogists, which has issued a finding aid to their collection (see the Bibliography). Local libraries in England are likely to have copies of such publications. In some cases the registers, accounts, board minutes, and other school papers have been deposited with the County Record Office. If nothing has turned up through readily available sources and the school still exists, you can write direct (see the current edition of *Whitaker's Almanac* or the telephone directory to obtain the address). For Oxford and Cambridge there are printed lists of students from earliest times to the end of the nineteenth century, and these are quite readily available at the FHL and on film through family history centers. For schools and universities look in the *Family History Library Catalog* (*FHLC*) under ENGLAND—SCHOOLS, ENGLAND, COUNTY NAME—SCHOOLS, and ENGLAND, COUNTY NAME, TOWN—SCHOOLS. Take a little more time to go back within each section, looking for directories and histories that might help.

Information on local schools can be found in the volumes of the *Victoria History of the Counties of England*, in directories and topographical dictionaries, in volumes of local history, and in special books such as *A Concise Description of the Endowed Grammar Schools in England and Wales* (Carlisle, 1818 and 1974).

For a review of records in England see *The Growth of British Education and its Records* (Chapman, 1991).

Apprentice and Guild Records

A boy or girl was bound to serve a master or mistress as an apprentice for a specified period in return for instruction, food, and lodging. These agreements were generally private and sometimes very informal, so documentation is difficult to find. The exceptions are parish apprenticeships, apprenticeships in towns or boroughs with livery companies, and those contracted during the period of the stamp duty (1710 to 1811).

For the one hundred years of the stamp duty, a tax was payable on the premium paid for the apprenticeship. The records show the name of the apprentice, name and trade of the master, date of indenture, and duty paid. Parents of the apprentice were listed up until the middle of the eighteenth century only. (Parish apprenticeships were not subject to the tax.) The records of this duty are preserved at the Public Record Office (PRO), Kew, and microfilm copies are in the FHL (under ENGLAND—TAXATION). The Society of Genealogists has partially indexed the apprenticeship stamp duty records to 1774, and this also has been filmed for the FHL.

Membership in a guild was acquired by apprenticeship, patrimony (son of a member), or redemption (purchase). Records of redemption are brief and only rarely include parental information. The number of guilds and whether they included one or many trades varied according to town size. Extensive records, including accounts and admissions to guilds, exist for London. These are in Guildhall Library, but a considerable number of books and microfilmed documents have been gathered by the FHL. For other towns, these resources are with the town or borough or the local record office.

Membership in a guild or livery company was usually linked to *freedom of a city*. This status conferred certain privileges, such as exemption from tolls and the right to vote in elections. Freedom registers or records of admissions can be means of discovering the guild to which someone belonged. For some counties and cities, lists of apprentices and freemen have been published. The Society of Genealogists is preparing a series of abstracts to apprentice registers for the London Livery Companies up to 1800 (ed. by Cliff Webb).

Further resources or information on apprentices, guilds, and freemen can be found in *Occupational Sources for Genealogists* (Raymond, 1996), *Tracing Your Ancestors in the Public Record Office* (Bevan, 1998), and in the *London Apprentices* series (Webb, 1996-97).

Armed Forces

Those of you who discover that an ancestor served in the army or navy can consider yourselves fortunate. The records of these men, and sometimes of their families, too, are extensive. Even two hundred years ago, the armed forces generated an extensive bureaucracy and the accompanying detailed records: muster lists, pay records, service records, physical descriptions, and pensions, to name a few. Records of the army, navy, and ancillary services are complex and vast. This section will introduce you to the most accessible and point you to further guidance.

It is easiest to trace officers of either service. If an ancestor reached an exalted rank such as admiral or general, be sure to check for an entry in the *Dictionary of National Biography*. Regimental histories frequently mention or list officers but typically name only a few enlisted men. There is a series of annual volumes for each service listing all officers, including appointment at the time and seniority. *Army Lists* begin in 1754 and

Navy Lists in 1718. Officers of the Royal Marines are usually in the *Army Lists* and Coast Guard officers in the *Navy Lists*. The *Army Lists* for the period 1779 to 1878 and *Navy Lists* for the latter half of the nineteenth century are available on microfilm in the FHL or through family history centers. There are other lists of commissioned officers; check the *FHLC* under GREAT BRITAIN—MILITARY RECORDS. In Canada, university libraries probably have at least partial sets of one or both *Lists*. The PRO at Kew and the Society of Genealogists library in London are other locations to check.

Naval Records

Information about naval officers can also be found in the Passing Certificates of master's mates and midshipmen qualifying as lieutenants. At the PRO the classification is Admiralty (ADM) 107; there is an index. The individual's training and career to that point is given, usually along with information about date and place of birth, character, and seamanship. If your naval ancestor was an officer during the long Napoleonic Wars he may appear in the series of surveys carried out by the Admiralty from 1817 to 1851. The complement of the navy had to be dramatically reduced when hostilities ceased. In order to determine which officers would be retained and which placed on half-pay (like a pension), an account of service was requested from each officer and from commissioned officers, masters, pursers, boatswains, gunners, and carpenters. These are mainly in ADM 6, 9, 10, and 11, and must be consulted at Kew. Other record groups for naval officers and noncommissioned officers are described in *Tracing Your Ancestors in the PRO* (Bevan, 1998) and in *Naval Records for Genealogists* (Rodger, 1998).

For sailors, the longest and most accessible source is the Continuous Service Engagement Books, 1853–1896 (ADM 139 and 188). These are in three series and are arranged by service number; however, there is an overall alphabetical index. Books and the index can be consulted through family history centers. Outside this period, the search must be taken to England. Application can be made to the Ministry of Defence at Hayes, Middlesex, for modern records; a fee applies (twenty pounds in 1997). For anyone who entered the navy before the middle of the nineteenth century, ship musters (ADM 36–41) and pay books (ADM 31–35) will provide useful information. It is necessary to know the name of the ship or to come to it by some roundabout research. You may know where the sailor served. If so, reference to the *Navy Lists* will indicate the ships attached to each naval station each year, thereby giving clues for a methodical search. Musters (about 1830) and pay books (about 1875) introduce partially alphabetical surname indexes sorted by initial letter; either of these may start you off on a search for the correct muster. The resource books listed above for officers will give further guidance.

Army Records

The first resource for officers, as has been mentioned, is the *Army Lists*. Next, consider whether War Office (WO) 42 would be worth a search. The alphabetical portion of this class, 1776 to 1881, is in the FHL. It contains certificates of birth, marriage, baptism, and death, with wills, administrations, statements of service, and personal papers of officers and their families where the officer died on service or on half pay. There will be some applications from widows for pensions, or for compassionate allowances for children. Records of Officers Services are in WO 76, also in the Family History Library. These are not extensive until the nineteenth century. Content varies, but they generally include service details and personal information about families.

Part of WO 25 is the Services of Officers on Full and Half Pay—
Returns to the Circular Letter of 22 October 1828. These
accounts, supplied by the officers themselves, are in the FHL, but
you must look under the item for Regimental Description and
Succession Books (also part of WO 25) to find them in the
FHLC. The catalog listing does not tell you that these are alphabetical, nor what part of the alphabet is on each film.

There are vital records for army personnel at the Family
Records Centre. The Indexes to Regimental Registers of Birth
1761–1924 (overseas events begin in 1791) are of particular
value because they include the name of the regiment. Beginning
with some information about the birth of a child, these could
lead to finding the soldier father and his regiment. Even if the
name is somewhat common, preparing a short list of possible
regiments from this index is a sensible way to narrow a search.
There are also registers of marriages from 1771 and of deaths
from 1776. Neither of these includes the regiment in the index.
The Index of Chaplains' Returns of Births, Marriages, and
Deaths 1796–1880 is also at the Family Records Centre. It does
not include regiments.

When searching for a soldier ancestor you will come to the
records of WO 97, Royal Hospital Chelsea Soldiers Documents
1760–1913. Up until 1883 these listed only those discharged to
pension; anyone killed on duty, deserters, and those discharged
without a pension will not be here. The name of the hospital
appears in the record title because, in the beginning, soldiers
lived either at Chelsea or at its counterpart in Ireland,
Kilmainham. When this system proved inadequate, payments
were made instead and retired soldiers resided elsewhere. The
records are arranged by regiment up until 1872, by branch of the
service (e.g., cavalry, infantry) to 1883, and thereafter in alphabetical order. In England a team of volunteers has recently completed an index to the years 1760 to 1854 (available at the PRO),

which eliminates the need to know the regiment. For common names you may have to search the records of more than one man.

There are other accessible pension records. Many soldiers took their discharge in North America, or left England after their army service. *British Army Pensioners Abroad 1772–1889* (Crowder, 1995) lists about twelve thousand of these. WO 120 is Royal Hospital Chelsea Regimental Registers 1715–1857, arranged by the regiment in which the soldier last served. WO 118, Registers of Out-Pensioners of the Army and Militia 1759–1863, relates principally to Kilmainham hospital pensioners; some years are indexed. These are in the FHL. If you need to deduce which is the most likely regiment, consult *In Search of the Forlorn Hope* (Kitzmiller, 1987), a guide to all regiments that indicates where and when they served.

A group of records called Description Books provide much interesting information, including physical descriptions (recorded in case of desertion), birthplace and date, trade, and reason for leaving the army. There are two types: Depot Description Books (WO 67) and Regimental Description and Succession Books (part of WO 25). The Depot Description books omit any soldiers who enlisted when the regiment was located somewhere other than its depot and any who transferred to the regiment. Those in WO 25 are better for the nineteenth century. Both these series are arranged by regiment, and both are, to some extent, found on film in the FHL (WO 25 is much more extensive).

Some of your ancestors were undoubtedly part-time soldiers; especially large numbers were recorded during the long period of the Napoleonic wars (1792 to 1815). The militia played an important role in home defense over the centuries, both before and after 1757, when they were organized on a national basis. Two finding aids, *Tudor and Stuart Muster Rolls*

(Gibson and Dell, 1991) and *Militia Lists and Musters 1757–1876* (Gibson and Medlycott, 1994), will guide you to surviving lists and indexes.

Tips and Strategy

Three additional tips may assist your military research. The easiest way to study the holdings of the FHL is to use the small separate section of fiche, within the locality listings, which is labeled Great Britain. If you discover that your ancestor was in the Indian Army or in the service of the Honourable East India Company, use the author/title section of the *FHLC* and search under India Office Library. In recent years a large collection of documents has been filmed, thereby making research into the British in India much easier. Finally, if your soldier or sailor died overseas and was owed back pay, he very likely will appear in the indexes of the Prerogative Court of Canterbury. This includes East India Company and merchant marine personnel. From 1800 to 1852 these men are listed separately within the indexes (see *Prerogative Court of Canterbury Will and Other Probate Records*, Scott, 1997).

Research Strategy

When beginning research on a member of the armed forces, gather as much information as possible. If you are short on facts try to use what information you have to narrow the search. For example, focus the geographical area to a theater of war, a battle, a naval station, or an army base. Read a little about the organization of the army and the navy and their rank structures. Do not neglect regimental histories or accounts of wars and sea battles, and take time to review the bibliographies in those books for further hints. *The Annual Register* (see chapter 4), available in many large libraries, contains dispatches (firsthand accounts) from army and navy officers.

Professions

If your ancestor was engaged in a profession, such as law, medicine, or the church, chances are some sort of governing authority regulated the profession and kept registers of practitioners. Many modern organizations hold records going back hundreds of years. The current edition of *Whitaker's Almanac* records the associations, as well as their annual lists. These exist not only for the professions already mentioned but for many others which acquired that stature later.

There is no consistency to what you may find, nor to the ease or difficulty in obtaining it. To research someone's professional career check what sources are close at hand, then methodically work your way through sources further afield. Begin with libraries as usual. (Do not assume that your library will hold only lists for Canada or the United States.) If there are no annual directories, check for biographical dictionaries in the appropriate field, and remember to look in the *Dictionary of National Biography* if you even suspect the individual achieved prominence. Next, look under ENGLAND—OCCUPATIONS in the locality section of the *FHLC*. There is a selection of books and films for such professions as architecture, medicine, the judiciary, and the foreign service. Books listing musicians and painters are also quite generally available. In addition, the FHL has *Crockford's Clerical Directory* back to the year it began (1858); it is the annual list of parishes and ministers of the Church of England. Other available church lists include a mixed selection of years for the Roman Catholic, Congregational, and Methodist churches. For further information on the ministers of dissenting churches, consult the series of booklets issued by the Society of Genealogists in their *My Ancestor...* series (see the Bibliography).

Consider whether the occupation which you regard as a profession may have been viewed differently in your ancestor's time. Some occupations required a license. The license may have been registered through the clerk of the peace and be in quarter sessions records. A few registered through the bishop's court, such as physicians, midwives, and school teachers, though the practice gradually died out over the nineteenth century. Read *My Ancestor Moved in England and Wales* (Camp, 1994) and *County Records* (Emmison and Gray, 1987) for additional background on quarter sessions and licensing.

Some occupational lists are included in *Marriage and Census Indexes for Family Historians* (Gibson and Hampson, 1996), and printed works are summarized in *Occupational Sources for Genealogists* (Raymond, 1996). A fine collection of professional lists and directories is held by the Society of Genealogists. The slim and inexpensive guide *Using the Library of the Society of Genealogists* is excellent for the simple reason that a verbal tour through the library's vast holdings produces many ideas for research, and there is a section on occupations.

Merchants, Tradesmen, and Laborers

It is probable that anyone in retail or wholesale trade or in manufacturing in the nineteenth century was listed in local directories. Occupations also appear on certificates of vital records, on census returns, and in probate records. Once you know the occupation, you can turn your attention to finding out about the job itself and to determining whether any records survive. Hundreds of job definitions appear in *Tracing Your Ancestors, The A to Z Guide* (Saul,1995) and *An Introduction to Occupations* (Culling, 1993). Check libraries and the *Periodical Source Index* (*PERSI*) for books and articles describing trades or manufacturing methods. Another source for useful articles is the twice-yearly journal of the Federation of Family History Societies,

Family History News and Digest, which abstracts articles of affiliated societies.

The records of many businesses and companies have survived, and a good overview of them is found in *Company and Business Records for Family Historians* (Probert, 1994). The National Register of Archives at the Royal Commission on Historical Manuscripts maintains a record of collections of business records. This can be a help when you are without the name of a company—the database can be searched for a type of business. County Record Offices will hold the papers of some local firms and factories, and records of others in business have survived because a license was required.

For the countless ancestors who toiled as unskilled laborers in the factories and on the farms, there is likely no record beyond an occasional pay list. It is much easier to find out about how these people and their families lived. Libraries can provide assistance in finding books, and travel guides will point you to museums of rural life, mining, etc. Sometimes the government took an interest in the distress of the working classes and conducted studies, usually followed by the issuing of a report—a Parliamentary paper. For a brief introduction to this source see *A Guide to Parliamentary Papers* (Ford, P. and G., 1972) or *Genealogical Research in England's Public Record Office: A Guide for North Americans* (Reid, 1996).

Railwaymen

Hundreds of railway lines and railway companies were operating in England in the nineteenth century. Railways are in themselves a great hobby interest, so there are innumerable books on the history of individual lines and others full of old railway photographs and descriptions of the engines and rolling stock. To find out if a record of service of a railway employee has survived,

978 AGE

TRADES.

Agents—Commission.

Craddock W. 24 Romford rd.Stratford E

Egan Edward, 42 Neville rd. Upton E

Freeman E. 16 Ealing rd. sth. Ealing w

Giles Hermann, 30 Surrey st.Plaistow E

Govus T. E. 1 Eveline villas, Leicester road, New Barnet

Mónro G.84 Cornwall rd.Sth.Tottenham

Shannon Mrs. M. 87 Lansdowne road, Dalston N E

Wellesley, Hunt & Co. 1 Melrose villas, Philip lane, Tottenham

Wells Alfred John, Vine cottage, Park lane, Teddington S.O

Wootton William Beaumont,3 Woodford New road, Walthamstow

Agents—Dyers'.

McIlwraith Mrs. Mary Ann, 77 High street, Harlesden N W

Venimore Carey (Pullar's), 29 Pembroke road, Walthamstow

Agents—Forwarding.

See also Carriers.

Great Eastern Railway Co.(Christopher Harradence, agent) (Joseph Young, local agent), Goods department, Royal Victoria & Albert Docks E; Silvertown Goods depôt (Joseph G. Whitehead, collector), North Woolwich road, Canning Town E & coal depôts, Barking road, Canning Town E; Carpenters' road, Stratford E & 33 Eleanor road, Waltham Cross

Great Northern Goods Department (Charles R. Bentley, local agent), Royal Victoria & Albert Docks E

Great Western Railway Co.(Chas. Goodrich, local agent), Royal Victoria & Albert Docks E; (Jeayes, Kasner & Co. agents), Goods & Parcels office, Promenade house, Uxbridge road, Ealing Dean w; Goods depôt (Geo.S.Wright, supt.), Brentford dock, Brentford; booking office, 174 Railway approach, Goldhawk road, Shepherd's Bush w

London Parcels DeliveryCo.Lim.(Ernest Gladwin, agent), High st.Southgate N

London & North Western Railway Goods Depôt (Alfred Kinch, local agent), Royal Victoria & Royal Albert Docks E; goods. & coal depôt (R. A. Jones, district superintendent), Barking rd. Canning Town E

London & South Western Railway Co.

Balme George, 355 Upton lane, Upton E

BarnesA.H.Clonbrock rd.Stk.NewngtnN

Bassett William John, jun. 6 Lorne terrace, Lea Bridge road, Leyton

Binnington Francis Thomas, South End road, Hampstead N W

Blanchard&Keyes,Archway rd.Highgt N

Blandford Angus, 22 Leyspring road, Leytonstone N E

Boddy Wm. 160 Downsell rd. Stratford E

BoltwoodWm.2 Frederick st.Walthmstw

Bonham Arthur, 87 Umfreville road, Harringay N

Bottomley Jsph. 25 Lillie rd. Fulham s w

Bowyer Alfred, Great Eastern buildings, Southbury road, Enfield

Boyer Wm. 5 Cardigan rd. Kilburn N w

Branson William, 56 Rylett road, Shepherd's Bush w

Brent Frederick Josiah, 3 Brompton villas, Lower Fore street, Edmonton

Brevetor Ernest Frederick, 7 West bank, Stoke Newington N

Brevetor Thomas, 11 Ashgrove, Mare street, Hackney N E

Bridges S. 7 Stanley rd. Sth. Tottenham

Brodie, Timbs & Baker, 1 Canfield gardens, Finchley road, Hampstd N w; 2 Southwood la. Highgate N & Lowlands rd. (adjoining the Met. Stat.), Harrow

Brougham W. F. & Co. 10 King's road & Crown rd.St. Margaret's,Twickenham

Brown & West, 6 Finsbury Park buildings, Station road, Finsbury Park N

Brown Hy. Station rd. Wood Green N

Bryham Richard, 1 Station road, Bowes park, Wood Green N

BuckJ.W.Elm dene,Southbury rd.Enfield

Bunch Jsph. B. 360 Mare st.Hackney N E

Burridge & Bendell, 27 Dionis terrace, Fulham s w

CanhamH.J.20 Sprowston rd.ForestGt E

Capel T. H.38 Brandon rd.Walthamstow

Carter G.49Glenwood rd.Sth.Tottenham

Castle Josiah, 139 Dawes road & 10 Rosaville road, Fulham s w

Chamberlain Charles,7 Rosedale terrace, Fulham road s w

Charles & Griffith, 433 West Green road, South Tottenham

Cheko Richard & Co. Beaconsfield house, Romford road, Manor Park

Child F. F.S.I. 1 Station rd. New Barnet

Clark Chas.116 Carlton vale, Kilburn NW

Clark J.L.298 Romford rd.Forest Gate E

Figure 8-1 Trades Index from *Kelly's Directory, Middlesex-Northern Suburbs* (Society of Genealogists).

you must begin with the name of the company or companies involved. Some old maps identify the railway lines by name. Topographical dictionaries include stations and railways, and old travel guides will tell you what company served a region.

Was Your Grandfather a Railwayman? (Richards, 1995) is an introduction to researching railway records. A comprehensive account of the records, their location (most are in the PRO), and how to use them can be found in *Railway Ancestors* (Hawking, 1993).

Merchant Seamen

Finding a record of a sailor, master, or mate serving in the merchant service requires some specific knowledge. The collections of records are in more than one location and only a few have been indexed. Prior to 1835, it is necessary to know the port from which a ship sailed; after 1860, you need the name of a ship, its number, and an approximate date to search. More readily accessible facts may come from census records if your seafaring ancestor was afloat at the right time (see pp. 61–62).

For 1835 to 1857 there are indexed records: Registers of Seamen. They include name, birthplace, age, and details of voyages. The originals are in the PRO (Board of Trade 112, 113, 116, 120) and microfilm copies are in the FHL. It is possible to trace ships' officers through certificates of competency; some of these are in the FHL. If the officer achieved command he should appear in *Lloyd's Captains Register.* The original is in the Guildhall Library, and copies are in the FHL (it does not circulate) and in the National Archives of Canada in Ottawa. The Society of Genealogists has produced an index to the register for 1869 which does circulate to family history centers and which can be purchased on microfiche. Although for one year only, it includes a large number of officers whose service began much earlier in the century.

The Society of Genealogists has made available another possible source: Trinity House Petitions, which survive from the 1780s to when they ceased in 1854. The society sells a calendar of the records on microfiche, and the FHL has filmed copies of the registers; look in the *FHLC* under GREAT BRITAIN—MERCHANT MARINE. It was possible for the widows and orphans of merchant seamen to appeal to the Corporation of Trinity House on Deptford Strand for financial assistance. This organization had a variety of other responsibilities, including looking after lighthouses and marker buoys.

Somewhat scattered, and thus less accessible, are the records of the merchant navy after 1860. Approximately 70 percent of crew agreements and ships' logs of British merchant ships, 1863 to 1938, are held by the Maritime History Archive, Memorial University of Newfoundland. There is no index, which is why you need to know the ship, its number, and a date. It may be possible to research these details but you will need access to *Lloyd's Register*. These volumes run from the late 1700s and list all ships in commission with their numbers; microfiche copies (1764 to 1880) can be accessed at LDS family history centers. Through *Lloyd's Registers* you may be able to produce a short list of ships in which a seaman served if you know some details of the routes he sailed and when. The remaining 30 percent of these records are at the PRO or the National Maritime Museum, Greenwich.

If you have sailor ancestors, keep in mind that they did not necessarily remain exclusively in the merchant service or the Royal Navy. Crew signed on for a voyage or a term of commission of a ship. During the Napoleonic Wars captains of Royal Navy vessels did everything possible to persuade men to join their crews, promising prize money and a chance to bash the French. When stronger measures were necessary the press gang "recruited" men ashore, and sailors were taken from merchant ships at sea. Search for elusive sailors in the records of the navy and the merchant marine. Books to introduce you to the subject are *Basic Facts About Using Merchant Ship Records for Family Historians* (Hogg, 1997) and *My Ancestor Was a Merchant Seaman* (Watts, M.J., and C.T. Watts, 1991).

Conclusion

If you are a thorough researcher you will go beyond the identification of the job, trade, or profession to find out about the nature of the work, the rate of pay, the tools, the clothing, and the diet of your ancestor. Some knowledge of historical background and the local economy may provide additional clues as to why a family suddenly moved or required parish assistance, for example. All of this effort will pay off. At the very least it will be interesting, and it may well produce solid genealogical facts.

Searching Occupational Records

1. Find the occupation from census returns, civil records, probate, directories, etc.

2. Select the date, geographic area, and name or names.

3. Check the *FHLC* and resource guides; note to what extent you can do the research through a family history center.

4. Check local libraries for directories, professional lists, and local, business or economic histories.

5. For records in England, decide on the likely location (PRO for government employees, County Record Office for local business) or obtain some assistance from the Royal Commission on Historical Manuscripts.

6. Prepare a plan for the records to be consulted—location, method of access.

9 ❧ LOCAL ADMINISTRATION AND JUSTICE

arish officers and local magistrates were responsible for the temporal affairs of a parish. In fact, their duties and responsibilities were inextricably mixed. Methods varied, as did personalities, and a made-in-the-parish solution could resolve an issue rather than a punishment called for under the law. There were visible examples of this mix of parish and civil matters. On the one hand, some cases brought parish officers into the court of quarter sessions, and on the other, temporal objects such as militia weapons, even the village fire engine, might be stored in the church.

This chapter sets out the essentials of local administration and justice. There is information about the poor, the courts, and the land, followed by first steps in locating the records and guidance for further study.

Parish Administration

Parish registers of baptism, marriage, and burial were by no means the only records stored in that "sure coffer" which Thomas Cromwell ordered every parish to possess. There was another variety of documents of varying genealogical significance, the sum total of which can enable the researcher to recreate the milieu in which an ancestor lived out his or her life. This came about because, as time went on, an increasing burden of civic administrative duties was assigned to the parish. During the sixteenth and seventeenth centuries several acts of Parliament legislated the transfer of secular matters from the manor courts to the parish. The records relating to these secular aspects of parish management were collected together in various ways: according to the parish as defined; by township in the huge parishes of the north; and in urban areas, as borough records of several parishes banded together. Part of the explanation of a parish in the *Local Historian's Encyclopedia* (Richardson, 1986) neatly summarizes these points.

> [The parish was] originally a township or group of townships possessing its own church and parson, to whom it paid its tithes and other ecclesiastical dues. A parish could contain one or several manors, and sometimes a manor was large enough to spread over more than one parish.

> Successive Acts of Parliament, particularly in the 16th and 17th centuries, encouraged the transformation of the parish into a secular authority through its meetings of the Vestry. The early parish already had the power to levy a church rate, but further legislation empowered the parish to levy a rate for poor relief and the repair of highways—two areas of activity which increased and so enhanced the importance of the parish. As this happened the functions of the

> manor courts … declined, although for a time there
> could be an overlap of powers between vestry and
> manor court.

As the above implies, meetings held to discuss parish business were called *vestries*. They were so named because, at least in the beginning, the meetings were assembled in the vestment room of the parish church. These vestries were the forerunners of local councils. Their minutes reveal the wide array of administrative matters which concerned the parish. Here can be found reference to poor relief, road repair, common land, lighting, education, peacekeeping, charities, maintenance of the fabric of the church, special taxes, apprentices, and even parliamentary investigations. Some parishes had *select* vestries (not elected—usually a small group of local landowners) while others were governed by *open* vestries. Open vestries were general meetings of all rate-paying inhabitants which sometimes, in large urban parishes especially, became very unruly.

It was the vestry which appointed the parish officers, such as the churchwardens. The vestry also made recommendations to the justice of the peace for such posts as the overseer of the poor, the surveyor of the highways, and the local constable. There is a very good chance that your ancestor took his turn as a parish officer, though, as we find to this day, volunteer posts tended to be filled by the same few people, over and over again. The men assuming these positions were unpaid, unskilled, and usually unwilling. Sometimes they paid money to avoid duty, or occasionally were fortunate enough to escape service through possession of a Tyburn Ticket, a certificate granted to anyone who had secured the prosecution of a criminal for a capital offense. The certificate exempted the holder from all parish offices within the parish where the offense was committed. The Tyburn Ticket was permitted to be sold once, and it commanded a good price. The act enabling this procedure was repealed in 1818.

If by some chance your ancestor did not serve as a parish officer, his name may well appear in the minutes as one receiving poor relief, repairing the church or the highway, or receiving the benefice of a local charity. Nineteenth-century vestry minutes often contain records of parish-assisted emigration schemes.

Parish Officers

Churchwardens. Among the most important officials elected by the vestry were the churchwardens; a parish generally had two to four. Their duties were extensive, ranging from areas of church operation such as repairs, assigning pews, and keeping up the registers, to secular chores which might include looking after parish arms and exterminating vermin. The churchwardens' account books record payments to all manner of laborers and craftsmen. At Great Barr near Birmingham in the late seventeenth century, churchwardens' accounts list payments for beer for the bellringers, and to the dog whipper (his name given) whose job was to ensure the good behavior of dogs brought into church (Gould 1983).

Constable. Another important parish official was the constable. His duties varied in different parishes and at different times in history, but for the most part he was concerned with keeping the peace and looking after travelers and vagabonds. There were many travelers on the roads without means of support. Many were soldiers and sailors going home on official passes. As one might suspect, these passes were often forged or stolen. A record was kept of the cost of providing for these transients. Vagabonds were escorted out of the parish to hurry them back to their own place of legal settlement (i.e., the location of their entitlement to poor relief). The ratepayers did not want a stranger to become a burden on their accounts; even less did they want illegitimate children born in the parish. Constables' accounts recorded expenses related to various other duties such as checking weights and measures, mustering the militia in time of crisis, preventing prize fights on the common, and attending to violations of the Sabbath (Richardson 1986).

Overseer of the Poor. In the beginning he was responsible for supervising charitable funds and endowments left for the benefit of the parish poor. After 1597 he was empowered to levy a poor rate and to see to the construction of a poorhouse. Overseers were to set to work the able-bodied poor, apprentice pauper children, and see to the removal of strangers from the parish. Like other officers the overseer kept accounts of his expenditures and submitted them to the vestry for approval. These accounts show payments for food, clothing, medical attention, and burial, and list the names of local rate payers.

Surveyor of the Highways. After 1691, this office was usually filled by rotation; before then the surveyor was elected by the parishioners or appointed, sometimes by the justices and sometimes by other officers. Duties included inspecting the roads at least three times a year and arranging the required local labor. Able-bodied men had to provide four day's labor (later increased to six) or send a substitute. Failure to do so resulted in a fine. It was not easy to enforce and supervise the road work, and local records reflect the difficulties. In this example one negligent citizen is none other than the mayor.

> Mr. Mayor G. Pley and Mr. T. Waltham having carted water to the injury of the streets and bridge, their cart wheels "being iron bound", were amerced [fined] 2s. each. Seventeen persons were amerced 4s. each (affeered to 2s.) for not coming or sending to repair the highways in "Whitesonweeke last" for four days. (October 13, 1651, III.120. *Minutes of the Borough Court, Weymouth and Melcombe Regis*)

The Poor Law, Settlement, and Illegitimacy

Up until the passing of the Poor Law Amendment Act in 1834, each parish was responsible for the care of its own poor and was correspondingly reluctant to assume responsibility for some other parish's pauper. Those born in a parish of a *settled* father had nothing to worry about. A newcomer to a parish had to qualify. This was achieved by paying the rate on a piece of land or property, by serving a seven-year apprenticeship to a settled man, by working without interruption for a year for a settled man, or by serving as a parish official. Parish officials were almost always chosen from the ratepayers. The churchwardens collected a poor rate from those who could afford to pay. It was then up to the overseer of the poor to distribute parish relief. Who received what, where and when, and even family relationships show up in the records.

Relief was either "indoor" or "outdoor"—that is, either to the poor residing in a parish-supported poorhouse or to those remaining in their homes. By the end of the eighteenth century most parishes had a poorhouse or workhouse of some sort even if it was only a cottage. A parish which could not afford even that might arrange to share in a poorhouse with another parish (the union of parishes for this purpose was encouraged under Gilbert's Act, 1782). Most relief was "outdoor." Everything was done to encourage some measure of self-support; women could spin or take in laundry, men could do useful manual labor about the parish. The clothing, food, medical attention, burial expenses, cash payments, and sometimes loans were all recorded. Payments would be made for the support of children, but useful work was found for them from about the age of seven. Older children were apprenticed to a local craftsman occasionally, but more likely worked as farm laborers or domestic help. There were generous parishes and considerate masters, but there was also much hardship and abuse. In the nineteenth century hundreds of children from South of England parishes were sent to work in the Lancashire mills.

Parishes took great care to ensure their welfare rolls did not increase and that they did not help anyone settled in another parish. The overseer of the poor was always ready to arrange for the examination and removal of undesirables. A series of acts in the late seventeenth century governed who could settle in a new parish. These regulations led to the creation of the various settlement papers: the certificate, the examination, and the removal order. When someone left his parish of legal settlement he had to obtain from parish officials a settlement certificate. This he would give to the officers of his new parish. When and if he became a burden on this parish, the magistrate was asked for a removal order which precipitated the examination. A settlement examination could reveal a life history; it would be kept either with the parish records or the quarter sessions records for future reference.

Illegitimate children were another potential drain on the overseer's resources. The baptismal record did not often include the name of the father. The mother was examined for information as to the child's paternity, and a warrant was sometimes issued to apprehend the father. Where possible the couple were compelled to marry; otherwise the father paid a bond, either lump sum or in regular amounts, for the maintenance of the child. It is evident how valuable these records could be to the genealogist. Even the accounts of the overseer of the poor can tell a story:

May 6, 1816	Certificate issued for the removal to Aldridge of Sarah Stackhouse, single and with child from Pelsell
Dec. 3, 1817	Order made by a J.P. for John Masefield of Beckby to pay £5 13s. 6d. and 1/8 weekly for the child of Sarah Stackhouse

July 22, 1818   Order made for Francis Slater of Pelsell
                  to pay £10 and 1/8 weekly for the
                  child of Sarah Stackhouse

April 3, 1822   Order for the removal from Barton
                  under Needwood to Aldridge of Sarah
                  Stackhouse, single and with child

(Gould 1983)

The growth in population, the end of the Napoleonic Wars, and hard times in the 1820s all put incredible stress on the parish system of poor relief. The payments over the whole country were becoming astronomical. Various changes were tried, Parliamentary commissions investigated, and the result, in 1834, was the New Poor Law. Parish-based relief disappeared, and administration was handed over to boards of guardians in roughly six hundred Poor Law Unions. Each had a workhouse where life was made as unattractive as possible. New residents gave up all their possessions, including clothing, and were given uniforms; the diet was boring and barely nourishing; families were separated; hours of work were long. The idea was to eliminate outdoor relief and make indoor relief something the poor would do everything possible to avoid. As under the old poor law, unions did not want to pay for support when someone else was responsible, so they actively sought those who had abandoned their families. Issues of the *Poor Law Unions' Gazette* survive at the British Newspaper Library; they attest to the irresponsibility of the named truants. The Poor Law Amendment Act of 1834 remained in place until 1929.

Church Courts

You will be aware of the structure of the courts of the established Church of England if you have researched probate records which predate 1858. These courts had many responsibilities: they looked after administrative matters such as tithes, spiritual discipline, and the manners and morals of parishioners (usually revolving around matrimonial disputes and slander). No criminal or debt cases came before these courts. Punishments were in the form of penance, fines, exclusion from the local church, and a more complete excommunication. Two books provide extensive information on the function of these courts. *Church Court Records* (Tarver, 1995) covers each category of business and how to use the records. *Hatred Pursued Beyond the Grave* (Cox, 1993) concentrates on the vivid tales that emerge from the pages of the cases heard at Doctors Common, the court of the Prerogative Court of Canterbury in London. A particularly interesting aspect of these records is the presentments made by parish churchwardens when the archdeacon or bishop made his visitation. Local parish matters were reported, such as adultery, illegitimacy, repairs to the fabric of the church, and those who failed to attend service.

Civil Courts

Much of the parish business discussed to this point was carried on in association with the justice of the peace in quarter sessions, and the clerk of the peace. The justice of the peace was usually a gentleman of some stature, and the clerk of the peace an attorney with a private practice. The latter had to have some formal legal training as he advised the justice of the peace on the law and acted as custodian of the records. Quarter Sessions, where the justices came together, were held at Easter, Midsummer (24 June), Michaelmas (29 September), and Epiphany (6 January), at one or more locations in a county. Trivial offences need not wait, as they could be dealt with in a summary trial at Petty Sessions—these records were retained by the Clerk of the Peace.

The workload of the justices and the clerks was burdonsome, and the surviving doumentation is vast.

The court of quarter sessions upheld the King's Peace. It dealt with the vast majority of breaches of the law, with the more serious offenses, such as treason, murder, forgery, and bigamy, being reserved for the assizes. These lesser offenses included such things as assault, theft, witchcraft, poaching, and failure to clear ditches or repair the road. Sometimes a parish was the defendant. Records of what went on in court can be found in session rolls and order books (the administrative account of proceedings).

The court played an active administrative role of maintenance, supervision, or licensing for many things, and acted as a depository for others. Some of the topics coming within its jurisdiction were: aliens, small traders, barges, charities, dissenters, meetinghouses, enclosure awards, freemasons, jails, prisoners, jurors, land tax, inns and alehouses, victuallers, weights and measures, oaths of allegiance, banks, vagrancy, and lunatics. It is the lists of various sorts and order books that are most useful because they have a better chance of being in the Family History Library (FHL) and because they are more likely to have indexes and finding aids.

The assizes, which dealt with more serious cases, were set up as traveling courts from the beginning, and by the 1400s they had an established pattern of dealing with criminal matters. A group of assize judges was responsible for a *circuit* which was made up of several counties. Some parts of the country, known as *palatinates,* were outside this system and had their own courts (e.g., Durham and Lancaster). Before 1733 the majority of the records are in Latin. Those found guilty of a criminal offense, and not executed or transported, were (until about 1800) sentenced to the stocks or pillory, a fine, or a whipping. Lockups or jails (*gaols* in England) were used for debtors and those awaiting trial or transportation. Prison hulks (no-longer-serviceable ships permanently tied up at a dock) came into being as a result of the American War of Independence when the loss of the Thirteen Colonies as a destination for transportees resulted in a buildup of people in local jails.

Land Records

Search for middle- and upper-class ancestors in the Land Tax Assessments. The maximum span of years is from the late 1600s to the middle of the twentieth century, but survival is best from 1780 until 1832. During those years Land Tax Assessments were used to establish voting qualifications. Copies were deposited with the clerk of the peace, so duplicates are found among quarter sessions records. Land Tax Assessments show owners and occupiers, provide some identification, perhaps even a description of the property, and the amount assessed. The information can be used to confirm location, to estimate someone's time in a community, and to compare with parish registers to help confirm family ties.

For the year 1798 there is a record for the entire country. As of that year the tax became a fixed sum and owners could make a lump sum payment which freed them from the annual charge. To ascertain what that lump sum should be it was necessary to prepare a record of all owners and occupiers. This national listing is arranged by parish. The records are at the Public Record Office (PRO), Kew, but they may also be viewed on film in the FHL and family history centers. To look up Land Tax Assessments in the *Family History Library Catalog* (*FHLC*), look in the locality section under ENGLAND—LAND AND PROPERTY and ENGLAND, COUNTY NAME—LAND AND PROPERTY.

Another type of land record found among quarter sessions and worthy of mention is the enclosure award. The transition of English agriculture from the old open field system of farming to modern methods can be followed by studying the enclosure movement. Enclosure had actually been going on slowly over a very long period of time, but the greatest change and the majority of enclosure awards occurred between 1795 and 1850. The English village before the middle of the eighteenth century was still an open-field one, not very different from that of the Middle Ages. Within a century this was all changed as the modern system of consolidated farms became firmly established. Procedure varied, particularly in the nineteenth century when Parliament acted to speed up the process. The significant feature for genealogists is that a copy of the award and an accompanying map were deposited with the clerk of the peace. Not every parish went through this process; of those that did, some involved only small pieces of land. However, in many cases the changes were extensive, and the documentation may include a detailed map of the entire parish with names of householders. For those with farming ancestors whose lives were influenced for good or ill by enclosure, an excellent description of the process and assessment of the impact can be found in *The Common Stream* (Parker, 1975). Other helpful sources of background material are *Men of Aldridge* (Gould, 1983) and the volumes of *The Victoria History of the Counties of England*. For a visual summary of agrarian change see *Historical Atlas of Britain* (Falkus and Gillingham, 1981). Records of Enclosure will usually be deposited with the County Record Office.

Beginning the Research

The practical approach is to ascertain what resources are in local libraries, or what can be borrowed from elsewhere, in whatever format. You may also want to know what records can be purchased. Follow these steps:

- In local libraries look for the *Victoria County History* of the county being studied, and for volumes of serial publications issued by historical societies, or the guides to what such groups have printed

- Review, using the *FHLC* locality section, the county and specific town/parish holdings in the FHL; at the county level, recommended headings are:

   ENGLAND, COUNTY NAME—CORRECTIONAL INSTITUTIONS

   ENGLAND, COUNTY NAME—COURT RECORDS

   ENGLAND, COUNTY NAME—POORHOUSES, POOR LAW, ETC.

   ENGLAND, COUNTY NAME—TAXATION

- Check the publications of the county family history society

The *Victoria County History* not only provides pertinent local details but also extensive references to documents in the County Record Office. For some counties there are volumes of bibliography providing more source ideas. The serial publications issued by organizations like the Norfolk Record Society and the Worcestershire Historical Society are volumes of printed documents. *Bibliographies, and Texts and Calendars* I and II (1958 and 1983) are two places to find listings of the publications of these groups. Test the name of a local group in the author/title section of the *FHLC*. Don't worry about knowing a specific name; in all probability it will be in the form of the county name followed by record society, historical society, or archeological society.

Once you've found the more accessible records, or when you've concluded that the work must be done in England, information must be obtained from the County Record Office and other local repositories. Direct letters of inquiry, a search of Web

```
**********************************************************************
ENGLAND, WILTSHIRE - COURT RECORDS
                                          +---------------+
Church of England.  Archdeaconry of Sarum.  Court.        |BRITISH        |
  Court records, 1572-1699. -- Salt Lake City : Filmed by the   |FILM AREA      |
  Genealogical Society of Utah, 1988. -- on 3 microfilm reels ;  +---------------+
  16 mm.

  Microfilm of original records at the Wiltshire County Record Office,
    Trowbridge.
  Text in Latin and English.
  High reduction (42X) microfilm.  Use high magnification reader.
  Wiltshire Record Office: D2/4/1-17; D2/5/1/1, 4-7; D2/5/2/1-2; D2/5/4/1,
    5; D2/6/1; D2/14-15

  Act books                       1572-1602 --------------- 1526566
                                                            item 10-14.
  Act books             1590-1620 ------------------------- 1526567
  Act books             1620-1666 ------------------------- 1526568
    Citations           1604-1699                           item 1-17
    Excommunications    1572-1633
    Purgations          1607-1639
    Miscellaneous       1588-1670
    Deposition book     1580-1605
    Matrimonial         1592
    Probate             1597-1639


**********************************************************************
ENGLAND, WILTSHIRE - COURT RECORDS
                                          +---------------+
Great Britain.  Court of Quarter Sessions of the Peace (Wiltshire). |BRITISH        |
  Ecclesiastical court records, 1614-1864. -- Salt Lake City :     |FILM AREA      |
  Filmed by the Genealogical Society of Utah, 1988. -- 2          +---------------+
  microfilm reels ; 16 mm.

  Microfilm of original records at the Wiltshire Record Office,
    Trowbridge.
  Wiltshire Record Office: D1/41/1/1-5; 41/2/1, 3, 4; 41/3/1-4; D28/21;
    A1/235-240, 242, 250, 255, 310.

  Citations,                      1631-1640 --------------- 1545038
    Excommunications,             1614-1641
  Libels,               1614-1619, 1624, 1638 ------------- 1545039
    Probate of wills,             1820-1825               item 1-9
  Nonconformist declarations against
    transubstantiation, (no actual dates given),
    ca. 1689-1690
  Names of persons subscribing oaths and
    declarations
  Oaths of allegiance, abjuration, supremacy, and
  Declarations against transubstantiation,
    1730-1864
  Oaths in leiu of sacramental certificates,
    1829
  Dissenting ministers and teachers oaths and --------------------- 1545039
    declarations, 1687-1829                              item 10-15.
  Quakers declarations of allegiance and
    supremacy, ca.1723
  Papist oaths of allegiance, 1778-1830
  Licences for dissenters' meeting houses,
    1695-1850


**********************************************************************
ENGLAND, WILTSHIRE - CORRECTIONAL INSTITUTIONS
                                          +---------------+
Great Britain.  Court of Quarter Sessions of the Peace (Wiltshire). |BRITISH        |
  Transportation of felons, 1728-1789. -- Salt Lake City : Filmed  |FILM AREA      |
  by the Genealogical Society of Utah, 1988. -- on 1 microfilm     |1545037        |
  reel ; 16 mm.                                                    | item 4-5      |
                                                                   +---------------+
  Microfilm of original records at the Wiltshire County Record Office,
    Trowbridge.
  High reduction film (42X); use high magnification reader.
  Contains bonds and contracts for the transporation of felons to the
    American colonies and plantations and elsewhere, 1728-1789.
  Wiltshire Record Office: A1/320/1-2
```

Figure 9-1 Various Local Court Records. These items, not consecutive in the *FHLC,* indicate the range of business conducted by church and civil courts. The collection of the FHL varies widely for different counties.

Reprinted by permission. Family History Library Catalog Copyright 1987, 1998 by Corporation of the President of The Church of Jesus Christ of Latter-day Saints.

sites, and/or the purchase of guides to holdings will provide the details. Addresses correct at the end of 1997 are in appendix D, including the address and Web site for the National Register of Archives and ARCHON (Archives On-Line) (sources of the most current address information).

The Benefits of Searching for Serial Publications

Surrey Record Society

Mitcham settlement examinations, 1784–1814. Edited ... by Blanche Berryman, 1973. Calendars of three books of examinations. In the introduction, a brief account of the process of examination and removal in general and as exemplified in the Mitcham records. Witnessing justices are listed in the appendix. (p.176)

Devon and Cornwall Record Society

Churchwardens' Accounts of Ashburton, 1479–1580. Edited ... by Alison Hanham, 1970. Transcript, the Latin translated, followed by several pages of memoranda, obits, agreements, etc. The introduction surveys the range of the accounts ('exceptional in being so full and in furnishing a nearly unbroken record over the hundred years from 1479'), comments on the use of West Country words and forms, and on the quality of the Latin. Glossary. (p.114)

These two listings from Texts and Calendars II *(Mullins, 1983) demonstrate the value, especially for the inexperienced, of searching for serial publications; the printed works are easier to read than films or original documents; sometimes the Latin has been translated, and usually they are easier to track down.*

Some of these records have been the subject of genealogical finding aids. These list collections and any indexes, with locations and any special instructions about access. Not only do they serve to guide your research in England, but they can be used as checklists against which the contents of the FHL can be compared. The Federation of Family History Societies (FFHS) has issued *Land and Window Tax Assessments* (Gibson, Mills, and Medlycott, 1998), *Quarter Sessions Records for Family Historians* (Gibson, 1995), and *Poor Law Union Records 1834–1930* (Gibson and Rogers, 4 parts, 1993). Also of interest from this publisher are the volumes in the Raymond bibliography series (e.g., *Cumberland and Westmorland*, 1993), which include a section on parochial and borough records.

Further Reading

Two books are regarded as classics when it comes to discussions of local records and obtaining maximum benefit from them. These are *The Parish Chest* (Tate, 1983) and *Village Records* (West, 1997). For the latter, there is a companion volume, *Town Records* (West, 1983). Several other books are listed in the Bibliography. Accounts of the experiences of other researchers in journal articles are referenced in *PERSI;* or check the article abstracts in each issue of *Family History News and Digest* (published two times a year by the Federation of Family History Societies).

Obtaining Records of Local Administration

1. Decide on the family or families, region, and time period of interest.

2. Consult how-to books for details on the records you plan to consult, and refresh your knowledge of local history.

3. Go carefully through the appropriate sections and entries of the *FHLC,* not forgetting the author/title listings.

4. Look for published records, others on microfiche, and record guides in nearby libraries. Consult the *Victoria County History.*

5. Locate and review the inventories and finding aids to contents of record offices in England to determine what is available overall, and what tools are there to assist your search.

6. Prepare a research plan.

10 ❧ EARLY ENGLISH RESEARCH—AN INTRODUCTION

n the context of this book, "early" means before 1730. Everyone reaches this point eventually, whether by a progression back from an ancestor who recently crossed to America, or by a sudden leap because of a colonial line. This book, thus far, has had quite a lot to say about records which are useful for early English research. The parish registers of the Church of England, for many parishes, have entries from the 1500s; wills start in the 1300s; some occupational documents predate 1730; and court and parish chest records also go back a long way.

There are new obstructions in early records, the most obvious being the use of Latin, handwriting, and missing records. To surmount the first two requires a little study and some practice, the other, record knowledge and strategy. Additional challenges include tougher access, and, for some researchers, reluctance to tackle an apparently difficult search. This chapter should remove that reluctance. There are many ways to gently introduce your-self to the early periods of English genealogical research.

Begin With Lists

There are many lists to choose from. They present fewer prob-lems of translation or interpretation, and many have been printed or microfilmed and deposited in the Family History Library (FHL). Furthermore, the ones surveyed here cover a broad geo-graphic area and include at least a significant proportion of the heads of households.

It will help if you study the context of the record to be con-sulted. Some of these records were related to a specific political situation, or an event, or to an urgent need for funding. When each was made, for what purpose, who recorded the details, on what basis the list was compiled—all these factors are important to getting the most benefit from the research.

Tax Lists

Poll Tax: This was paid by those not receiving poor relief; every-one over the age of sixteen was assessed 1 percent of the value of their estate. It was first collected in the thirteenth century, and there were six levies in the 1600s: 1641 (poorest survival), 1660, 1666, 1677, 1694, 1698. The records are in the Public Record Office (PRO) in class E179. Those for London, 1694, are among the printed lists.

Subsidies: Parliament granted the monarch, by statute, the authority to collect a subsidy. It most cases, it was assessed on movables with certain items being exempt (e.g., a knight's armor). There was a distinction between lay subsidies, levied on the general citizenry, and clerical subsidies, assessed on church property. The subsidy rolls (PRO: E179) are arranged by counties and parishes, and list taxpayers; there are good returns late in the thirteenth century, several in the fourteenth, and for 1542 to 1545 (during the reign of Henry VIII). Four collections were made in the 1600s but not all contain lists of names. An entire community was assessed a sum and details of who paid how much were not always recorded. *Subsidy* is used as a general term for different taxes, so several types may be listed under this heading in other source books.

Hearth Tax: First collected at Michaelmas of 1662 and abolished in England in 1689, it was charged to the occupant rather than the owner of a property. This tax caused a great deal of discontent, and its overall unpopularity led to evasion. Some stopped up their hearths, and others connived to have the count reduced. The penalties of higher payment or a month in jail did not deter people from avoidance. There were exemptions for the impoverished. In the years where government took responsibility for collections, returns are better (the best is Lady Day 1664), but when collection was farmed out to contractors, the survival of records declines. The records are in the PRO (E179) and in some County Record Offices. Printed lists, which record the head of the house and the number of hearths, exist for many counties; countywide in a single volume and published to date are: Bedfordshire, Cornwall, Derbyshire, Devon, Dorset, Hampshire, Leicestershire, Norfolk, Nottinghamshire, Oxfordshire, Rutland, Shropshire, Somerset, Staffordshire, Suffolk, Surrey, Westmorland, and Yorkshire.

Window Tax: In 1696, to help cover the cost of reminting the coinage of the realm, a tax on windows was legislated. The way it was levied changed over the years and it was not abolished until 1851. Again, people tried evasion, stopping up windows to pay a lower rate or to be exempt. A large part of the population, living in small cottages, would never have been assessed. The lists are in the PRO (E181) and in County Record Offices.

Matters of Loyalty

Protestation Returns: 1641–1642: In 1641 Parliament passed a bill requiring all Englishmen (over eighteen) to sign a statement that they would "promise, vow, and protest to maintain and defend…the true reformed Protestant religion." This was at the beginning of the conflict between King Charles I and Parliament, which resulted in the Civil War and the eventual triumph of Oliver Cromwell. Anyone refusing to take the oath was rendered incapable of holding public office. Lists record those who complied and those who did not. They are in the House of Lords Record Office. Some have been printed, and for some counties many have survived.

Collection in Aid of Distressed Protestants in Ireland 1641: This was a rare act of unity of king and Parliament on the eve of the Civil War, but the strife and atrocities in Ireland attracted much attention and sympathy. There was a need to help those who lost their homes, crops, animals, etc., as well as a need to raise a force to go to Ireland. This act of Parliament authorized local officials to collect charity and gifts; names of donors were listed. Returns exist for more than twenty counties, with some notable differences from the surviving Protestation Returns (in the PRO, E179 and SP28). A full survey with a comment on the value of knowing the details of surviving lists for both of these records is in "The Collection for Distressed Protestants in Ireland, 1642" (Webb, 1985); for example, Leicestershire has no Protestation Returns, but there are lists of collections from 256 parishes.

Free and Voluntary Present to King Charles II: In 1661, immediately following the Restoration, the king had a cash-flow problem. Parliament voted him a "free and voluntary present" as a temporary expedient. The lists of contributors drawn up by local commissioners survive for about thirty counties. Some are published and some are in County Record Offices, but most are in the PRO (E179). If a hearth tax return cannot be located, look for this.

Association Oath Rolls: A parliamentary act of 1696 imposed penalties on open supporters of James II (the king over the water). All office holders, civil, military, and naval personnel in receipt of a pension, and members of London Livery Companies were required to swear loyalty and be recorded in the Association Oath Roll. Quakers could make a declaration. What is particularly interesting is that the rolls were open for all to sign. In most places all males were encouraged to do so, and many women added their names to the lists. Survival varies (PRO: C213); some rolls were made in Virginia, New York, and the West Indies, and have been printed.

Recusant Rolls: *Recusancy* is the failure to attend the services of the established church. It came to be a term applied to Roman Catholics, but lists include some Protestant nonconformists, although they do not state individual religious convictions. Religion was considered an indication of loyalty; people were expected to conform. Fines were imposed for noncompliance by Acts of Uniformity in 1559 and 1581, and goods and property could become forfeit. Recusant Rolls, 1592 to 1691, list the names with the fines or forfeitures. These are in the PRO (E376–77) and are the annual lists made by county sheriffs. Some have been published by the Catholic Record Society.

Military Lists

Muster Rolls: These are lists of able-bodied men within the statutory age limits (usually sixteen to sixty) who could be called upon for defense of the realm, or to quell local riots (in which case the force was called the *posse comitatus*). The authorities were nervous about large numbers of armed men gathering in one spot, so a local official would simply draw up a militia list.[1] The majority of these records are in the PRO; some are in County Record Offices.

Monmouth Rebels: In July 1685 about five thousand rebels assembled on the field at Sedgemoor in support of James, Duke of Monmouth. It was known as the "Pitchfork Rebellion," for the army was made up of a ragged bunch, mostly from the West Country. Afterwards, those who had not died in battle were hunted down, to be later transported or executed, sentenced by the notorious Judge Jeffries, at the "Bloody Assizes." A roll call of these men has been compiled: *The Monmouth Rebels 1685* (Wigfield, 1985) records their names, homes, and eventual fate.

Locating the Records

There are three key elements to finding records described in this section: several volumes in the series of finding aids known as Gibson Guides; the locality section of the Family History Library Catalog (*FHLC*); and those records which have appeared in a printed form. The first becomes a means of looking in and for the other two:

The Protestation Returns 1641–1642 (Gibson and Dell, 1995) includes The Protestation Returns, The Collection in Aid of Distressed Protestants in Ireland, a subsidy, and a poll tax.

The Hearth Tax, Other Later Stuart Tax Lists and the Association Oath Rolls (Gibson, 1996) includes the hearth tax, some subsidies and poll taxes, the free and voluntary present, and the Association Oath rolls.

Land and Window Tax Assessments (Gibson, Medlycott, and Mills, 1994) includes the window tax and the land tax records (discussed in chapter 9).

Tudor and Stuart Muster Rolls (Gibson and Dell, 1991) includes lists of local militia.

Take what you have learned about the records which survive for the county of interest and search the appropriate section of the *FHLC*. As recommended in the previous chapter, experiment with a search in the author/title section on fiche, looking for an agency or society name. Using these two parts of the *FHLC* should flush out any filmed copies of the records and any printed volumes. In addition, look for printed volumes and even microfiche versions of some of these documents in university libraries. Once these options have been exhausted, the research will have to be done in England.

Records of the Manor

An interest in manorial records should develop before your research reaches this early period. For several hundred years the manors of England, and the structure of life they created, were important aspects of the lives of our ancestors. The records they generated reveal much detail that is not confined to the times which predate parish registers. In fact, manorial documents will be easier to use if you first study some from the more modern period, in English and with simpler handwriting.

Manorial records are divided into two types: the court records and the records of administration. The courts dealt with land holding and with infractions against the common good of the community. There were two—the court leet (which had lost much of its significance by the 1600s) and the court baron. The latter dealt with minor disputes, debts, and trespass and recorded the change in tenure of land. Administrative records are predominantly accounts of the income of the lord, as well as surveys of land and obligations, which name the tenants, the land held, and services to be rendered.

To get the fullest advantage of the time and effort put into searching records of the manor, be sure to do some initial background reading and gain an understanding of the system. There are two excellent, reasonably-priced guides: *My Ancestors Were Manorial Tenants* (Park, 1994) and *Using Manorial Records* (Ellis, 1997). Some manorial records are in the FHL, and others have been printed. Beyond that, finding what survives is an easy matter of contacting the Manorial Documents Register at the Royal Commission on Historical Manuscripts. The commission has a cross-referenced list of parishes and manors, arranged by county. This is another place to check for an obscure place name that could be the name of a manor. The commission also keeps track of the location and description of manorial documents. This came about when copyhold land tenure was abolished in 1925; it was necessary to preserve the records of lands formerly held in that way. An inquiry can be made to the commission by letter, or through a visit to the Web site. The information contained in the Manorial Documents Register is gradually becoming available via the Internet.

About Latin

Latin can be managed. Achieving some level of confidence requires repetitive work, but several hours of self-study should be enough to get you started. Parish registers are a good beginning because they contain a limited vocabulary of about fifty words (other than the Latin forms of names). The transition is not sudden; you will come across a little Latin in the 1700s and somewhat more in the late 1600s, but the Interregnum or Commonwealth (mid-century), when everything was done in English, resulted in a decline after 1650.

More Latin words and more grammatical constructions emerge in other records. Manor court rolls maintained the use of Latin into the 1700s. Marriage licenses, deeds, and probate records (wills are in English from the mid-1500s) vary in their retention of Latin, but, like manor records, the vocabulary is more complex than in parish registers. This need not stop you from attempting to read documents. More than 40 percent of the English vocabulary is derived from Latin, so many words are easy to recognize. Also, clerks, not highly trained in Latin, thought in English and sometimes simply Latinized an English word for want of an accurate translation. If you know some English grammar, Latin grammar will not seem so difficult to grasp.

Several key characteristics make Latin look difficult: there is no *the* or *a* in Latin; the ending of a Latin word, rather than its place in the sentence, determines its function; and there is extensive use of abbreviations. Anyone who took high school Latin will remember terms like declension (Latin nouns fit into five of these), conjugation (Latin verbs fit into four), and cases, such as genitive, accusative, and ablative. For an excellent self-study course, see *Latin for Local and Family Historians* (Stuart, 1995).

You must develop skill in reading old handwriting as your research goes further back and as you attempt to read any documents in Latin. The last of the pre-Italic styles was Secretary Hand, used from 1550 to 1700. The other style used at this time was Court Hand, usually by lawyers and their clerks. Here are some suggestions for improving your ability to read old documents:

- Read a document slowly, looking at every letter.

- Transcribe line by line with a space between to jot other possible interpretations of each letter.

- Return to the difficult spots after reading further and watching for similar constructions which can be interpreted.

- Capital letters express individuals' writing styles, so pick out the obvious ones and mark them throughout the document.

- If making a guess, be sure every letter can be accounted for.

- Expect the same word or name to be spelled more than one way in the same document.

Translation and interpretation are skills which require development, but unless you read old handwriting regularly, it will be necessary to have reference books handy. In addition to the titles mentioned in chapter 1 and above, *The Record Interpreter* (Martin, first pub. 1919; very good for Latin abbreviations), *Village Records* (West, 1997), *How to Read Local Archives* (Emmison, 1983), and *Reading Tudor and Stuart Handwriting* (Munby, 1988) all provide assistance.

Strategy and Tactics

Researchers who plunge into English research in the 1600s, or those who reach 1700 but then lose the line, face similar problems. To pick up the trail, begin by reassessing the facts that are the foundation of the search. Then, work through the indexes and finding aids that suit your parameters, beginning with the most broadly based (usually the International Genealogical Index [IGI]). Make a list, and note the dates and geographic regions for the search—yours and those of the finding aid. The problem may be as fundamental as a gap in the index caused by a gap in the record. Probate indexes at the highest level, the Prerogative Court of Canterbury, and at the diocesan level offer scope but exclude a significant part of the population. If IGI and will searches produce nothing, make some calculated assumptions about where and when, and begin to work your way through as many of the lists described in this chapter as seems necessary. Record what you do and verify the thoroughness of your work. Then go to the records themselves; an index alone is not sufficient.

Use these records and those discussed in chapter 9 to amplify and support what you find in the first round of work in more-basic records. So-called "lost" families may not be lost. Keep in mind that some of these records were collected by hundreds or townships, so also take time to understand the boundary or jurisdiction in effect at the time of collection (you may not be looking in quite the right spot). Chapter 1 offers some suggestions for reading on this topic.

Note

1. Gibson and Dell, 1991, 4.

First Steps in Pre-1730 Research

1. Check the IGI first; where a geographic region can be selected, even if several counties, note the extent of coverage of that area by the IGI.

2. Look for probate indexes for the area; consider whether a PCC index search is worthwhile (remember that for the years 1653 to 1660 all probate, without exception, was handled by the London court).

3. Check for the existence of lists, and an indication of completeness, for the geographic area and time period of interest; begin by consulting a finding aid such as one of the Gibson guides.

4. Once the record type has been selected, determine whether the index and/or the record has been printed as a book or microform.

5. Check for availability through an LDS family history center, a local library, or by purchase.

6. It may be possible to use the Internet to locate a record and up-to-date information on finding aids.

7. Consider repeating this process for a slightly different time period and area if results are negative. When seeking to confirm the presence of a family in a particular parish or region, be sure to use generous parameters and to compare the extent of one source to the others.

8. If basic records have gaps or become unavailable, investigate the survival of manorial records and records of local administration (see chapter 9).

9. Do this work in conjunction with knowledge of the availability of parish registers in the County Record Office and in the collection of the FHL.

11 ❧ WORKING IT OUT

istory is frequently an attempt to find the cor-
rect answer to equations which have been half
erased. Family history is no different. Your
research into a line of ancestry is not likely to
be a "textbook" case. You will rarely find that
your studies can be neatly organized in the
way the chapters of this book have been. Great-Grandfather was-
n't home on census night; the crucial years of a parish register are
missing; perhaps you didn't start with the right facts.

The Ocean Crossing

There are no formal records of arrival or naturalization in the
United States before 1820. For Canada, passenger arrival lists
begin much later (1865) and no naturalization was required up
until 1947, as Englishmen and -women were British subjects.
This leaves several methods to determine, or at least surmise as a
basis for study, an ancestor's place of origin in England. It may

take more than one method; in fact, the wise genealogist will do all these things.

- Look in printed lists because the place or region, and its inhabitants, may have been researched and recorded (this is true for many early colonial settlers).

- Study the local history of the ancestor's first place of settlement (there may be a pattern, the majority having similar origins).

- Search early records in the U.S. or Canada.

- Study the origins and distribution of an uncommon surname in England.

- Use wide-ranging indexes to find the ancestor or to select a group of likely candidates for study (e.g., civil registration, the International Genealogical Index [IGI], several probate indexes, the 1881 census index, some early tax lists).

It is entirely possible that a stage in an ancestor's life or a generation or two in the family line are missing—unknown to you. The Englishman in Illinois may have spent fifteen years in Ontario before he moved on. Many of the English in British Columbia came via an interval in California or even South America. The gap might have occurred back in Britain—some years in Scotland or Wales, or overseas with the army. The thoroughness of your research before attempting the ocean crossing will reduce the chances of your being fooled; also maintain a receptive outlook and be willing to try the odd hypothesis.

Finding Answers

Problem-solving in genealogy, rather like detective work, depends on a mixture of methodical plodding, inspired guesswork, and luck. However, you may still have difficulty unless you have studied the sources and gained some research experience. I am inclined to believe, as well, that you must be willing to gamble occasionally—to risk time and/or money on a long shot.

Methodical plodding is best undertaken by you. If you hire someone else to search through endless rolls of census films, for example, the cost becomes prohibitive. The preparatory work of investigating accessibility, checking for finding aids, and discovering how the records are organized should always be done. It is also advisable to consult maps of the area to ensure familiarity with the place-names and with the boundaries of the various jurisdictions. Then plan your search on a basis that suits your objective, the geography, and the records themselves.

Inspired guesswork tends to be accompanied by an unexplained gut feeling. *Guesswork* may not be the best word, because this sort of success generally arises from first-class historical and geographical knowledge, from an easy familiarity with the records, or from a flash of memory. None of these things will occur unless you work consistently to build up your knowledge base.

Luck comes because you created an opportunity. For example, you may have sent your entries to a genealogical directory or to a family history society surname index. Perhaps you responded to someone else's notice in one of those resources, or took a chance and wrote or telephoned a complete stranger when you spotted a name from your family tree. Luck can also surface when you browse in used-book stores or drop into public libraries on your travels. Plodding, guesswork, luck, coincidence, serendipity—whatever you choose to call it, there is no doubt that the more you know, the more likely it is these things will happen.

Problem-solving can be simplified if you can identify common problems. Assuming you score 100 percent for good research habits (look again at chapter 1), there are seven common

Roadblocks

*For each roadblock, use the solutions suggested or
choose your own strategy.*

1. The base information you are working from may be inaccurate. (B, C, G)

2. You may not have gathered enough of or the right sort of information for the record. (G, I, J)

3. There may be a gap in the records for the particular time and place. (The records may have been damaged or destroyed, may not have been kept for a time, or may be in private hands.) (A, E, H, L, M)

4. After you've checked for survival and availability, the record may still be missing. Perhaps an individual entry was never made or there was a human error (e.g., name copied incorrectly into an index, name missed when the transcript was made), or your research was hurried. (A, E, F, H)

5. Your research may have turned up several possible solutions. (H, I, J, K)

6. The scale of the search may be too large (too many years to cover, too large an area, too common a name, or a combination of these). (D, H)

7. There may be a technical problem involving language, handwriting, or organization (e.g., only chronological, not completely alphabetical, or haphazard geographical arrangement). (D, L, M)

Solutions

A. Check the alternate sources which provide similar information.

B. Expand the geographical area of your search.

C. Expand the time span of your search.

D. Check that all indexes and finding aids have been identified and checked.

E. Examine another copy of the same source in a different location.

F. Repeat the search.

G. Double-check your base information.

H. Carry out the same search for a sibling or other close relation.

I. Try to supplement your base information through additional sources.

J. Improve your historical and geographical background knowledge, create a hypothesis, and work it through.

K. Trace downward from all possible solutions.

L. Check books and periodicals for case studies and talk to other researchers.

M. Hire a professional.

roadblocks to further research (see page 180). Each roadblock mentioned is followed by letters suggesting solutions, a key to which appears on the facing page.

This list is a useful guide—design your own checklist of difficulties and options. The object of the exercise is to encourage you to look critically at why research has bogged down, and to formulate a new strategy. Do not forget to note the elements of any genealogical resource (listed in chapter 1) for each new source you consider using. In fact, it is helpful to jot down six short questions and have them handy any time you consider finding out about a new resource or when you visit an archive or library.

What time period does the record cover?

What geographical area does the record cover?

How is the record organized?

What information is needed to access the record?

What new information will the record supply?

Where and how can the record be consulted?

Sources and Evidence

Much earlier in this book it was suggested that you be aware of the nature of your sources, whether they could be described as primary or secondary, and what degree of authority could be ascribed to them. Do you consider the evidence to be direct or circumstantial, original or hearsay? Consider this carefully when problems arise. Take time to test the chronology and the facts against other records and reliable accounts of historical events. Sometimes it is best to verify from another source before continuing a line of inquiry. Build up lots of evidence.

A marriage certificate provides a good example. You can feel quite confident that the date and place of the marriage have been recorded correctly. However, everything else should be regarded as no more reliable than a clue, dependent upon the accuracy of the informant's response. Addresses are commonly temporary, ages often vague or inaccurate, the condition (spinster, bachelor, widow, etc.) of the parties may or may not be correct, and you cannot be sure accurate information about the fathers was supplied. Often you must work from these facts for want of other information, but do not blindly accept them as true until new information proves them to be so. A good genealogist applies a healthy dose of skepticism.

Other qualities of the family historian are curiosity, optimism, and a commitment to not only finding the truth but to leaving a thoroughly referenced account of what has been done. Cite your sources in a professional manner, and if you accept information based on work done by others, ask for their sources, or find them yourself. The essential guide to citation and to demonstrating reliability of genealogical research is *Evidence! Citation and Analysis for the Family Historian* (Mills, 1997).

It is important to sense that we are well-rooted in the past— to know who we are and where we have come from. Family history produces these roots, and offers bonuses besides: unusual skills, fascinating reading, places to visit, new friends and relations, adventures in technology. As Jane Austen seems to imply through the words of Catherine Morland in *Northanger Abbey*, the history of history books is a bore; history on another plane must be superior.

> *But history, real solemn history, I cannot be interested in …*
> *I read it a little as a duty but it tells me nothing that does*
> *not either vex or weary me. The quarrels of popes and kings,*
> *with wars or pestilences, in every page; the men all so good-*
> *for-nothing, and hardly any women at all.*

A

THE
FAMILY HISTORY LIBRARY
CATALOG

Half the questions posed by participants in a typical genealogy course need never have arisen if library catalogs—in particular, the *Family History Library Catalog (FHLC)*—were used to
full effect. An effective search allows the patron to navigate into
the depths of a library collection. It takes experience, a little skill,
and certainly a sound knowledge of the organization of the catalog to make the most of its offerings.

The *FHLC* describes the contents of the Family History
Library (FHL) in Salt Lake City. It exists in two formats: microfiche and CD-ROM. This discussion focuses first on the microfiche catalog, for several reasons: all topical arrangements of the
listings can be viewed on microfiche; the hierarchy of catalog
organization is apparent; in most family history centers fiche
readers are less heavily booked; and sections of the fiche catalog

can be purchased. Features, advantages, and disadvantages of the CD-ROM version follow.

The *FHLC* has four main sections: locality, surname, author/title, and subject. There is a fifth part—a native-language version of the locality section with all headings in the language of the country concerned. The *FHLC* is updated on a fairly regular basis; you can see the date of issue at the top of each fiche or on each full display in the CD-ROM format, which is revised more frequently. Information about each item includes:

- Author or issuing authority
- Title
- Publishing details (company or agency, where, when)
- Notes on contents including number of pages or films; sometimes fairly extensive descriptions about organization of a collection of records
- Book and/or microfilm and/or microfiche call numbers and location in the FHL
- Computer number
- Headings under which the item is listed (often several)

In the microfiche edition of the catalog, every item in the FHL is listed in the author/title section. It is rare for an item to appear in all four arrangements, but it will definitely appear in two.

Experience will demonstrate that the most useful and most frequently consulted part of the *FHLC* is the locality section. It is organized by geographic units, in descending order. Before you get to the record listings—in the current edition on the fourth fiche—you will see the list of "Pointers." It indicates every place for which there is an entry, with its exact locality section format. In the case of England this means that records created by the national government at Westminster, or pertaining to the country as a whole, are listed first (see figure A-1). Next comes records which relate to the county level (figure A-2) for the first county in England (Bedfordshire), followed immediately by local records (figure A-3) for each of the parishes of the county (for which there is at least one item) arranged in alphabetical order. The last place in Bedfordshire is followed by the county level holdings for Berkshire, the parish level holdings for Berkshire, and so on through all the counties to the last parish in Yorkshire. The county names are those in use before 1974. Within the geographic sections, whether national county or parish, the records are arranged by type.

The headings for the types of records are taken from a standard list. Occasionally, where a unique record does not fit these categories, a new heading must be created. There are more than eighty headings under which records and books are classified; a partial list appears in Table A-1. As you scan down the columns of a microfiche you will follow a pattern in the headings:

- ENGLAND—RECORD TYPE

- ENGLAND—RECORD TYPE—DESCRIPTIVE (e.g., INDEXES)

- ENGLAND—COUNTY NAME—RECORD TYPE

- ENGLAND—COUNTY NAME—RECORD TYPE—DESCRIPTIVE

- ENGLAND, COUNTY NAME, PARISH/TOWN—RECORD TYPE

- ENGLAND, COUNTY NAME, PARISH/TOWN—RECORD TYPE, DESCRIPTIVE

Practice this, watching for the changes in headings and picking up the pattern. For many small places only one type of record will be listed (usually church records or the census). Within the sections for each record type, where there is more than one item, they appear in alphabetical order according to author's surname or the name of the issuing authority. If there is any question about where an item ought to be listed, it will in

TABLE A-1

FHLC Subject Heading

Archives and Libraries	Maps
Bibliography	Military History
Biography	Military Records
Business and Commerce	Names—Geographic
Cemeteries	Names—Personal
Census	Newspapers
Church Directories	Nobility
Church Records	Obituaries
Church Histories	Occupations
Civil Registration	Pensions
Court Records	Periodicals
Description and Travel	Politics and Government
Directories	Poor Houses
Emigration and Immigration	Probate Records
Gazetteers	Public Records
Genealogy	Schools
History	Social Life and Customs
Indexes	Taxation
Inventories and Registers	Vital Records
Land and Property	Voting Registers

all probability appear in both locations. A group of records or a book, such as a regional directory, which pertains to several counties should appear under each county and perhaps the national section as well.

The author/title section is a strictly alphabetical listing of every single item in the FHL according to author names and book titles; they are intermingled and some things may appear in this index more than once. Probate records, for example, appear within this section under the name of the authority responsible, the Church of England or the Principal Registry of the Family Division. To better understand what this arrangement of records can do, select one from the locality section, preferably with an archive or agency as the author, and look it up here. All items in the collection generated by that agency will be together; this could generate some ideas for problem-solving.

The subject section is more limited in scope than the locality and author/title sections. Subjects are based on those used by the Library of Congress, and they are mainly religious, political, and ethnic groups. Some of the headings link the group to a country or region (e.g., METHODISTS—ENGLAND). There are other subjects based on topics like occupations, libraries, and language. Looking in this section is a good way to find background information.

From time to time, look up the new names in your growing family tree in the surname section. It is a source of information on work already done by others. It is organized alphabetically by the surname (not by author). If the book discusses other families, the entry will show up to seven additional names. There are also indications of dates and geographic area to narrow your selection.

Not all of these index formats are available on the CD-ROM version of the *FHLC*. It can be used for surname search and for locality browse or locality search. Locality browse helps with identification of a place—for example, to find the proper spelling or the county it is in. Input what you know, and a list of possibilities will appear on the screen. If you know country, county, and place, then use the locality search. It can present you with too many possibilities, but if this happens, type F3 followed by a record type or place name; the search will immediately go to that spot. Within a place and record category, there may still be numerous entries; scan them first by author, marking those that require a closer look. This is quicker than going through each listing in full display. The computer does warn you if a collection is very large. From the full display screen, the enter key will produce a listing of the location of the record, including all family history centers where it is on indefinite loan (this information is only as reliable as the staff members who are expected to submit it annually).

CD-ROM is an excellent way to search the surname section of the *FHLC*. For common names, additional facts will speed up the search. Interesting entries can be marked and placed in a holding file for printing to paper or disk. "Wild card" searches are possible: type in part of a name and an asterisk; the computer will display anything that fits the part of a name entered. This can also be done with places in locality browse. Both surname and locality search allow for use of key words, details which will limit the selections found. You could request Colwoods linked to New York, or Loyalist to draw out only those Colwood families which fit the key words.

Author/title and subject searches are not available on the CD-ROM version. It does have a section which lists all items in the FHL according to their computer numbers, and you can search on computer by fiche, film, or computer number. This can be useful for making a quick check of the contents of a record and to discover whether it is in a family history center on indefinite loan. On fiche, the computer number (RN for record number) can be found on each entry in the author/title set of fiche.

The best way to get the full advantage of the *FHLC* is to use it in all its forms. Some searches work better with the fiche, others with CD-ROM. You will develop your own preferences. It can be faster to scan a fiche than to wait for the computer to search for an item, but key word and wild card searches on computer are powerful tools. If you are some distance away from a family history center, consider purchasing a copy of the *FHLC* for England or just several counties. That way you are free to study listings at home or in another, perhaps closer, library.

Study the *FHLC*. When research turns up a new name or a new place, assess the holdings of the FHL. Explore the possibilities with the author/title listings. Here you can find out most about the extensive fiche collections issued by Chadwyck-Healey of Cambridge. This company produces the *National Index of Documentary Sources in the United Kingdom*. The finding aids of many archives and libraries are in it as well, so their contents can be assessed. The locality section has the listings under the appropriate heading, but a scan of them all together might be useful. Also in the author/title section are the entries for *British and Irish Biographies 1840–1940,* which contains thousands of biographical and professional directories. There is a master name index of the individuals in those volumes (*The Index to British and Irish Biographies*); however, only the first edition (105 fiche) circulates to family history centers.

Important as the *FHLC* is, it is the catalog for only one library. Vast as its holdings are, the FHL does not have everything that could be useful to your research. A review of what can be studied through LDS resources must be accompanied by a review of what is available overall. Such a review ensures that your research is thorough and that you can plan the most effective way to carry out a search.

Clear steps to using the catalog effectively are contained in several publications available at family history centers or from the LDS church's Family History Department.

> *Getting Started: Family History Library Catalog* (on CD-ROM)
>
> *Family History Library Catalog* (on CD-ROM)
>
> *Family History Library Catalog* (on microfiche)
>
> *Using the Family History Library Catalog*

```
*****************************************************************************
ENGLAND - TAXATION
                                                        +--------------+
Great Britain.  Board of Inland Revenue.                |BRITISH       |
   Land tax assessments, England and Wales, 1798-1801. -- London, |FILM AREA     |
   England : Filmed by the Public Record Office, 1988. -- 64      +--------------+
   microfilm reels

   Microfilm copy of original records at the Public Record Office in
   London.
   Records are organized by counties.  Each county is organized by
   hundreds.  (York is first divided into ridings, then hundreds.)
   Each hundred is organized by parishes.  Each parish contains
   records of taxes assessed to each property owner.  An index
   of page numbers precedes each county and each hundred.  Dates vary
   from 1798 to 1808.
   Public Record Office of London no.: IR 23/1-121.

   Bedfordshire                           1798-1799 --------------- 1483001
     Berkshire (1-286)                    1798-1800
   Berkshire (286-400)                    1798-1800 --------------- 1483002
     Buckingham, Vol. 1                   1798
     Buckingham, Vol. 2 (1-196)          1798
     (Some records are faded.)
   Buckingham, Vol. 2 (197-234)           1798 ------------------- 1483003
     Cambridge                            1798-1800
     Chester (Cheshire) (1-27?)           1798
   Chester (Cheshire) (280-628)           1798-1800 --------------- 1483004
     Cornwall (1-215)                     1798-1799
   Cornwall (215-295)                     1798-1799 --------------- 1483005
     Cornwall Vol. 2 (296-613)           1798-1799
     Cornwall (1-141)                     1799-1800
   Cornwall (142-408)                     1799-1800 --------------- 1483006
     Cornwall, Vol. 2 (409-719)          1799-1800
     (Some records are faded.)
   Cornwall Vol. 2 (720-741)              1798-1800 --------------- 1483007
     Cumberland (1-333)                   1798
     Cumberland Vol. 2 (342-523)         1798
   Cumberland, Vol. 2 (524-613)           1798 ------------------- 1483008
     Derby, Vol. 1 (1-359)                1798-1800
     Derby, Vol. 2 (363-456)             1798-1800
   Derby, Vol. 2 (457-659)                1798-1800 --------------- 1483009
     Devon, Vol. 1 (1-348)                1798-1800
   Devon, Vol. 1-3 (349-894)              1798-1800 --------------- 1483010
   Devon, Vol. 3-4 (895-1227)             1798-1799 --------------- 1483011
     Devon, City of Exeter (1-211)        1798-1800
   Devon, city of Exeter, (213-222)       1798-1800 --------------- 1483012
     Dorset, Vol. 1-2 (1-550)             1798-1800
   Dorset, Vol. 2 (550-584)               1798-1800 --------------- 1483013
     Durham, Vol. 1-2 (1-515)             1798-1800
   Durham, Vol. 2-3 (516-950)             1798-1800 --------------- 1483014
     Cambridge, Isle of Ely (1-117)       1798-1800
   Cambridge, Isle of Ely (113-121)       1798-1800 --------------- 1483015
     Essex, Vol.1-3 (1-532)               1798-1800
   Essex, Vol. 3 (533-725)                1798-1800 --------------- 1483016

     Gloucester, Vol. 1 (1-363)           1798-1800
   Gloucester, Vol. 1-2 (364-795)  .      1798-1800 --------------- 1483017
     Hereford, (1-126)                    1798-1800
   Hereford (127-419)                     1798-1800 --------------- 1483018
     Hereford, Vol 2. (1-259)             1798-1800
     Borough of St. Albans (11-23)        1798-1800
     (Borough of St. Albans included in Hereford,
     Vol. 2.)
   Hertford (260-393)                     1798-1800 --------------- 1483019
     Borough of Huntingdon (1-250)        1798-1800
     Kent, Vol.1 (1-160)                  1798-1800
   Kent, Vol. 1-3, (160-740)              1798-1800 --------------- 1483020
   Kent, Vol. 3-4 (740-1218)              1798-1800 --------------- 1483021
     Lancashire, Vol.1 (1-75)             1798-1800
   Lancashire, Vol. 1-2 (77-630)          1798-1801 --------------- 1483022
   Lancashire, Vol. 2-3 (631-1185)        1798-1800 --------------- 1483023
   Lancashire, Vol. 3-4 (1186-1730)       1798-1800 --------------- 1483024
   Lancashire, Vol. 4 (1731-1742)         1798-1800 --------------- 1483025
```

Figure A-1 Locality section on microfiche. Note the heading, COUNTRY, followed by RECORD TYPE, indicating the section listing national records. In this case the "author" is a government department.

```
*************************************************************************
ENGLAND, ESSEX - VITAL RECORDS
                                                     +-------------+
Church of England, Diocese of London. Consistory Court.   |BRITISH      |
   Marriage bonds and allegations, 1665-1817. -- Salt Lake City : |FILM AREA  |
   Filmed by the Genealogical Society of Utah, 1951. -- 18   +-------------+
   microfilm reels ; 35 mm.

   Microfilm of originals at Essex Record Office.
   Jurisdiction: Essex County.

   Marriage bonds and allegations,    1665-1680 ------------------- 0091192
   Marriage bonds and allegations,    1681-1731 ------------------- 0091193
   Marriage bonds and allegations,    1732-1734 ------------------- 0091194
   Marriage bonds and allegations,    1735-1739 ------------------- 0091195
   Marriage bonds and allegations,    1740-1742 ------------------- 0091196
   Marriage bonds and allegations,    1743-1745 ------------------- 0091197
   Marriage bonds and allegations,    1746-1751 ------------------- 0091198
   Marriage bonds and allegations,    1752-1754 ------------------- 0091199
   Marriage bonds and allegations,    1755-1760 ------------------- 0091200
   Marriage bonds and allegations,    1761-1764 ------------------- 0091201

   Marriage bonds and allegations,    1765-1768 ------------------- 0091202
   Marriage bonds and allegations,    1769-1772 ------------------- 0091203
   Marriage bonds and allegations,    1773-1777 ------------------- 0091204
   Marriage bonds and allegations,    1778-1782 ------------------- 0091205
   Marriage bonds and allegations,    1783-1792 ------------------- 0091206
   Marriage bonds and allegations,    1793-1802 ------------------- 0091207
   Marriage bonds and allegations,    1803-1817 ------------------- 0091208
   Marriage bonds and allegations,    1818-1853 ------------------- 0091209

*************************************************************************
ENGLAND, ESSEX - VITAL RECORDS
                                                     +-------------+
D'Elboux, R. H.                                        |BRITISH      |
   The monumental brasses of Essex / by Miller Christy, W. Wade |BOOK AREA  |
   Porteous, and E. Bertram Smith ; edited by R. H. D'Elboux. -- |1942       |
   Ashford, Kent : Monumental Brass Society, 1948. -- 47 p. : |A1        |
   ill.                                               |no.  258   |
                                                     +-------------+
   Part 1, Alphamstone to Berden.

*************************************************************************
ENGLAND, ESSEX - VOTING REGISTERS
                                                     +-------------+
Bramfill, Champion.                                   |BRITISH      |
   The poll for knights of the shire to represent the county of |FILM AREA  |
   Essex : taken at Chelmsford, on Tuesday the 7th day of May, |1594313    |
   1734 / by Champion Bramfill. -- Salt Lake City : Filmed by | item 6    |
   the Genealogical Society of Utah, 1989. -- on 1 microfilm +-------------+
   reel ; 35 mm.

   Microfilm of original published: London : [s.n.], 1734.  181 p.
   Contains lists of knights' names, their town or city, and their
      freeholds.
   Waltham Forest Archives no.: 146.

*************************************************************************
ENGLAND, ESSEX - VOTING REGISTERS
                                                     +-------------+
Clay, Richard Lomax.                                  |BRITISH      |
   The Poll for knights of the shire to represent the county of |FILM AREA  |
   Essex, taken at Chelmsford on Tuesday, March 29, 1768 / by |1594313    |
   Richard Lomax Clay. -- Salt Lake City : Filmed by the | item 8    |
   Genealogical Society of Utah, 1989. -- on 1 microfilm reel ; +-------------+
   35 mm.

   Microfilm of original published:  Chelmsford [England] : by authority of
      the high sheriff, 1768.  xvi, 183 p.
   Includes index.
   Contains freeholders names, places of abode and where freeholders lie.
      Also includes freeholders from out of the country.
   Waltham Forest Archives no.: 146.
```

Figure A-2 Locality section on microfiche for the county of Essex. The heading is now COUNTRY, COUNTY, – RECORD TYPE, and the listings reflect this.

```
***********************************************************************
ENGLAND, ESSEX, WENNINGTON - CHURCH RECORDS

Church of England.  Parish Church of Wennington (Essex).          +--------------+
   Bishop's transcripts, 1715. -- Salt Lake City : Filmed by the  |BRITISH       |
   Genealogical Society of Utah, 1965. -- on 1 microfilm reel ;   |FILM AREA     |
   35 mm.                                                         |0413719       |
                                                                  | item 3       |
   IN Copies of parish registers brought in at visitations, various dates /
      Church of England.  Diocese of London.                     +--------------+
   Microfilm of original records at the Guildhall Library, London.
   Record contains baptisms, burials, 1715 (51st parish).

   Another filming.                                               BRITISH

                                                                  FILM AREA
                                                                  0566146
                                                                  item 1

***********************************************************************
ENGLAND, ESSEX, WENNINGTON - CHURCH RECORDS

Church of England.  Parish Church of Wennington (Essex).          +--------------+
   Bishop's transcripts, 1800-1866. -- Salt Lake City : Filmed by |BRITISH       |
   the Genealogical Society of Utah, 1991. -- on 1 microfilm      |FILM AREA     |
   reel ; 16 mm.                                                  |1702676       |
                                                                  | item 3       |
   Microfilm copy of original at Essex Record Office in Chelmsford,+--------------+
      England.
   High reduction (42x) microfilm.  Use high magnification reader.
   Contents:  Baptisms, burials, 1800-1824, 1844-1866; marriages,
      1800-1824, 1851.
   Essex Record Office, Chelmsford, no.: D/CR 405.

***********************************************************************
ENGLAND, ESSEX, WEST BERGHOLT - CENSUS

Great Britain.  Census Office.                                    +--------------+
   Census returns for West Bergholt, 1841-1891. -- on 5 microfilm |BRITISH       |
   reels ; 35 mm. & 16 mm. + 3 microfiches                        |FILM AREA     |
                                                                  +--------------+
   IN Census returns 1841 ... [et al.] / Great Britain.  Census Office.
   A film or fiche set may contain more than one parish.

   1841 --------------------------------------------------------- 0241372
   1851 p. 630-657 --------------------------------------------- 0207431
   1861 --------------------------------------------------------- 0542754
   1871 --------------------------------------------------------- 0829971
   1881 --------------------------------------------------------- 1341434
   1891 RG 12/1416 (3 fiches) --------------------------------- 6096526

***********************************************************************
ENGLAND, ESSEX, WEST BERGHOLT - CHURCH RECORDS

Church of England.  Parish Church of West Bergholt (Essex).       +--------------+
   Bishop's transcripts, 1639-1640. -- Salt Lake City : Filmed by |BRITISH       |
   the Genealogical Society of Utah, 1965. -- on 1 microfilm      |FILM AREA     |
   reel ; 35 mm.                                                  |0413721       |
                                                                  +--------------+
   IN Copies of parish registers brought in at visitations, various dates /
      Church of England.  Diocese of London.
   Microfilm of original records at the Guildhall Library, London.
   Record contains baptisms, marriages, burials, 1639-1640 (13th parish).
```

Figure A-3 Locality section on microfiche for Wennington and West Bergholt in Essex. The headings now indicate COUNTRY, COUNTY, PARISH—RECORD TYPE. Within each county section, local records follow county records.

```
                    Family History Library Catalog 04 Mar 1998        Page 1
                              **Full Display**

AUTHOR
Great Britain.  Census Office.

TITLE
Census returns for West Bergholt, 1841-1891.

FORMAT
on 5 microfilm reels ; 35 mm. & 16 mm. + 3 microfiches

NOTES
IN Census returns 1841 ... [et al.] / Great Britain.  Census Office.
A film or fiche set may contain more than one parish.
                                                             BRITISH
CONTENTS                                                     FILM AREA
1841 ------------------------------------------------------- 0241372
1851  p. 630-657 ------------------------------------------- 0207431
1861 ------------------------------------------------------- 0542754
1871 ------------------------------------------------------- 0829971
1881 ------------------------------------------------------- 1341434
                                                             BRITISH
                                                             FICHE AREA
1891  RG 12/1416  (3 fiches) ------------------------------- 6096526

·THIS RECORD FOUND UNDER
    1. England, Essex, West Bergholt - Census
```

Figure A-4 *FHLC* WEST BERGHOLT, ESSEX—CENSUS. This is the full
display from the locality search on CD-ROM.
Compare to figure A-3.

Reprinted by permission. Family History Library Catalog Copyright 1987, 1998 by
Corporation of the President of The Church of Jesus Christ of Latter-day Saints.

B

THE INTERNATIONAL
GENEALOGICAL INDEX

The International Genealogical Index (IGI) is an important
tool for any English genealogical research. A logical approach to
understanding the potential value and possible shortcomings of
the IGI is to answer a series of questions about it.

What Is It?

The IGI, created by the Family History Department of the LDS
church, is an index to more than 280 million events worldwide,
the majority being christenings and marriages. The names
indexed are from original records, or from submissions by members of the LDS church, or those of deceased members of the
LDS church. No living person is included among the names
taken from original sources, so most entries predate 1875. The
IGI is not complete—the scale of the undertaking is difficult to
imagine—and the on-going project will never finish. For

Figure B-1 Sample Page from the IGI.

Reprinted by permission. "International Genealogical Index." Copyright 1980, 1992 by Corporation of the President of The Church of Jesus Christ of Latter-day Saints.

England, there is a large number of entries and many entries from the extraction program.

Extracted records are from the parish registers of the Church of England, or from the bishops' transcripts where the registers were not available. Sometimes already-prepared indexes or lists, such as Phillimore's Marriages, have been included. The IGI also incorporates names from the nonconformist registers held by the Public Record Office (PRO).

Researchers can examine the IGI on microfiche and on CD-ROM in LDS family history centers. Fiche editions will also be found in some other libraries and archives in North America and in England. In the Family History Library (FHL) in Salt Lake City, researchers access the main computer system so there is no need to move disks in and out of a drive. More recent supplements are also available. It is usually possible to make copies of the pages from microfiche using a reader-printer, and computer entries can be collected in a holding file and then downloaded to disk or printed.

Two ancillary finding aids are in family history centers. One is the Batch Number Index, a key to the numbers in the two right-hand columns of each frame on a microfiche. These numbers reveal the microfilm location where the original source, whether parish record or individual submission, can be found. The CD-ROM version of the IGI indicates this source information on a separate screen in response to a keystroke. The other aid is the Parish and Vital Records List. In it, countries are listed in alphabetical order and then broken down geographically, as in the IGI. For England, this is by pre-1974 county. Within each county section, parishes are in alphabetical order. The Parish and Vital Records List provides the name of the church or churches, denomination (if not the Church of England), whether the entries came from bishops' transcripts, outside dates (some longer gaps in records will be revealed), and the film number.

What Does It Contain?

The best way to explain the IGI's content is to illustrate one frame or page from the microfiche format and discuss each heading or column in turn (see Figure B-1). The top line of the page gives the country, the county, the edition of the IGI, and the page number (useful when identifying pages to be copied). Immediately below that are the headings for each of the eleven columns across the page.

The names are always listed alphabetically by surname. There is a system of standard spellings, which means that if your spelling is not the standard, you will usually be able to find the variation by referring to the standard spelling. This may not always happen where your version is especially rare or where pronunciation or other difficulties have altered the name more than you suspect. Within the same surname, individuals are then listed alphabetically by Christian name exactly as given (e.g., Brown, Henry would appear before Brown, Hy.). Where several individuals have the same surname and Christian name, the entries appear in chronological order. If "Σ" appears beside a name it means some part of the entry has been evaluated and may have been altered. Other symbols (#, @) indicate that relatives are named in the source.

The next column identifies the sex of the individual as male or female (for baptisms or births) or husband or wife (for marriages).

The second narrow column beside this is the type of event. There are nine possibilities:

A   adult christening

B   birth

C   christening

D   death or burial

F   birth or christening of first child in place of marriage date

M   marriage

N   census

S   miscellaneous

W   will or probate

The fifth column indicates the date of the event, and the sixth the parish. The place entry may also give the church and/or denomination if relevant. The next three columns provide dates of LDS events.

The final two columns on the right provide the key to identifying the original source of the information. The batch number allows you to differentiate between those entries submitted by private individuals and those obtained from the names extraction program. Names taken from the latter have batch numbers which begin with *C* or *P* (usually birth entries), *J*, *K*, or *M* (usually marriage entries, but not M17 or M18), *E*, 725, 744, 745, and 754. Entries submitted by individuals have batch numbers which are all digits, the third one being smaller than four. Any index entries taken from LDS temple records begin with *A*, M17, or M18. Where a number begins with an *F* the date is calculated or approximate.

Using the numbers in the last two columns and the Batch Number Index, the precise source of the information can be identified. The serial sheet number is the page number for the sheet on which an entry appears.

The CD-ROM version provides the same information (in fact, a bit more) arranged differently. Names appear in alphabetical order, but in separate listings for baptism and marriage. Scrolling through them you see the essential names, dates, and places. When you submit the facts required to launch a search, all entries for England, Scotland, Wales, and Ireland are searched

```
Main International Genealogical Index 4.00--British Isles      16 MAR 1998
Esc=Exit  F1=Help  F2=Print/Holding File  F4=Search

 ┌─ F6=Individual Search ─┐  ┌─ F7=Marriage Search ─┐  ┌─ F8=Parent Search ─┐

      ┌─ PgDn PgUp=Move ─┐  ┌─ Enter=Details ─┐  ┌─ F9=Search Addendum ─┐

(-Name Group-)——Name————————Event Type————————Year——Place—Father/Mother/Rel
-CALEY-
Thomas CALEY ...........   C         1765    IMan   Fa:Michael CALEY
Thomas CALEY ...........   C         1766    Lond   Fa:John
Thomas James CALLEY .....  C         1771    Warw   Fa:George CALLEY
Thomas CALEE ...........   C         1773    IMan   Fa:Thos CALEE
Thomas CALEY ...........   C         1773    IMan   Fa:Thos CALEY
Thomas CALEY ...........   B         1775    IMan   Fa:Michael CALEY
Thomas CALEY ...........   C         1775    IMan   Fa:Michl CALEY
[Thomas] Thos CALEY .....  C         1775    IMan   Fa:Wm CALEY
Thomas CALEY ...........   C         1777    Lanc   Fa:Thomas CALEY
Thomas CALEY ...........   C         1778    IMan   Fa:John CALEY
Thomas CALLEY ..........   C         1779    Lanc   Fa:Wm. CALLEY
Thomas CALLEY ..........   C         1780    Devo   Fa:Wm CALLEY
Thomas CALLEY ..........   B   Abt   1780    Wilt   Re:John T. CALLEY
[Thomas] Thos CALLEE ....  C         1781    Linc   Fa:John CALLEE
```

Figure B-2 Sample screen, Individual Search, from the IGI on CD-ROM.

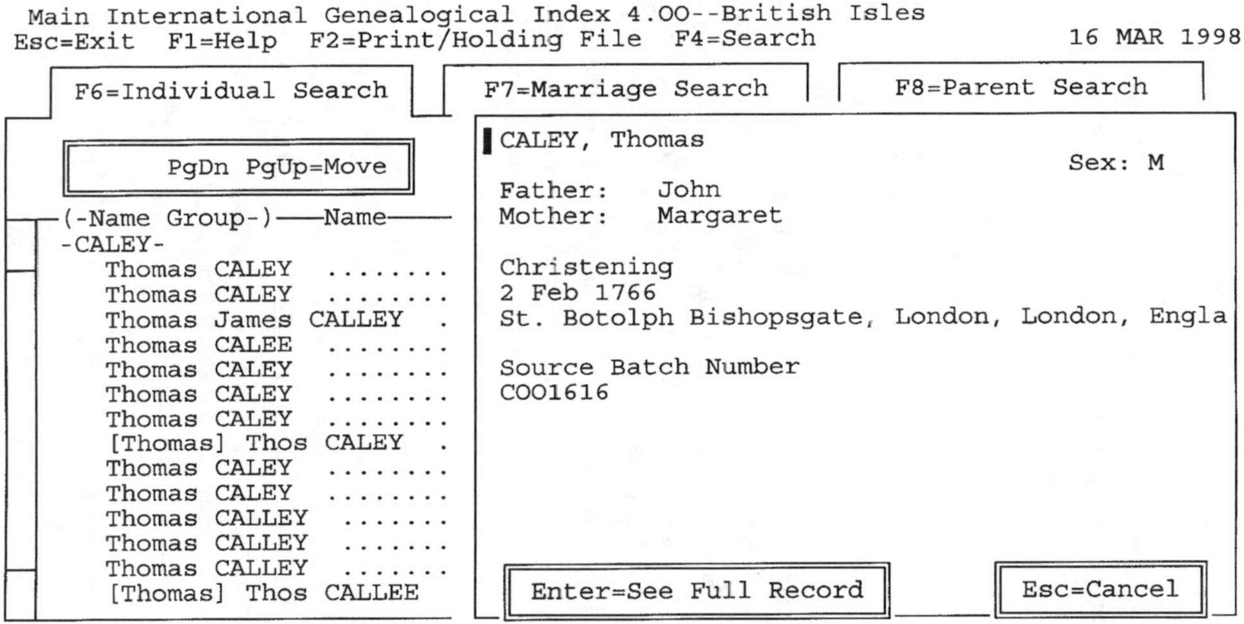

Figure B-3 Sample screen with detail. One of the entries from the list in figure B-2 is highlighted and it appears on top.

unless you specify a county or counties. On CD-ROM, the use of standard spellings has been introduced for some given names (e.g., Catherine and Katherine), and middle names are not taken into account for the alphabetical order. The command to see details will produce the source, making it unnecessary to look at the Batch Number Index.

What Are Its Benefits?

The greatest benefit of the IGI is its potential to save time and money. Depending on whether you have access to the CD-ROM or microfiche edition, you can check the entire country for a particular name in a matter of minutes or a few hours. Consider how long it would take to read through the registers of many parishes, or how much it might cost to have an agent carry out such a search. If your information about the English place of origin is vague, and if the name is not too common, you can use the IGI as a survey tool, for it will indicate the county or counties where the name appeared. You can also trace the spread of a name from, or back to, its place of origin (see figure B-2).

The computer format of the IGI allows for some flexibility in your search and for some helpful combinations. In addition to applying geographic limitations to a search, date ranges can be specified, as can a preference for exact spelling only. When doing a marriage search, it is possible to link the full name of one individual to another, or even to only the first name of the other—for example, any John Hardings who married a Mary. Another benefit of the computer format is the parent search feature. A couple of keystrokes requests all children of parents of the names indicated. If more than one set of parents had the same names, it may be necessary to sort out the families. The computer searches for the name combinations without knowing one family unit from another. Because there is no geographic breakdown, this search may also reveal a child born in another county.

What Are Its Shortcomings?

It is always necessary to keep in mind the fact that the IGI is incomplete. In other words, it does not represent 100-percent coverage of all the counties of England from the middle of the last century back to the first parish registers in the sixteenth century. Some counties, such as Somerset and Norfolk, have very poor representation, while other areas, such as Lancashire and Greater London, have excellent coverage. Other counties may have good coverage for one area and poor coverage for another. Yorkshire is a case in point; the western area, especially around Leeds, is very well covered, but the North Sea coast (e.g., Scarborough) is not.

Always check the coverage of the IGI for the area of, and around, your search. Then take time to compare this to the overall survival of Church of England and nonconformist records for the same area (see chapter 5). The parishes included in the IGI, with outside dates, can be found listed in the Parish and Vital Records List, the locality section of the *Family History Library Catalog (FHLC)*, and in *The Atlas and Index of Parish Registers* (Humphery-Smith, 1995). When looking at a listing in the *FHLC* on microfiche, look to the right of the entry; an *X* indicates that the particular item has been included; *P* means part of the film is in the IGI; *I* means the film is being indexed.

It is also worth bearing in mind that the IGI does not identify infant burials or any linkages between events. Do not focus on a likely entry without being certain that the individual listed actually lived to adulthood. There will be no clue to indicate whether a marriage entry and a birth entry showing the same name (and a logical span of years between) actually refer to the

Figure B-4 A survey of the origins and distribution of Howlands in England (based on the IGI).

+ = Pre–1600 listings
o = 1600–1700 listings

Not only is it possible to plot the distribution of a name in a country or region, but by the use of a code it is also possible to depict the spread of a family. This map shows that in Tudor times, when parish registers were first kept, Howlands were found in north-west Essex and in London. The earliest entries were in Essex. In the next century the name spread further afield (and to North America). Even where coverage is incomplete, such surveys can indicate where to focus research efforts. (Each symbol on the map does not necessarily equal one IGI entry.)

---

same person, or coincidentally to two different people with identical names.

Finally, never forget that the IGI is only an index and that it is subject to error. Always order the film of the original parish register to be sure the IGI information is correct, and to check for additional facts. If you do not find what you want in the IGI, be prepared to order the appropriate film anyway. Sometimes entries in the parish registers were missed by the indexers. In other instances, poor handwriting or faded ink led to incorrect interpretations which have put a name in the wrong part of the alphabet. Indexers have also transposed names, especially where the first or second name is a recognized surname.

Further information on the layout and interpretation of the IGI can be found in the following clearly written LDS guides.

Family Search: International Genealogical Index (on CD-ROM)
Finding an IGI Source
International Genealogical Index (on microfiche)

C

LORD HARDWICKE'S ACT

Philip Yorke, first Earl of Hardwicke, was responsible for the act of Parliament which bears his name. The act is more correctly described as "An Act for the Preventing of Clandestine Marriages." Genealogists have reason to be grateful for Yorke's accomplishment.

Yorke was the son of a country attorney, an equity lawyer of justified reputation who rose to be both solicitor general and attorney general. Subsequently he served as Lord Chief Justice, and in 1737 he was made Lord Chancellor. Yorke's reputation is somewhat marred by the fact that he was mainly responsible for the harsh measures introduced for the pacification of Scotland after the 1745 rebellion and for the execution, by firing squad, of Admiral Byng in 1756 over the loss of Minorca.

Lord Hardwicke's Marriage Act decreed that no marriage would be considered valid unless the banns had been read on three successive Sundays in the parish church or unless a special license had been obtained. In the case of those under twenty-one, the consent of parents or guardian was required. The marriage had to take place in a church or chapel that was customarily used for such a purpose, and the event had to be recorded in a special register according to a specified format. The registers came in three styles: books with pages for recording the banns at the front and marriages after; books which noted the banns and marriage for each couple as one entry; and as separate volumes for each. There is, as a result, much better survival of records of banns from 1754. These listings are valuable; some are the only indication that a marriage took place outside the parish, and others are the source of information on the home parish of the groom. Some separate banns books are in the Family History Library (FHL).

By the middle of the eighteenth century, clandestine and illegal marriages had reached scandalous proportions. A significant element of society was deeply disturbed by the fact it had little recourse should its offspring contract an unsuitable alliance. The aristocracy and the merchant classes wanted to be able to forge profitable and powerful alliances without fear that the young people involved would run off, or be carried off, in the meantime. But the scandal touched all classes. Purveyors of hasty marriages openly advertised their services. They married anyone willing to pay. Navy men, whenever their ships came in, and often when they were drunk, were married by the hundreds.

It was all too easy. Up until this time the consent of the parties alone was required before the marriage took place; no permission of parents or registration of any kind was needed. In the eyes of the church, the age of consent was twelve for women and fourteen for men. Any ordained priest could conduct the wedding at any time or place, and the marriage was indissoluble. A stamped license was supposed to be taken out, but failure to do so was merely a minor form of fraud and did not invalidate the marriage. The church did impose penalties on the bride and groom and on the minister. Such censure was meaningless, however, when English common law recognized such unions and particularly when the clergyman had neither money nor benefice to forfeit.

So it was that the Fleet Prison in London became a marriage factory. By the eighteenth century it was used mainly as a debtors' prison. Many younger sons of noble or wealthy families studied for holy orders without ever accepting a parish. Frequently they found themselves in prison for debt. Sometimes, too, they were there for already abusing the marriage laws of the church as this item from the *Grub Street Journal* of 29 July 1739 illustrates:

> The same day, the Master of the Rolls committed a Clergyman to the Fleet, for marrying a young gentleman, about 17, and intitled (sic) to 150l. per ann. to a servant maid; and at the same time committed the person who gave her in marriage. . . . By carrying on the trade of marrying in the Fleet, this clergyman, I suppose, will turn his punishment into preferment.

Whatever the reason for their imprisonment, Fleet parsons were under "the Rules of the Fleet," which essentially meant they could come and go as they pleased within its precincts. In the beginning the marriages were performed in the prison, but they soon moved out as the parsons made lucrative arrangements with area tavern keepers. A room was fitted out as a chapel, and the parson and tavern-keeper shared the profits of fees, food, and drink. In one four-month period (ending mid-February 1705) 2,954 marriages were performed. On the last day before the new law came into force, 25 March 1754, 217 marriages were recorded at the Fleet. Surprisingly, these marriages were recorded in large numbers in the register of the Fleet Chapel. They can be seen at the Public Record Office (PRO) in RG 7, or on microfilm through family history centers. It would be fair to say that these records make up a very significant number of weddings for London and the bordering parishes, for rich and poor alike. It is true that false names were used and some dates are incorrect, but this should not deflect any search of London marriage records from this resource.

Besides the Fleet Prison, marriages took place in the slightly more respectable Rev. Alexander Keith's Chapel in Curzon Street, and the lawless or marriage shop churches. The "Mayfair Marriages" of the Reverend Keith were estimated to number as high as six thousand per year. As for the lawless churches, several parishes claimed exemptions from the authority of the local bishop, thereby giving them the right to marry couples at once without banns or license. The best known of these were Holy Trinity Minories, St. James Duke Place, The Mint-Southwark, Lincoln's Inn Chapel, and, out of London, Dale Abbey Chapel and the Chapel of Peak Forest. This last chapel attracted about sixty couples a year for a bonus of about one hundred pounds for the parson.

Lord Hardwicke's Act was vehemently attacked in the House of Commons. Some claimed it was outside Parliament's legislative powers, others that it was contrary to the Gospel. One Charles Townshend expressed the real sentiments when he stated that it was unfair to debar younger sons from running off with heiresses. This was not entirely true, for elopement was still possible, though much more difficult. The act did not apply in Scotland or the Channel Islands. Authors take note: for an historical romance set after 1754 it becomes necessary for the hero to carry his love off to Gretna Green.

From 1754 until the the introduction of civil registration in 1837, the only legal marriages in England and Wales were Anglican, Jewish, or Quaker. As part of the introduction of civil registration, superintendent registrars were empowered to issue licenses for marriage in the office of a registrar, or in a nonconformist church.

The story behind Lord Hardwicke's Marriage Act demonstrates two important aspects of good genealogical research. First, background to the records themselves often contains key facts which may be important in guiding research. Second, what you learn about the record and its making is often as interesting as your own family story, and, in a sense, is part of it.

References

The material contained in this appendix is based upon the sources listed below, all of which provide much additional useful and interesting information.

Benton, Tony. *Irregular Marriages in London Before 1754*. London: Society of Genealogists, 1993.

Cox, J. Charles. *The Parish Registers of England*. London: Methuen, 1910.

Kent, William. *An Encyclopaedia of London*. London: Dent, 1951.

Turberville, A. S. *English Men and Manners in the Eighteenth Century*. New York: Galaxy, 1964.

D

ADDRESSES

This list provides at least one address for each county or major metropolitan area, and there is a list of World Wide Web sites at the end. If a letter goes astray—changes continue to occur since the 1996–98 reorganization of local government—write the National Register of Archives, or check the ARCHON web site.

Association of Genealogists and
  Record Agents
29 Badgers Close
Horsham West Sussex RH12 5RU
*Will supply a list of qualified profes-
sional researchers—specify area.*

Bath and NE Somerset Record
  Service
Guildhall
Bath BA1 5AW

Bedfordshire and Luton Archives
  and Record Service

County Hall
Cauldwell Street
Bedford MK42 9AP

Berkshire Record Office
Shire Hall
Shinfield Park
Reading RG2 9XD

Birmingham City Archives
Central Library
Chamberlain Square
Birmingham B3 3HQ

Bristol Record Office
'B' Bond Warehouse
Smeaton Road
Bristol BS1 6XN

British Directories Project
Scriptorium Family History Centre
386 Ferrars Street
Albert Park 3206
Australia

British Library, Newspaper Library
Colindale Avenue
London NW9 5HE

British Library, Oriental and India
  Office Collections
96 Euston Road
London NW1 2DB

Buckinghamshire Record Office
County Hall
Aylesbury Bucks HP20 1UU

Cambridgeshire County Record
  Office
Shire Hall
Castle Hill
Cambridge CB3 0AP

Cambridgeshire COUNTY
  RECORD OFFICE-Huntingdon
Grammar School Walk
Huntingdon PE18 6LF

Catholic Central Library
47 Francis Street
London SW1P 1QR

Cheshire Record Office
Duke Street
Chester Cheshire CH1 1RL

Church of England Records Centre
15 Galleywall Road
South Bermondsey
London SE16 3PB

Cornwall Record Office
County Hall
Truro Cornwall TR1 3AY

Corporation of London Record
  Office
P.O. Box 270
Guildhall
London EC2P 2EJ

Countryside Books
Highfield House
2 Highfield Avenue
Newbury Berkshire RG14 5DS

Cumbria Record Office
Carlisle Headquarters
The Castle
Carlisle CA3 8UR

Cumbria Record Office
County Offices
Kendal LA9 4RQ

Cumbria Record Office
140 Duke Street
Barrow-in-Furness LA14 1XW

Cumbria Record Office
Scotch Street
Whitehaven CA28 7BJ

Derbyshire Record Office
New Street
Matlock Derbyshire DE4 3AG

Derby Library Local Studies Dept.
25 Irongate
Derby DB1 3GL

Devon Record Office
Castle Street
Exeter Devonshire EX4 3PU

North Devon Library and Record
   Office
Tuly Street
Barnstaple EX31 1EL

West Devon Area Record Office
Unit 3, Clare Place, Coxside
Plymouth Devonshire PL4 0JW

Dorset Record Office
Bridport Road
Dorchester Dorset DT1 1RP

Dr. William's Library
14 Gordon Square
London WC1H OAG

Durham County Record Office
County Hall
Durham DH1 5UL

Essex Record Office
PO Box 11 County Hall
Chelmsford Essex CM1 1LX

Colchester and NE Essex Branch
   ERO

Stanwell House, Stanwell Street
Colchester Essex CO2 7DL

Southend Branch ERO
Central Library
Victoria Avenue
Southend-on-Sea Essex SS2 6EX

Family History Department
50 East North Temple Street
Salt Lake City, UT 84150

The Family History Library
35 West North Temple
Salt Lake City, UT 84150

Family Records Centre
1 Myddelton Street
London EC1 1UW

Federation of Family History
   Societies
Administrator
Benson Room
Birmingham and Midland Institute
Margaret Street
Birmingham B3 3BS
*Will provide names and addresses of
   current membership secretaries for all
   affiliated societies—include return
   postage.*

Federation of Family History
   Societies
Publications
2-4 Killer Street
Ramsbottom, Bury
Lancashire BL10 9BZ

General Register Office
Office for National Statistics
Postal Application Section
Smedley Hydro
Trafalgar Road, Birkdale
Southport PR8 2HH

Gloucestershire Record Office
Clarence Row, Alvin Street
Gloucester GL1 3DW

Guildhall Library
Aldermanbury
London EC2P 2EJ

Guild of One Name Studies
14 Charterhouse Buildings
Goswell Road
London EC1M 7BA

Hampshire Record Office
Sussex Street
Winchester Hampshire SO23 8TH

Hereford Record Office
The Old Barracks, Harold Street
Hereford HR1 2QX

Hertfordshire Archives and Local
  Studies
County Hall
Hertford SG13 8EJ

House of Lords Record Office
House of Lords
London SW1A 0PW

Imperial War Museum
Department of Documents
Lambeth Road
London SE1 6HZ

Huguenot Society
Huguenot Library
University College
Gower Street
London WC1E 6BT

International Society for British
  Genealogy and Family History
PO Box 3115
Salt Lake City, UT 84110
*Maintains a list of vendors of British
genealogical publications in the USA
and Canada; quarterly journal.*

Institute of Heraldic and
  Genealogical Studies
Northgate
Canterbury
Kent CT1 1BA

Institute of Genealogy and
  Historical Research
Samford University
Harwell G. Davis Library
800 Lakeshore Blvd.
Birmingham, AL 35229-7008
*Offers courses on British research at the
annual June campus program and
summer study tours to Britain.*

Isle of Man Record Office
23 Apple Street
Douglas IOM

Isle of Wight County Record
  Office
26 Hillside
Newport PO30 2EB

Jewish Genealogical Society of GB
32 Tavistock Street, Covent Garden

London WC2E 7PD

Canterbury City and Cathedral
  Archives
The Precincts
Canterbury Kent CT1 2EH

Centre for Kentish Studies
County Hall
Maidstone Kent ME14 1XQ

Lancashire Record Office
Bow Lane
Preston Lancashire PR1 2RE

Leicestershire Record Office
Long Street
Wigston Magna Leicestershire LE18
  2AH

Lincolnshire Archives
St. Rumbold Street
Lincoln LN2 5AB

NE Lincolnshire Archives
Town Hall
Town Hall Square
Grimsby DN31 1HX

Liverpool Record Office and Local
  History Service
Central Library
William Brown Street
Liverpool L3 8EW

Merseyside Record Office
Central Library
William Brown Street
Liverpool L3 8EW

London Metropolitan Archives
40 Northampton Road
London EC1R 0HB

Manchester Local Studies Unit
  Archives
Central Library
St. Peter's Square
Manchester M2 5PD

Greater Manchester County
  Record Office
56 Marshall Street, Newcross
Manchester M4 5FU

Maritime History Archive
Memorial University of
  Newfoundland
St. John's NF A1C 5S7 Canada

Methodist Archives and Research
  Centre
Manchester University
John Rylands Library
150 Deansgate
Manchester M3 3EH

Metro Toronto Reference Library
789 Yonge Street
Toronto ON M4W 2GH

National Army Museum
Royal Hospital Road
London SW3 4HT

National Maritime Museum
Romney Road
Greenwich
London SE10 9NF

National Register of Archives
Quality House
Quality Court, Chancery Lane
London WC2A 1HP

Norfolk Record Office
Gildengate House
Anglia Square
Upper Green Lane
Norwich NR3 1AX

Northamptonshire Record Office
Wootton Hall Park
Northampton NN4 8BQ

Northampton Central Library
Abingdon Street
Northampton NN1 2BA

Northumberland Record Office
Melton Park
North Gosforth
Newcastle upon Tyne NE3 5QX

Berwick upon Tweed Record
  Office
Council Offices
Wallace Green
Berwick upon Tweed
Northumberland TD15 1ED

Nottinghamshire Archives
County House
Castle Meadow Road
Nottingham NG2 1AG

Ordnance Survey
Romsey Road
Southampton SO16 4GU

Oxfordshire Archives
County Hall, New Road
Oxford OX1 1ND

Phillimore and Company Ltd.
Shopwyke Manor Barn
Chichester West Sussex PO20 6BG

Principal Probate Registry of the
  Family Division
First Avenue House
42 – 48 High Holborn
London WC1V 6HA
  (postal requests to York Probate Sub-
  Registry, Duncombe Place, York YO1
  2EA)

Public Record Office
Ruskin Avenue, Kew
Richmond, Surrey TW9 4DU

Public Record Office
Census Reading Rooms
1 Myddelton Street
Islington
London EC1R 1UW

Royal Commission on Historical
  Manuscripts
Quality House
Quality Court, Chancery Lane
London WC2A 1HP

Society of Friends
Library of the Religious Society of
  Friends
Friends House
Euston Road
London NW1 2BJ

Society of Genealogists
14 Charterhouse Buildings
Goswell Road
London EC1M 7BA

Shropshire Records and Research
  Centre
Castle Gates
Shrewsbury SY1 2AQ

Somerset Archive and Record
  Service
Obridge Road
Taunton Somerset TA2 7PU

Staffordshire Record Office
County Buildings
Eastgate Street
Stafford ST16 2LZ

Suffolk Record Office
Bury St. Edmunds Branch
Raingate Street
Bury St. Edmunds IP33 2AR

Suffolk Record Office
Ipswich Branch
Gatacre Road
Ipswich IP1 2LQ

Suffolk Record Office
Lowestoft Branch
Central Library
Clapham Road
Lowestoft NR32 1DR

Surrey History Center
130 Goldsworth Road
Woking, GU21 IND

East Sussex Record Office
The Maltings
Castle Precincts
Lewes BN7 1YT

West Sussex Record Office
postal inquiries:
County Hall
Chichester PO19 1RN
actual location:
Sherburne House
3 Orchard Street
Chichester

Warwickshire County Record
  Office
Priory Park
Cape Road
Warwick CV34 4JS

Wiltshire and Swindon Record
  Office
County Hall
Trowbridge BA14 8JG

Wirral Archives Service
Birkenhead Reference Library
Borough Road
Birkenhead, L41 2XB

Wolverhampton Archives and Local
  Studies
42-50 Snow Hill
Wolverhampton WV2 4AB

Worcester Record Office
Headquarters Branch
County Hall
Spetchley Road
Worcester WR5 2NP

Worcestershire Record Office
St. Helen's Branch
Fish Street
Worcester WR1 2HN

North Yorkshire County Record
  Office
postal inquiries:
County Hall
Northallerton DL7 8AF
actual location:
Malpas Road
Northallerton

Sheffield Archives
52 Shoreham Street
Sheffield S1 4SP

Teeside Archives
Exchange House
6 Marton Road
Middlesborough TS1 1DB

Tyne and Wear Archives Service
Blandford House
Blandford Square
Newcastle upon Tyne NE1 4JA

West Yorkshire Archives Service
15 Canal Road
Bradford, BD1 4AT

West Yorkshire Archives Service
Central Library
Northgate Houe, Northgate
Halifax, HX1 1UN

West Yorkshire Archives Service
Central Library
Princess Alexandra Walk
Huddersfield, HD1 2SU

West Yorkshire Archive Service
Headquarters
Registry of Deeds
Newstead Road
Wakefield WF1 2DE

West Yorkshire Archives Service
Chapeltown Road
Sheepscar
Leeds LS7 3AP

York City Archives Department
Art Gallery Building
Exhibition Square
York, YO1 7EW

York University, Borthwick Institute
  of Historical Research
St. Anthony's Hall
Peasholme Green
York YO1 2PW

East Riding of Yorkshire Archive
  Office
County Hall
Beverly HU17 9BA

WEB SITES

The sites listed here provided links to hundred of others (URLs are all preceded by http://). The majority of record offices have Web sites, all of which are accessible through ARCHON.

ARCHON
Archives On-Line
www.hmc.gov.uk/archon/
archon.htm

BRITISH LIBRARY PORTICO
portico.bl.uk/

BRITISH TOURIST AUTHORITY
www.bta.org.uk

FEDERATION OF FAMILY HISTORY SOCIETIES
www.ffhs.org.uk

GENEALOGY—UK
www.genuki.org.uk

GUILD OF ONE NAME STUDIES
www.one-name.org

HISTORY IN THE UK
www.ihrinfo.ac.uk

INSTITUTE OF GENEALOGY AND HISTORICAL RESEARCH
www.samford.edu/schools/ighr/
ighr.html

ORDNANCE SURVEY
www.ordsvy.gov.uk/

PUBLIC RECORD OFFICE
www.pro.gov.uk/
Has two very valuable resources: Research Information Leaflets which can be downloaded; and access to the Online Catalogue which lists the contents of the record classes at Kew.

ROYAL COMMISSION ON HISTORIC MONUMENTS OF ENGLAND
www.rchme.gov.uk/homepage.html

SOCIETY OF GENEALOGISTS
www.sog.org.uk/

VICTORIA COUNTY HISTORIES
ihr.sas.ac.uk/vch/linka.asc.html

BIBLIOGRAPHY

To obtain recently published how-to books and finding aids, (1) you can obtain a list of vendors of British genealogy books in the USA and Canada from the International Society for British Genealogy and Family History; (2) the Society of Genealogists and the Federation of Family History Societies supply books by mail order; and (3) most English family history societies sell their own guides and finding aids as well as some other titles. See the address list for where to write, and the list of Web sites.

Books are generally listed in the section for which they are the most useful. All the general guides are worth a look for each different type of record. A few titles are listed more than once, but the comments differ.

General Reference

Blatchford, Robert, and Geoffrey Heslop. *The Genealogical Services Directory*. York: GR Specialist Information Services, 1999. In three years this publication has grown significantly and received wide recognition as a very useful compendium of research services, suppliers, societies, archives, museums, etc.

Cheney, C. R. *Handbook of Dates for Students of English History*. London: Royal Historical Society, 1978.

Cole, Jean, and John Titford. *Tracing Your Family Tree*. Newbury, Berks: Countryside Books, 1997. The best features of this comprehensive guide are the background to records and the hints/reminders at the end of each chapter.

Evans, Ivor H. *Brewer's Dictionary of Phrase and Fable*. 2nd rev. ed. London: Cassel, 1981.

Falkus, M., and J. Gillingham. *Historical Atlas of Britain*. New York: Continuum, 1981. Copiously illustrated with all sorts of maps—a pleasant way to review English history as well as obtain needed information.

Fitzhugh, Terrick V. H. *The Dictionary of Genealogy*. Edited by Susan Lumas. 3rd ed. London: A & C. Black, 1998. A reference work with a genealogical perspective.

Friar, Stephen. *The Batsford Companion to Local History*. London: Batsford, 1991. More than two thousand entries from a few words to short essays on all aspects of history including genealogy. With cross-references.

Harvey, Richard. *Genealogy for Librarians*. London: LAPL, 1992. Originally published in 1983, this excellent book tells librarians how to answer the wide range of questions asked by genealogists. Expensive, but you may find it in a reference library. Contains an especially helpful section on occupations.

Herber, Mark D. *Ancestral Trails*. Baltimore: Genealogical Publishing Co., 1998. First published in England; nearly 700 pages, just about every type of record is described. Best used as a reference book.

Hey, David. *Family History and Local History in England*. London: Longman, 1987. Provides a helpful perspective on the importance of linking genealogy and history.

——. *The Oxford Guide to Family History*. Oxford: Oxford University Press, 1993.

————. *The Oxford Companion to Local History*. Oxford: Oxford University Press, 1996. Another dictionary-style reference work (they are all slightly different).

Hoskins, W. G. *The Making of the English Landscape*. London: Penguin Books, 1985. First published in 1955, this very readable book traces the historical evolution of the landscape and thereby enhances our understanding of the surroundings of our ancestors.

Humphery-Smith, Cecil. *The Atlas and Index of Parish Registers*. 2nd ed. Chichester, Sussex: Phillimore, 1995. Recently updated; an indispensable tool. Remember that dates given for survival of registers are a range from the earliest entry of any type to the most recent. There are no clues as to missing sections.

Iredale, David, and J. Barrett. *Discovering Your Family Tree*. 3rd ed. Princes Risborough, Bucks: Shire, 1996. An inexpensive and useful introduction for anyone planning a trip.

Lewis, Samuel. *Topographical Dictionary of England*. 2 vols. Baltimore: Genealogical Publishing Co., 1996. This is a reprint of Lewis's first edition (1831), which predated many changes in the ecclesiastical boundaries of the Church of England.

McLaughlin, Eve. *First Steps in Family History*. 2nd ed. Newbury, Berks: Countryside Books, 1998. Pulls together a number of the small guides to basic nineteenth-century records by this author.

————. *Further Steps in Family History*. 2nd ed. Newbury, Berks: Countryside Books, 1998. A further collection of information on record sources, for researching before civil registration.

Mills, Elizabeth Shown. *Evidence! Citation and Analysis for the Family Historian*. Baltimore: Genealogical Publishing Co., 1997. Clearly written guidelines for assessing and citing sources.

Richardson, John. *The Local Historian's Encyclopaedia*. Chichester: Phillimore and Co., 1986. Reprint. 1993. The addresses need an update, but most of this excellent book provides very useful answers to all sorts of questions.

Rogers, Colin D. *Tracing Missing Persons: An Introduction to Agencies, Methods and Sources in England and Wales.* Manchester: Manchester University Press, 1986.

—————. *The Family Tree Detective.* 2nd ed. Manchester: Manchester University Press, 1997 (Published in the United States by St. Martin's Press and in Canada by UBC Press). Many ideas for research strategy from the problem-solving approach of this book.

Room, Adrian. *Dictionary of Place-Names in the British Isles.* London: Bloomsbury, 1988.

Saul, Pauline. *Tracing Your Ancestors: The A to Z Guide.* 5th ed. Newbury, Berks: Countryside Books, 1995. Provides information on records, definitions of terms, details of genealogical organizations, and much more in a dictionary format. Good for quick reference. Published in paperback as *The Family Historian's Enquire Within.*

Smith, Frank. *Genealogical Gazetteer of England.* Baltimore: Genealogical Publishing Co., 1987. Every genealogical society library should have this book. It covers location, ecclesiastical jurisdiction, and mid-nineteenth-century population for approximately forty thousand places.

Smith, F., and D. E. Gardner. *Genealogical Research in England and Wales.* Vol. 2. Salt Lake City: Bookcraft, 1959.

Titford, John. *Writing and Publishing Your Family History.* Newbury, Berks: Countryside Books, 1996. How to collect and arrange your material with good ideas about the perspective for the narrative.

Todd, Andrew. *Basic Sources for Family History Back to the Early 1800's.* Bury: Allen and Todd, 1987. Particularly helpful with civil registration and census research.

Whitaker's Almanac. London: Published annually by J. Whitaker and Sons since 1868. Information on local government and legal matters, plus addresses for schools, associations, and guilds.

Winchester, Angus. *Discovering Parish Boundaries*. Princes Risborough, Bucks: Shire, 1990. A practical handbook to help sort out the terminology and the context for use of all sorts of civil and ecclesiastical divisions.

Names and Biographies

Barrow, G. B. *The Genealogist's Guide: An Index to Printed British Pedigrees and Family Histories 1950–1975*. Chicago: Research Publishing Co., 1977.

Burke, John. *A Genealogical and Heraldic History of the Commoners of Great Britain and Ireland*. London, 1837.

Burke's Family Index. London: Burke's Peerage Ltd., 1976. A name index to the most up-to-date narrative pedigrees of each family in all Burke's publications since 1826.

Dictionary of National Biography. 17 vols. Oxford: Oxford University Press, 1900. Decennial supplements have been issued since 1900.

Dod, Robert P. *The Peerage, Baronetage and Knightage of Great Britain and Ireland*. London: Whitaker, 1857. Includes bishops and justices of the peace; published into the twentieth century.

Filby, P. William. *American and British Genealogy and Heraldry*. American Library Association, 1985. A compendium of printed sources.

Guppy, Henry B. *Homes of Family Names of Great Britain*. Baltimore: Genealogical Publishing Co. (for Clearfield Co.), 1996. Originally published in 1890. Organized on a county basis for England and Wales with a short section on Scotland, this book provides distribution listings and meanings.

Hanks, P., and F. Hodges. *A Dictionary of Surnames*. Oxford: Oxford University Press, 1988.

Johnson, K. A., and M. R. Sainty, eds. *Genealogical Research Directory*. Annual editions since 1985. Available in the United States from Mrs. J. Jennings, 3324 Crail Way, Glendale, CA 91206; available in Canada from Mrs. J. Tyson, 94 Binswood Avenue, Toronto, Ontario M4C 3N9.

Leeson, Francis L., ed. *Directory of British Peerages from Earliest Times to the Present Day*. London: Society of Genealogists, 1984. Useful summary by surname and title.

Marshall, G. W. *The Genealogist's Guide*. 1903. Reprint. London: Heraldry Today, 1967. Lists pedigrees which have appeared in print.

Reaney, P. H., and R. M. Wilson. *A Dictionary of English Surnames*. 3rd ed. Oxford: Oxford University Press, 1995.

Register of One-Name Studies. 12th ed. London: Guild of One-Name Studies, 1996. Puts on record the interests of those individuals who research one specific surname; only one person may register a surname (one-name societies have a representative listed).

Thomson, T. R. *A Catalogue of British Family Histories*. Chicago: Research Publishing Co., 1976.

Whitmore, J. B. *A Genealogical Guide: An Index to British Pedigrees in Continuation of Marshall's Genealogist's Guide*. London: Walford, 1953.

Guides to Published Records and Archives

Baxter, I. A. *India Office Library and Records: A Brief Guide to Biographical Sources*. 2nd ed. London: India Office Library, 1990.

Bevan, Amanda, ed. *Tracing Your Ancestors in the Public Record Office*. Kew: PRO Publications, 5th ed., 1999. For anyone using British government records this is an essential planning tool (even if you never go to London).

Cerny, J., and J. Elliott. *The Library: A Guide to the LDS Family History Library*. Salt Lake City: Ancestry, 1988. Now out of print but available on CD-ROM with some other Ancestry reference titles. Remains a useful basic introduction to LDS resources.

Cole, Jean, and Rosemary Church. *In and Around Record Repositories in Great Britain and Ireland*. 4th ed. Ramsey, Cambs.: ABM Publishing, 1998. A concise and affordable guide, including address, phone, e-mail, URL, services, fees, and a brief outline of main collections.

Cox, Jane. *New to Kew?* London: PRO Publications, 1997. This is an essential guide to making the most of a visit to the PRO. It is exceptionally clear and helpful. If you go to Kew there is a wide selection of instructive free pamphlets (collectively titled *Records Information*). The PRO will not post them but they can be obtained via the Web site.

Cox, Jane, and Stella Colwell. *Never Been Here Before?* London: PRO Publications, 1997. The book describes in depth the collections of the new Family Records Centre and how to use them.

Foster, Janet, and Julia Shepherd. *British Archives: A Guide to Archive Resources in the United Kingdom*. 3rd ed. London: Macmillan, 1995.

Gibson, J. S. W,. and Pamela Peskett. *Record Offices: How to Find Them*. 7th ed. Birmingham: Federation of Family History Societies, 1996.

Giusseppi, M. S., et al. *Guide to the Contents of the Public Record Office*. London: Her Majesty's Stationery Office, 1963–68. In some libraries. The descriptions of classes of early records remain useful.

Gross, Charles. *Bibliography of British Municipal History*. 2nd ed. Leicester: Leicester University Press, 1968.

Harvey, Richard. *A Guide to Genealogical Sources in the Guildhall Library*. London: Guildhall, 1988. One of a series of booklets, all very useful. If you are in London, the Guildhall Library has a wonderful bookshop.

Irvine, Sherry. "The Monuments and Manuscripts of England." *Ancestry* 15 (3) (May–June 1997). This article explains the resources of the Royal Commission on Historical Manuscripts and the National Monuments Record Centre.

Lumas, Susan. *Basic Facts About Using Archives.* Birmingham: Federation of Family History Societies, 1997. A useful introduction for those intending to visit archives in England for the first time.

Milne, A. T. *Guide to the Publications of the Royal Historical Society and the Former Camden Society.* London: Royal Historical Society, 1968.

Mullins, E. L. C. *Texts and Calendars: An Analytical Guide to Serial Publications.* London: Royal Historical Society, 1958 and 1983. Updates to *Text and Calendars* now appear on the Historic Manuscripts Commission web site rather than in print.

Raymond, S. *Cumberland and Westmorland, A County Genealogical Bibliography.* Birmingham: Federation of Family History Societies, 1993. Just one of a series of lists of published works on the counties of England.

Record Repositories in Great Britain: A Geographical Directory. 10th ed. London: Her Majesty's Stationery Office, 1998.

Reid, Judith Prowse. *Genealogical Research in England's Public Record Office: A Guide for North Americans.* Baltimore: Genealogical Publishing Co., 1996. If you do not have ready access to PRO and List and Index Society publications, this is a helpful summary of the main classes of records most useful to North American researchers.

Royal Commission on Historical Manuscripts. *Guide to the Location of Collections Described in the Reports and Calendars Series, 1870–1980.* London: Her Majesty's Stationery Office, 1982.

———. *Survey of Historical Manuscripts in the United Kingdom.* 2nd ed. London: Her Majesty's Stationery Office, 1994.

Using the Library of the Society of Genealogists. London: Society of Genealogists, 1999. This excellent booklet is regularly updated to reflect changes in the ever-growing collections. Because of this diversity, there are many ideas for research.

Wareham, Heather and Roberta Thomas. *Guide to the Holdings of the Maritime History Archive.* St. John's: Memorial University of Newfoundland, 1991.

History and Description

The Compleat Parish Officer. Devizes: The Wiltshire Family History Society, 1996. This is a reprint of the seventh edition, published in 1734. Reveals a great deal about parish life through this guide to the duties of parish officials.

Currie, C. R. J., and C. P. Lewis. *A Guide to English County Histories.* Stroud, Glos: Sutton, 1997. This work of reference is an historiographic survey of published county histories of England.

Gould, Jim. *Men of Aldridge.* Gloucester: Alan Sutton, 1983. The story of the people of a place near Birmingham, through local documents.

Mee, Arthur, ed. *Essex.* One of over forty volumes of *The King's England.* London: Hodder and Stoughton, 1942. The series describes the villages and towns of the counties of England. Pre-1950 editions are best.

Nurse, Bernard, Joy Pugh, and Imogen Mollet. *A Village in Time: The History of Newport, Essex.* Newport: The Newport News, 1995. This book won a prize for local history. Many such histories can be found, in and out of print, in new- and used-book shops. Two publishers of local series are Phillimore of Chichester, Sussex, and Countryside Books of Newbury, Berkshire.

Parker, Roland. *The Common Stream.* New York: Holt, Rinehart and Winston, 1975 (and Academy Chicago, 1994). The history of Foxton in Cambridgeshire told through documentary evidence. Beautifully written.

Pevsner, Nikolaus. *The Buildings of England.* 2nd ed. Vol. 1. London: Penguin, 1962. First volume in a series for the country. You may find the home of an ancestor featured, for humble as well as grand buildings are described.

Stephen, W. B. *Sources for Local History*. Chichester: Phillimore, 1985. Much more than a narrative bibliography; filled with interesting background to records and society.

The University of London Institute of Historical Research (various editors). *The Victoria History of the Counties of England*. Oxford University Press has published since 1903. An ongoing project since the turn of the century. The following topics are covered for each county: natural features; antiquities; Domesday; political, ecclesiastical, social, economic, architectural, artistic, industrial, and biographical history. Details supplied for each parish. Twelve counties have been completed: Bedfordshire, Berkshire, Buckinghamshire, Hampshire, Hertfordshire, Huntingdonshire, Lancashire, Rutland, Surrey, Warwickshire, Worcestershire, Yorkshire (general), and Yorkshire (North Riding). Volumes for remaining counties are dormant or in progress. Northumberland and Westmorland have yet to be started.

Record Categories

Civil Registration and the Census

Chapman, Colin R. *Pre-1841 Censuses and Population Listings in the British Isles*. 4th ed. Dursley: Lochin Publishing, 1994. A narrative account of inhabitants lists of all sorts, large and small.

Churchill, Else. *Census Copies and Indexes in the Library of the Society of Genealogists*. 3rd ed. London: Society of Genealogists, 1997. This includes a broad range of surviving pre-1841 returns and many other early inhabitants lists.

Collins, Audrey. *Basic Facts About Using the Family Records Centre*. Birmingham: Federation of Family History Societies, 1997. Concise introduction for the first-time user, helpful refresher for those who go occasionally.

Baptism, Marriage, and Burial

Allen, C. E. and R. J. Thompson. *Bedfordshire Contiguous Parishes.* London: Cart Publications, 1997. There are 24 English counties and 11 Welsh now in print. Each booklet lists the adjacent parishes for each and every parish.

Benton, Tony. *Irregular Marriages in London Before 1754.* London: Society of Genealogists, 1993. Explains how records of irregular marriages might fill in gaps in eighteenth-century London research.

Bourne, Susan, and Andrew H. Chicken. *Records of the Church of England.* 2nd ed. Maidstone: Prospect Litho, 1991. Concise explanations of all types of records of the established church.

Boyd, Percival. *Marriage Index 1538–1837.* London: Society of Genealogists. Complete copies are held by the Society of Genealogists and the College of Arms in London, and by the Genealogical Society of Utah. This index contains 6 to 7 million entries, about 15 percent of all marriages performed during this time period.

Breed, Geoffrey R. *My Ancestors Were Baptists: How Can I Find Out More About Them?* 3rd ed. London: Society of Genealogists, 1995.

Chapman, Colin, and Litton P. Chapman *Marriage Laws, Rites, Records and Customs; Was Your Ancestor Really Married?* Dursley, Glos: Lochin Publishing, 1996.

Clifford, David J. H. *My Ancestors Were Congregationalists in England and Wales: How Can I Find Out More About Them?* London: Society of Genealogists, 1992. Reprint with addenda, 1995.

Collins, L., ed. *Monumental Inscriptions in the Library of the Society of Genealogists.* Parts I and II. London: the society. Part I (Southern England) 1984. Part II (Northern England and elsewhere) 1987.

Cox, J. Charles. *The Parish Registers of England.* Totowa, N.J.: Rowman and Littlefield, 1974. Originally published around the turn of the century, this is a fascinating review of what is to be discovered in parish registers.

Crockford's Clerical Directory 1995–1996—A Directory of the Serving and Retired Clergy of the Church of England, The Church in Wales, The Scottish Episcopal Church and The Church of Ireland. London: Oxford University Press, 1995. First published in 1858.

Friar, Stephen. *A Companion to the English Parish Church.* Stroud, Glos: Sutton, 1996. Could also have been termed an encyclopedia; covers a vast range of topics. Illustrated.

Gandy, Michael. *Catholic Missions and Registers 1700–1880.* London, 1993. A series of six volumes, 1 to 5 covering regions of England.

————, ed. *Catholic Parishes in England, Wales and Scotland: An Atlas.* London, 1993.

General Register Office. *List of Non-parochial Registers: Main Series and Society of Friends' Series.* London: List and Index Society, 1969.

Gibbens, Lilian. *Basic Facts About Using Death and Burial Records for Family Historians.* Birmingham: Federation of Family History Societies, 1997.

————. *An Introduction to Church Registers.* Birmingham: Federation of Family History Societies, 1994.

Gibson, J. S. W. *Bishops' Transcripts and Marriage Licences, Bonds and Allegations: A Guide to Their Location and Indexes.* 4th. ed. Birmingham: Federation of Family History Societies, 1997.

Gibson, J. S. W, and E. Hampson. *Marriage and Census Indexes for Family Historians.* 7th ed. Birmingham: Federation of Family History Societies. 1998. Description, format, and access for all marriage indexes.

Leary, W. *My Ancestors Were Methodists: How Can I Find Out More About Them?* 2nd ed. London: Society of Genealogists, 1990. Reprint. 1993.

List of Parishes in Boyd's Marriage Index. 6th ed. London: Society of Genealogists, 1987. Corrected reprint, 1994.

Litton, Pauline M. *Basic Facts About Using Baptism Records for Family Historians*. Birmingham: Federation of Family History Societies, 1996.

Milligan, Edward H., and Malcolm J. Thomas. *My Ancestors Were Quakers.* London: Society of Genealogists, 2nd ed., 1999.

Mordy, I. *My Ancestors Were Jewish: How Can I Find Out More About Them?* London: Society of Genealogists, 1995.

Pallot's Marriage Index, 1780–1837. Held by the Institute of Heraldic and Genealogical Studies. Parishes represented are listed in *The Atlas and Index of Parish Registers*.

Parish Register Copies in the Library of the Society of Genealogists. 11th ed. London: Society of Genealogists, 1995. This collection holds copies of some registers that no longer survive.

Phillimore, W. P. W., ed. *Hertfordshire Parish Registers*. London: Phillimore, 1914. This is just one of the many volumes of marriage transcripts in the Phillimore parish register series. The number of parishes included varies from county to county; they are in the FHL.

Ruston, Alan. *My Ancestors Were English Presbyterians/Unitarians: How Can I Find Out More about Them?* London: Society of Genealogists, 1993.

Shorney, David. *Protestant Nonconformity and Roman Catholicism: A Guide to Sources in the Public Record Office.* PRO Publications, 1995. Provides background church history and a class-by-class description of the non-parochial records, which are now stored at Kew with many microfilm copies accessible at Myddelton Place.

Steel, Don. *The National Index of Parish Registers, Volume One, Sources for Birth, Marriage and Death Before 1837.* London: Society of Genealogists, 1976. Twenty-two volumes in the series have been issued: vol. 2 is *Sources for Nonconformist Genealogy and Family History;* vol. 3 is *Sources for Roman Catholic and Jewish Genealogy.* Eight titles are out of print; check reference libraries, which may have standing orders.

Tarver, Anne. *Church Court Records*. Chichester: Phillimore, 1995. Church courts were used by ordinary folk to settle differences over matrimony, probate, defamation, etc; often rich in family detail.

Wolfston, Patricia S. Revised by Clifford Webb. *Greater London Cemeteries and Crematoria*. 4th ed. London: Society of Genealogists, 1997.

Worrall, E. S. *Returns of Papists, 1767*. 2 vols. London: Catholic Record Society, 1980 and 1989.

Probate

Camp, Anthony J. *An Index to Wills Proved in the Prerogative Court of Canterbury 1750–1800*. 6 vols. London: Society of Genealogists, 1976–92. As volumes have gone out of print they have been made available on microfiche.

Cox, Jane. *An Introduction to Wills, Probate and Death Duty Registers*. Birmingham: Federation of Family History Societies, 1993.

————. *Hatred Pursued Beyond the Grave*. London: Her Majesty's Stationery Office, 1993. A fascinating and vivid account of family disputes, slander, etc., heard in cases at the church courts, Doctors Commons, London.

————. *Wills, Inventories, and Death Duties—A Provisional Guide*. London: Public Record Office, 1988.

Gibson, J. S. W. *Probate Jurisdictions: Where to Look for Wills*. 4th ed. Birmingham: Federation of Family History Societies, 1994. Updated 1997.

Hill, Ronald A. "Maximizing Probate Research: An Analysis of Potential, Using English Records from Cornwall." *National Genealogical Society Quarterly* 84 (4) (December 1996). Clearly shows why probate searches should go beyond one specific individual.

Humphery-Smith, Cecil. *The Atlas and Index of Parish Registers*. 2nd ed. Chichester, Sussex: Phillimore, 1995. The maps clearly set out the boundaries of all the probate jurisdictions.

Newington-Irving, Nicholas. *Will Indexes and Other Probate Material in the Library of the Society of Genealogists*. London: Society of Genealogists, 1996.

Pratt, David H. *Researching British Probates, 1454–1858, Volume 1, Northern England, Province of York*. Wilmington: Scholarly Resources, 1992.

Public Record Office. *Prerogative Court of Canterbury Inventories, Series II: Part II 1734–1782, with Index*. London: List and Index Society and Swift, vol. 86, 1973.

Scott, Miriam. *Prerogative Court of Canterbury Wills and Other Probate Records*. London: PRO Publications, 1997. A guide to the probate records held by the PRO including clear explanations of Death Duty Registers and probate inventories.

Webb, Cliff. *An Index to Wills Proved in the Archdeaconry Court of London 1700–1807*. London: Society of Genealogists, 1996. Follows up on the published wills and administrations issued by the British Record Society, to the final entries at this court.

Occupations (Including Military) and Education

Army List. London. Annual since 1754.

Barriskill, D. *A Guide to Lloyd's Marine Collection at Guildhall Library and Related Marine Sources*. London: Guildhall Library, n.d.

Baxter, I. A. *India Office Library and Records: A Brief Guide to Biographical Sources*. 2nd ed. London: British Library, 1990. A useful yardstick for judging the usefulness of items available through family history centers.

Bevan, Amanda, ed. *Tracing Your Ancestors in the Public Record Office*. Kew: PRO Publications, 5th ed., 1999. Contains descriptions and lists of all military and naval record groups.

Carlisle, Nicholas. *A Concise Description of the Endowed Grammar Schools in England and Wales*. Richmond, Surrey: Richmond Pub., 1974. Originally published in two volumes, 1818.

Chapman, Colin. *The Growth of British Education and its Records*. Dursley, Glos: Lochin Publishing, 1991.

City Livery Companies and Related Organisations: A Guide to Their Archives in Guildhall Library. 3rd ed. London: Guildhall Library, 1989.

Cook, Frank, and Andrea Cook. *The Casualty Roll for the Crimea: The Casualty Rolls for the Siege of Sabastopol and Other Major Actions During the Crimean War 1854–1856*. London: Hayward, 1976. Indexed.

Crowder, Norman K. *British Army Pensioners Abroad 1772–1899*. Baltimore: Genealogical Publishing Co., 1995. Lists of those overseas in receipt of a pension—about twelve thousand names.

Dalton, Charles. *The Waterloo Roll Call With Biographical Notes and Anecdotes*. London: William Clowes, 1890.

Dwelly, E. A. *Muster Roll of the British Non-commissioned Officers and Men Present at the Battle of Waterloo*. Edinburgh, 1934.

Foster, J. *Alumni Oxonienses*. Oxford: Parker & Co., 1891.

Fowler, Simon. *Army Records for Family Historians*. Kew: PRO Publications, 2nd ed.,1999.

Fowler, Simon, William Spencer, and Stuart Tamblin. *Army Service Records of the First World War*. Kew: PRO Publications, 1996.

Gibson, J. S. W,. and M. Medlycott. *Militia Lists and Musters 1757–1876*. 3rd ed. Birmingham: Federation of Family History Societies, 1994.

Hailey, John. *Maritime Sources in the Library of the Society of Genealogists*. London: Society of Genealogists, 1997. Lists, indexes, journal articles, and much more have all been organized in categories; much of the material could also be found in North America.

Hamilton-Edwards, Gerald. *In Search of Army Ancestry*. Chichester: Phillimore, 1977.

Hawkings, David T. *Railway Ancestors*. Stroud, Glos: Sutton, 1995. An immensely detailed account of railway records with lists of all British railways.

Hogg, Peter L. *Basic Facts About Using Merchant Ship Records for Family Historians*. Birmingham: Federation of Family History Societies, 1997. Complements *My Ancestor Was a Merchant Seaman*. Focuses on finding the ship.

Kitzmiller, John M. *In Search of the Forlorn Hope: A Comprehensive Guide to Locating British Regiments and Their Records, 1640 to World War I*. Salt Lake City: Manuscript Publishing Foundation, 1987. Indicates where and when each regiment served.

Lloyd's Captains' Register 1869–1948. Compiled from the records of Lloyd's underwriters. At the Guildhall Library, London, with copies also at the National Archives of Canada.

Lloyd's Register of Shipping. London: Lloyd's Registry. First published in 1760; issued yearly listing British ships to 1889 and all ships thereafter.

Morton, Ann. *Education and the State*. London: PRO Publications, 1997. A guide to the contents of records of education for all levels of learning, with case studies.

Navy List. London: Her Majesty's Stationery Office, et al., 1814–.

Probert, Eric D. *Company and Business Records for Family Historians*. Birmingham: Federation of Family History Societies, 1994.

Raymond. Stuart A. *Occupational Sources for Genealogists, a Bibliography*. 2nd ed. Birmingham: Federation of Family History Societies, 1996.

Richards, T. *Was Your Grandfather a Railwayman?* 3rd ed. Birmingham: Federation of Family History Societies, 1995.

Rodger, N.A.M. *Naval Records for Genealogists*. Kew: PRO Publications, 2nd editions, 1998.

School, University and College Registers and Histories in the Library of the Society of Genealogists. 2nd ed. London: Society of Genealogists, 1996.

Spencer, William. *Records of the Militia and Volunteer Forces 1757–1945.* Rev. ed. London: PRO Publications, 1997. Includes lists of units with PRO references.

Stewart, Charles H. *The Service of British Regiments in Canada and North America.* Ottawa, 1962.

Trinity House Petitions: A Calendar of the Records of the Corporation of Trinity House, London, in the Library of the Society of Genealogists. London: Society of Genealogists, 1987. An index to about 5,400 surnames.

Thomas, Garth. *Records of the Royal Marines.* Kew: PRO Publications, 1994.

Venn, J., and J. A. Venn. *Alumni Cantabrigienses.* Cambridge: Cambridge University Press, 1922.

Wareham, Heather, and Roberta Thomas, eds. *A Guide to the Holdings of the Maritime History Archive.* St. John's: Memorial University of Newfoundland, 1991.

Watts, M. J., and C. T. Watts. *My Ancestor Was in the British Army: How Can I Find Out More About Him?* London: Society of Genealogists. Reprinted with addendum, 1995.

————. *My Ancestor Was a Merchant Seaman: How Can I Find Out More About Him?* London: Society of Genealogists. Reprinted with addendum, 1991.

Webb, Cliff. *London Apprentices, Vol. 1, Brewers' Company 1658–1800.* London: Society of Genealogists, 1996. Volumes are being added to the series regularly. More than two dozen companies are represented—fanmakers, glass-sellers, gunmakers, needlemakers, and others.

Local Administration and Justice

Cale, Michelle. *Law and Society: An Introduction to Sources for Criminal and Legal History from 1800.* London: PRO Publications, 1996. Helps the layman understand a complex group of records.

Camp, Anthony J. *My Ancestors Moved in England and Wales: How Can I Trace Where They Came From?* London: Society of Genealogists, 1994. Immensely useful overview of dozens of sources. Relevant for eighteenth-century research.

Cornwall, Julian. *Reading Old Title Deeds.* 2nd ed. Birmingham: Federation of Family History Societies, 1997.

Ellis, Mary. *Using Manorial Records.* 2nd ed. London: PRO Publications, 1997. Clear help with content, access, and use.

Emmison, F. G., and I. Gray. *County Records.* London: Historical Association, 1987. Gives an itemized description of what is in quarter sessions records.

Gibson, J. S. W. *Land and Window Tax Assessments 1690–1950.* Birmingham: Federation of Family History Societies, 2nd ed., 1998.

————. *Quarter Session Records for Family Historians.* 4th ed. Birmingham: Federation of Family History Societies, 1995.

Gibson, J. S. W., and Colin Rogers. *Coroners' Records in England and Wales.* Birmingham: Federation of Family History Societies, 2nd ed., 1997.

————. *Poor Law Union Records in England and Wales.* 4 vols. Birmingham: Federation of Family History Societies, 1993. Three volumes are regional listings of surviving records with their locations; vol. 4 is a gazetteer.

Hawkings, David T. *Criminal Ancestors: A Guide to Historical Criminal Records in England and Wales.* Stroud, Glos: Sutton, 1996. Comprehensive and informative with many practical examples.

Iredale, David, and John Barrett. *Discovering Your Old House.* 3rd. ed. Princes Risborough, Bucks: Shire Publications, 1991. Reprint. 1994. Lots of useful information for researching a house—with application to genealogy.

May, Trevor. *The Victorian Workhouse.* Princes Risborough, Bucks: Shire Publications, 1997. A short general description and history.

McLaughlin, Eve. *Annals of the Poor.* 5th ed. Aylesbury, Bucks: Varneys Press, 1994.

————. *Illegitimacy.* 6th ed. Aylesbury, Bucks: Varneys Press, 1995.

Park, Peter B. *My Ancestors Were Manorial Tenants: How Can I Find Out More About Them?* 2nd ed. London: Society of Genealogists, 1994.

Reid, Andy. *The Union Workhouse.* Chichester: Phillimore (for the British Association for Local History), 1994. This study guide covers historical background, location, and use of sources.

Tate, W. E. *The Parish Chest.* 3rd ed. Chichester: Phillimore, 1983. Remains the classic account of all forms of records of the parish.

West, John. *Village Records.* 2nd ed. Chichester: Phillimore, 1997. Detailed advice about the material available for the study of local records.

————. *Town Records.* Chichester: Phillimore, 1983.

Early English Research—An Introduction

Bristow, Joy. *The Local Historian's Glossary and Vade Mecum.* 2nd ed. Nottingham: University of Nottingham, 1994. This general work of reference defines many items not found in similar volumes. Very helpful for early English research.

Buck, W. S. B. *Examples of Handwriting.* Reprint. London: Society of Genealogists, 1996. Numerous samples for every letter, large and small—keep it handy.

Ellis, Mary. *Using Manorial Records.* 2nd ed. London: PRO Publications, 1997. An excellent plain-language explanation of manor courts, tenure, custumals etc.

Emmison, F. G. *How to Read Local Archives.* London: Historical Association, 1983. A practical guide to secretary hand.

Gandy, Michael. *Basic Approach to Latin for Family Historians.* Birmingham: Federation of Family History Societies, 1995.

Gandy, Wallace. *The British Plantations Association Oath Rolls.* 1922. Reprint. Baltimore: Clearfield Co., 1993. Lists of those in New York, Virginia, and the West Indies who took the oath in 1696.

Gibson, J. S. W. *The Hearth Tax and Other Later Stuart Tax Lists and the Association Oath Rolls.* 2nd ed. Birmingham: Federation of Family History Societies, 1996.

————. *Land and Window Tax Assessments 1690–1950.* Birmingham: Federation of Family History Societies, 2nd ed., 1998.

Gibson, J. S. W. , and Alan Dell. *The Protestation Returns 1641–42 and Other Listings.* Birmingham: Federation of Family History Societies, 1995. Includes maps showing boundaries of hundreds.

————. *Tudor and Stuart Muster Rolls.* Birmingham: Federation of Family History Societies, 1991.

Hoyle, Richard. *Tudor Taxation Records.* London: PRO Publications, 1994. A practical manual to lay subsidies and other less-well-known records.

McLaughlin, Eve. *Reading Old Handwriting.* 3rd. ed. Aylesbury: Varneys Press, 1995.

Martin, C. Trice. *The Record Interpreter.* 1919. Reprint. Chichester: Phillimore, 1994. Remains a useful reference, especially for archaic terms, names, and Latin abbreviations.

Morris, Janet. *A Latin Glossary for Family Historians.* Birmingham: Federation of Family History Societies, 1989. Reprint. 1997.

Munby, Lionel. *Reading Tudor and Stuart Handwriting*. Chichester: Phillimore, for the British Association for Local History, 1988. A student's guide.

Park, Peter B. *My Ancestors Were Manorial Tenants: How Can I Find Out More About Them?* 2nd ed. London: Society of Genealogists, 1994.

Stuart, Denis. *Latin for Local and Family Historians*. Chichester: Phillimore, 1995. Essentially a well-constructed course in basic Latin.

Tate, W. E. *The Parish Chest*. 3rd ed. Chichester: Phillimore, 1983. An exhaustive study of all records of the parish that will prepare you for research in earlier documents.

Webb, Cliff. "The Collection for Distressed Protestants in Ireland, 1642." *Genealogists' Magazine* 21 (9) (March 1985).

West, John. *Village Records*. 2nd ed. Chichester: Phillimore, 1997. Organized into four sections, each a period of time. The record types are described fully, including how each one can be utilized. Originals are illustrated and transcripts given (most examples are from Worcestershire)

Wigfield, W. McD. *The Monmouth Rebels*. Stroud, Glos: Sutton, 1985. This is also vol. 79 of the publications of the Somerset Record Society. Lists the names, residence, and fate of five thousand West Country rebels in 1685.

Emigrants

Bailyn, Bernard. *Voyagers to the West*. New York: Random House, 1988. Focuses on those who came to America on the eve of the revolution.

Coldham, Peter Wilson. *American Wills and Administrations in the Prerogative Court of Canterbury 1610–1857*. Baltimore: Genealogical Publishing Co., 1992.

————. *American Wills Proved in London 1611–1775*. Baltimore: Genealogical Publishing Co., 1992.

————. *The Complete Book of Emigrants*. 4 vols. Baltimore: Genealogical Publishing Co., 1990–93. Covers the period 1607–1776.

————. *The Complete Book of Emigrants in Bondage 1614–1775*. Baltimore: Genealogical Publishing Co., 1988.

————. *Emigrants from England to the American Colonies*. Baltimore: Genealogical Publishing Co., 1988.

————. *Emigrants in Chains. A Social History of Forced Emigration to the Americas…1607–1776*. Baltimore: Genealogical Publishing Co., 1994.

————. *Supplement to the Complete Book of Emigrants in Bondage 1614–1775*. Baltimore: Genealogical Publishing Co., 1992.

Colletta, John P. *They Came in Ships*. Rev. ed. Salt Lake City: Ancestry, 1993. A very useful guide to printed and manuscript records of arrival.

Filby, P. William, with Mary K. Meyer. *Passenger and Immigration Lists Index: A Guide to Published Arrival Records of About 500,000 Passengers Who Came to the United States and Canada in the 17th, 18th and 19th Centuries*. Detroit: Gale Research, 1981. There have been a number of supplements.

Filby, P. William. *Passenger and Immigration Lists Bibliography 1538–1900: Being a Guide to Published Lists of Arrivals in the United States and Canada*. Detroit: Gale Research, 1981.

French, Elizabeth. *List of Emigrants to America from Liverpool 1697–1707*. 1913. Reprint. Baltimore: Genealogical Publishing Co., 1983.

Fischer, David H. *Albion's Seed*. Oxford: OUP, 1989. An in-depth study of four groups which came to the United States in the seventeenth and eighteenth centuries.

INDEX

Abbreviations
  expansion of, 4
  in Latin records, 173, 174
Abstracts. *See* Extracts
Access to records. *See* Availability
Account books
  of churchwardens, 151
  of overseer of the poor, illegitimate
    children in, 154, 155
Act books of probate courts, 122, 128
Acts. *See* Laws
Acts of Uniformity
  recusant rolls under, 169
  religious dissent suppression by, 98
Addresses. *See also* Residence
  of archives and associations, 211–18
Administrations (probate records), 128
  indexes to, 123–25
  in War Office, 136
Administrative records
  local, 148–64
    in early English research, 176
  of manors, 171
Admiralty records, 135, 136
Admons (letters of administration), 104
  indexes to, 107, 124, 125
Adoption records, 32, 34, 38

Adultery, in church court records, 156
Age
  in burial register, 94
  in census records, 47, 48
  of consent for marriage, 207
  for making will, 114
  in marriage records, 30, 96
  in Registers of Seamen, 144
Agents (record agents). *See* Professional
  genealogists
Aircraft, records of births and deaths
  on, 38
Air Force death records, 38
Allegations, marriage, 95, 96
Allen County Public Library (Fort
  Wayne, Indiana), 80
Ancestral File, 5
Anglican church. *See* Church of
  England
Annual Register, The (periodical), 80
  military dispatches in, 139, 140
Annuity records of Bank of England,
  117, 118
Apprentices
  orphaned, as foster children, 34
  in poor relief records, 153
  records of, 133, 134

Archbishop's court, probate in, 113
Archdeacon's court, probate in, 113, 114, 122
Archeological societies, serial publications of, 160
Arches, Court of the, will litigation in, 115
Archives, 8, 9. *See also* County record offices; Public Record Office (PRO)
    addresses, 211–19
    bibliography, 225–28
    business records in, 142
    online, 162, 219
    school records in, 132
ARCHON (Archives On-Line), 162, 219
Armed forces, records of, 134–40
Army records, 134–40
    vital, 38
Arrival lists, in Canada and United States, 177
Assizes (criminal courts), law enforcement by, 157
Association Oath Rolls, 169, 170
Atlases, 14
Authoritativeness of sources, 4, 5
Authors, Family History Library Catalog of, 185, 187
Availability
    of early census records, 50
    of early records, 165
    of manorial records, 172
    of parish registers, 89, 90
    of records for overseas research, viii, ix
    of records in Family History Library Catalog, 188, 189
    of twentieth-century census records, 49
Bank of England Will Extracts, 115, 117, 118, 125
Banns
    reading of, Lord Hardwicke's Act on, 206, 207
    required for marriage, 84

Baptismal records. *See also* Birth records; Vital records
    Church of England, 93, 94
    in IGI, 195
    nonconformist, 99
    standardization of parish, 86
    in War Office, 136
Baptist Church, 99, 100
Barracks, census enumeration in, 61
Batch Number Index to IGI records, 197, 199
Beneficiaries of wills, indexes to, 123
Bible Christian Church, 99
Bibliographies, 7
    of local government and parish records, 163
    of serial publications, 160
BigR (British Isles Genealogical Register), 6
Biographies and biographical dictionaries, 7, 224, 225
    in Family History Library Catalog, 189
    of military officers, 134
    of professionals, 140
Birth data
    in Army Description Books, 138
    census index sorted by birthplace, 54
    in census records, 47, 48
        inaccuracies in, 59
    on death certificates, 30
    in naval records, 135
    in Registers of Seamen, 144
    in school records, 131
Birth records, 32, 34, *illus.* 33. *See also* Vital records
    for births in aircraft, 38
    incompleteness of, 28
    of nonconformist churches, 100
    in War Office, 136
Bishops' courts
    occupational licenses from, 141
    probate in, 113, 114

Bishops' transcripts, 83
in IGI, 89, 197
Bishops' visitations, probate jurisdiction in relation to, 114
Bonds
investments, Bank of England records of, 117, 118
marriage, 95, 96
probate, 128
Books, reference, 25, 220–24
Boroughs
apprenticeship records, 133
court minutes, 152
of Greater London, *table* 19
parishes in relation to, 149
Boundaries
changes in, record location in relation to, 15, 17
of parishes, 87–89
Boyd's Marriage Index, 90, 96
British Directories Project, 69
British Isles Genealogical Register, 6
British Library, newspapers at, 79
Burgess rolls, 74
Burial records, 97. *See also* Death records
Church of England, 93, 94
kept by overseer of the poor, 152, 153
standardization of parish, 86
Business records, 142
in county record offices, 147
Calendar
Gregorian, adoption of, vii, 22, 23, 84
probate, 107, 123
Cambridge University, lists of students, 132
Canterbury
dioceses of Province of, *map* 120, 121
Prerogative Court of. *See* Prerogative Court of Canterbury (PCC)

Catalogs
of Family History Library, 5, 184–90
of newspaper collections, 79
Catalogue of British Family Histories, A (Thompson), 7
Catholic Church
clergy of, 140
records of, 100
Catholics, on recusant rolls, 169
CD-ROM
Family History Library Catalog on, 187, 188
IGI on, 197, 199, 202, *illus.* 200, 201
techniques for efficient use of, 91, 92
Cemetery records. See Burial records
Census place, census index sorted by, 54
Census records, 47–65
bibliography, 229, 230
of Catholics, 100
in Family History Library Catalog, *illus.* 194
at Family Records Centre, 27
of merchant marine, 144
occupation in, 141
recording of information from, 4
Certificates. *See also* Vital records
of competency of ships' officers in merchant marine, 144
of settlement in parish, 154
Chancery, Court of, will litigation in, 115
Channel Islands, marriage in, Lord Hardwicke's Act (1754) in relation to, 209
Chapel of ease, parish conversion to, 85
Chapelry, marriage at, 85
Chaplains' Returns of Births, Marriages, and Deaths, 38, 137
Charles II, "free and voluntary present" to, donor lists for, 168

Children
    of Army officers, records of, in War
        Office, 136
    association with parents in IGI on
        CD-ROM, 92
    of merchant seamen, welfare records
        of, 145
    names of, problems in, 43
    in poor relief records, 153
    in probate act books, 128
    support of illegitimate, 154
Children's Act (1975), on birth records
    of adoptees, 34
Christening records. *See* Baptismal
    records; Birth records
Chronology, evidence in relation to, 182
Church courts. *See* Church of
    England; Prerogative Court of
    Canterbury (PCC)
Church of England
    bishops' transcripts, 83
        in IGI, 89, 197
    clergy
        census data collection from, 58
        directories, 140
    courts of, 155, 156. *See also*
        Prerogative Court of Canterbury
        (PCC)
        occupational licenses from, 141
        probate of wills in, 105, 112–14
    dioceses and provinces of, *map* 120,
        121
    hierarchical organization of, 87
    marriages in, recognition of, viii, 84,
        209
    parishes. *See* Parishes (Church of
        England)
    property of, taxes on, 166
    records of, 82–97, 100–102. *See also*
        Parish records (Church of England)
Church of Jesus Christ of Latter-day
Saints
    family history centers of, 9
    research resources of, 5, 6

    temple records of, as source of IGI
        records, 199
Church records, 82–102. *See also*
    Church of England; Parish records
    (Church of England)
    in Family History Library Catalog,
        illus. 193
    nonconformist, at Family Records
        Centre, 27
Churchwarden, 150, 151, 153
Circuit courts, 157
Citation of sources, 183, 222
Cities
    address location in, 60
    directories, 68, *illus.* 72, 73
    maps, 15
Civil courts, 156, 157, 171
    borough, minutes of, 152
    manor, records of, 171, 172
    probate litigation in, 115
    records of
        in Family History Library
            Catalog, *illus.* 161
        time span of, 165
Civil divisions of England, *map* 20, 21,
    table 18, 19
Civil parishes
    administrative records of, 149, 163
    boundaries of, changes in, 15, 17
    in census records, 62
    maps of, in enclosure awards, 159
Civil records. *See* Birth records; Civil
    parishes; Death records; Marriage
    records; Vital records
Civil registration, 26–46
Civil War (1642–49)
    church recordkeeping during, 83
    loyalty oaths in relation to, 168
Clandestine marriages, prevention of,
    by Lord Hardwicke's Act, 206–9
Clergy
    census data collection from, 58
    directories, 140

Clerical subsidies, 166

Clerk of the peace, 71, 141, 156, 158, 159

Clipping files from newspapers, 79

Coast Guard, records of officers in, 135

Codicil to will, 104

Collateral relatives, 67, 104, 110

Collection in Aid of Distressed Protestants in Ireland (1641), lists of donors to, 168, 170

Colleges, peculiars in, probate jurisdiction of, 114

Colonies, Association Oath Rolls in, 169

Commissary court, probate in, 113

Commonwealth (1649–60)
church recordkeeping during, 83
Latin use decline during, 172
probate courts during, 124
probate inventories destruction in, 126

Company records, 142

Computers in research database searching, 3

Condition. *See* Marital status

Confidentiality of twentieth-century census records, 49

Congregational Church, clergy of, 140

Consent for marriage, 207

Consistory court, probate in, 113, 114

Consolidated Will Index (1750–1800), 124

Consols (consolidated annuities) in will extracts, 118

Constables, 150, 151

Consular Births, Marriages, and Deaths, 38

Continuous Service Engagement Books, naval records of sailors in, 135, 136

Correspondence with archives and libraries, 9

Counties, *map* 16, 17, *table* 18, 19
directories, 68
histories, 65, 228, 229
IGI coverage of, weakness in, 203
records, in locality section of Family History Library Catalog, 186

County record offices
addresses, 211–18
business records at, 142, 147
census records at, 53
electoral rolls at, 74
enclosure awards at, 159
parish registers at, 90
rate books at, 75
school records location through, 132
tax lists at, 166, 167
will litigation at, 115
wills at, 122

Court baron, 171

Court leet, 171

Court of Chancery, probate litigation in, 115

Court of the Arches, probate litigation in, 115

Courts
church. *See* Church of England; Prerogative Court of Canterbury (PCC)
civil. *See* Civil courts
ecclesiastical. *See* Church of England; Prerogative Court of Canterbury (PCC)

Crematory records. *See* Burial records

Crew agreements in merchant marine, 145

Criminal courts, 157

Cromwell, Thomas, 83

Dade registers, baptism and burial, 94

Databases, 5–7
of business records, 142
Family History Library Catalog, 184–94

Databases (*cont.*)
    IGI, 195–205
    of personal research, 3
Dates. *See also* Birth data; Death data
    adoption of Gregorian calendar
        effect on, viii, 22, 23, 84
    dictionaries of, 12
    filtering of, in computerized
        searches of IGI, 92
Death data
    in probate act books, 128
    in wills, 104
    of women, 106
Death records, *illus.* 31. *See also* Burial
    records; Vital records
    Death Duty Registers, 109, 118
    for deaths in aircraft, 38
    at Family Records Centre, 27
    incompleteness of, 28
    indexes to, 125
    in War Office, 136
    wills in, 115–17
Decipherment of early English
    records, 173, 174
Depot Description Books (Army), 138
Description Books (Army), 138
Dewey decimal classification system, 8,
    table 10
Dictionaries
    biographical, 7
        military officers in, 134
        professionals in, 140
    of dates, 12
    of place names and surnames, 21
    topographical. *See* Gazetteers
Diocesan courts
    occupational licenses from, 141
    probate in, 113, 114
Dioceses (Church of England), *map*
    120, 121
Directories, 68–71
    bibliography, 231
    city, 13, *illus.* 72, 73

in Family History Library Catalog,
    189
genealogical, 179
of genealogical societies, 6
occupational, 141, *illus.* 143
professional, 140
of schools, 132
trade, addresses in, 60
Dissenting churches. *See*
    Nonconformist churches
District boundaries under Poor Law
    (1834), changes in, 15
District probate registry, 104, 108
Divorce, 43, 44
Doctors Common (church court), 156
Dod's Peerage, Baronetage and Knightage, 7
Donor lists for poor relief to
    Protestants in Ireland, 168, 170
Dr. William's Registry of births in
    nonconformist churches, 100
Early English research, 165–76
    bibliography, 241–43
East India Company records, 139
Ecclesiastical courts
    probate by, 105, 112, 113, 119, *table*
        113
    probate jurisdiction of, 121, 122
Education, 130–33
    in genealogy, 24
Electoral rolls, 71, 74
    addresses in, 60
    Land Tax Assessments as, 158
Emigration
    bibliography, 243, 244
    parish records of, 151
    of relatives, in wills, 104
    routes of, 178
Enclosure awards, 157–59
Epidemics, in burial register, 94
Equity courts, will litigation in, 115
Errors
    in census records, 59, 64
    in IGI, 205

in marriage records, 209
in probate records, 111
in records, 180, 183
Event codes in IGI records, 198, 199
Evidence, direct and circumstantial,
182
Examination for settlement in parish,
life history in, 154
Executor
duties of, 104
relationship to testator, 104, 107,
128
residence of, probate jurisdiction in
relation to, 114, 119
in will extracts, 118

Extracts
of apprentice registers, 134
of bishops' transcripts and parish
records, IGI records from, 197, 199
of wills, 106, 115, 117, 118, 125,
illus. 106
Extraparochial parishes. *See* Peculiars
(extraparochial parishes)
Family history, 130
books on, 5–7
vs. genealogy, 12, 13
Family History Library
catalog, 5, 184–94
Anglican parish registers and
bishops' transcripts in, 89
local court records in, *illus.* 161
census records at, 50, 51
civil records indexes at, 34
probate records at, 122
Family History News and Digest (periodical), 142, 163
Family history societies. *See*
Genealogical societies
Family names. *See* Surnames
Family Records Centre (London), 27,
36–38
census records at, 51

Death Duty Registers at, 109, 116
vital records of army personnel at,
137
will indexes at, 123
wills at, 116
Family relationships
in census records, 47–49, 64
collateral, 110
in Death Duty Registers, 109
of executor, in will indexes, 107
in letters of administration, 105
in wills, 103
FamilySearch, 5
Federation of Family History Societies
(FFHS), 6, 24, 213, 219
publications of, 163
FFHS. *See* Federation of Family
History Societies (FFHS)
Filtering in computerized searches of
IGI, 92
Financial records
account books
of churchwardens, 151
of overseer of the poor, illegitimate children in, 154, 155
of Bank of England, 117, 118
pay records
of armed forces, 134
for laborers, 142
naval records of sailors in, 136
Finding aids. *See also* Indexes
for Army records, 138
bibliography, 225–28
for burial records, 97
in census research, 53, 62
for clergy, 140
for Death Duty Registers, 109
for early English research, 170, 176
in Family History Library Catalog,
189
for government reports, 142
for local government and parish
records, 163

Finding aids (*cont.*)
  for marriage records, 96
  for militia records, 138, 139
  for naval records, 135
  for newspapers, 78
  for occupations, 141
  for Parliamentary papers, 142
  for railway records, 144
  for school records, 132
  for sources of IGI records, 197
  for wills, 116, 119, 123
First Avenue House, Principal Probate
  Registry at, 105
Five Mile Act, 98
Fleet Prison (London) as marriage
  mill, 208, 209
Foster children, 34
Fraud in marriage records, 207–9
Freedom registers, 134
Freeholders, lists of, 71
Freemen, lists of, 134
Gaols, 157
Gazetteers, 14
  in parish record research, 88, 89
  probate jurisdictions in, 121
  railways in, 144
Genealogical Guide, A (Whitmore), 7
Genealogical Research Directory, 6
Genealogical societies, 24
  addresses, 211–19
  libraries, 9
  ordering civil record certificates
    through, 26, 36
Genealogies, compiled, 5, 6
Genealogists, professional, 25, 35, 108
  addresses, 211
*Genealogist's Guide: An Index to Printed
  British Pedigrees and Family Histories*
  (Barrow), 7
Genealogist's Guide (Marshall), 7
General Register Office, 26
Gentleman's Magazine (periodical), 80
Geography, genealogy in relation to,
  14, 15, 17, 19

Gibson Guides
  in early English research, 170, 176
  to newspapers, 78, 79
  to probate jurisdictions, 122
Gilbert's Act (1782), poorhouse sharing
  by parishes under, 153
GOONS (Guild of One Name
  Studies), 6, 214, 219
Government, local
  Anglican parish as unit of, 86
  parish officers and magistrates in,
    148
  records of
    in early English research, 176
    in locality section of Family
      History Library Catalog, 186
    research in, 159, 160, 162, 163
Government employees
  on Association Oath Rolls, 169
  records of, in Public Records
    Office, 147
Government reports, 142
Grammar, Latin, 173
Grandparents
  in baptism and burial registers, 94
  illegitimate children fostered by, 34
Gravestone inscriptions, 97
Greater London Boroughs, *table* 19
Gregorian calendar, adoption of, viii,
  22, 23, 84
Guildhall Library (London)
  directories at, 70
  guild records at, 133
Guild of One Name Studies, 6, 214,
  219
Guild records, 133, 134
Handwriting
  decipherment of, 22
  in early records, 165, 173, 174
Hearth tax, 167, 170
Highway repair
  parish taxes for, 149, 150
  surveyor of highways responsible
    for, 152

Historical societies, serial publications of, 160
History
 of Church of England records, 83
 family, books on, 5, 6
 genealogy in relation to, 12, 13
 local, books on, 65, 228, 229
 regimental, military officers in, 134
History of the Commoners of Great Britain and Ireland (Burke), 7
Holographic wills, 115
Hospitals
 census enumeration in, 61
 soldiers' records in, 137
Household, number of families in, in census records, 49
IGI (International Genealogical Index), 195, 197–99, 202, 203, 205
 Anglican parish registers and bishops' transcripts in, 89
 on CD-ROM, 197, 199, 202, *illus.* 200, 201
 in early English research, 174, 176
 on microfiche, 196
 for place of residence identification in census research, 60, 61
 techniques for efficient use, 91–93
Illegitimacy, 32, 85, 154–56
Illustrated London News (periodical), 80
Independent (Congregational) Church, 99, 100
Indexes. *See also* Finding aids
 to administrations, 107, 108
 to apprenticeship records, 133
 to census records, 53–57, illus. 52
 to civil records, 26, 34, 35, 37, 38, 41
 to Death Duty Registers, 109, 116
 to documentary sources in United Kingdom, 189
 to *Gentleman's Magazine*, 80
 for identification of immigrant ancestor, 178

IGI, 195–205
 to marriage records, 90, 95, 96
 to merchant marine records, 144
 to naval records, 136
 to newspapers, 79
 to nonconformist church records, 99
 to parish records, 90
 Periodical Source Index (PERSI), 80
 to Regimental Registers of Birth, 137
 to Royal Hospital Chelsea Soldiers Documents, 137
 street, in census research, 51
 of surnames, 6, 179
 to will extracts, 117, 118
 to wills, 107, 108, 116, 119, 123, *illus.* 106
Indian Army records, 139
Indian Service, vital records of, 38
Individual submission of IGI records, 199
Indoor poor relief, 153
Inheritance of guild membership, 133
Inheritance tax, 109, 117
Institutions
 census enumeration in, 61
 records of. *See* Military records; School records
International Genealogical Index. *See* IGI (International Genealogical Index)
International Society for British Genealogy and Family History, 24
Internet
 in census research, 53
 in early English research, 176
 Manorial Documents Register on, 172
 name lists on, 7
Interregnum. *See* Commonwealth (1649–60)

Intestate estates
    in Death Duty Registers, 109, 116,
        125
    distribution of, rules for, 104, 105
Inventories (probate records), 126, 128
Investment records of Bank of
    England, 117
Ionian Islands Births, Marriages, and
    Deaths, 38
Ireland
    poor relief for Protestants in, lists of
        donors to, 168, 170
    property in, probate jurisdiction in
        relation to, 114
Irregular marriages, 206–10
Jails, 157
James, Duke of Monmouth, rebellion
    in support of, 170
Jewish marriages, recognition of, viii,
    84, 209
Jewish records, 100
Julian calendar, 23
Jurisdiction
    of district probate offices, 104
    early English research in relation to,
        175
    locality records in Family History
        Library Catalog listed by, 186
    for probate, 105, 121, 122
        in ecclesiastical courts, 113, 114
Justice of the peace, 150, 156
Keith, Rev. Alexander, marriages by,
    209
Laborers, records of, 142
    in churchwarden account books, 151
    kept by surveyor of highways, 152
    in poor relief records, 153
Land. *See also* Property
    description of, in wills, 103, 104
    records, 158, 159, 171–73
    taxes on, 71, 157, 158
        early, 170
        inheritance, 109, 117

    settlement in relation to, 153
Landowners in select vestry, 150
Latin
    church records in, translations of,
        162
    court records in, 157
    early records in, 165, 172–74
    in English documents, viii
Lawless churches, marriages by, 209
Laws
    Acts of Uniformity, 98, 169
    Children's Act (1975), 34
    enforcement of
        by civil courts, 157
        by constables, 151
    Five Mile Act, 98
    Gilbert's Act (1782), 153
    Legitimacy Act (1926), 34
    Lord Hardwicke's Act (1754), viii,
        84, 206–10
    Married Women's Property Act
        (1882), 105, 106
    Poor Law Amendment Act (1834),
        153, 155
    Population Act (1840), 58
    Rose's Act (1813), 86
    Succession Duty Act (1853), 117
Lay subsidies, 166
LDS Church
    family history centers of, 9
    research resources of, 5, 6
    temple records of, as source of IGI
        records, 199
Legacy tax, 109, 117
Legitimacy Act (1926), 34
Letters of administration, 104
    indexes to, 107, 124, 125
Libraries, 8, 9
    addresses, 211–18
    catalogs of, 184
    newspapers in, 79
    professional directories in, 140
    school records in, 132

Library of Congress Classification System, 187, *table* 11
Licenses
  business, 142
  from civil courts, 157
  marriage, 84, 95, 210
    Lord Hardwicke's Act on, 206, 207
  occupational, 141
Linkage
  of events, IGI weakness in, 203
  of names, on IGI, 202
Lists, 67–81
  in civil court records, 157
  in early English research, 176
  of early records, 166
  of freemen, 134
  occupational, 141
  of serial publications, 160
  of students at universities, 132
  of taxpayers, 152
Litigation over wills, location of records of, 115
Livery companies, 134
  apprenticeship records of, 133
  members of, on Association Oath Rolls, 169
Lloyd's Captains Register, merchant marine records in, 144, 145
Local Census Listings 1522–1930 (Gibson and Medlycott), 50
Local government
  Anglican parish as unit of, 86
  records of
    bibliography, 240, 241
    in locality section of Family History Library Catalog, 186
    research in, 159, 160, 162, 163
Local history books, 65
Localities
  Family History Library Catalog of, 185, 187, 188, *illus.* 191–94
  filtering of, in computerized searches of IGI, 92

Parish and Vital Records List arranged by, 197
Local Newspapers 1750–1920: A Select Location List (Gibson), 78
Lockups, 157
Log books of schools, 131
London, boroughs of Greater, *table* 19
London Metropolitan Archives, directories at, 70
Lord Hardwicke's Act (1754), viii, 84, 206–10
Loss
  of early records, 165
  of inventories during Commonwealth (1642–1660), 126
  of rate books, 75
Loyalty oaths, 168, 169
  in civil courts, 157
Magistrates, local, 148
Manorial Documents Register, 172
Manors
  courts in, transfer of responsibilities of, to parishes, 149, 150
  peculiars in, probate jurisdiction of, 114
  records of, 171–73
Maps
  in census research, 49, 57, 60
  city, 15
  in directories, 68
  in enclosure awards, 159
  railways on, 144
  in research, 14, 15, 17, 179
  topographical, in parish record research, 88, 89
Marine Births and Deaths, 38
Marital status
  in census records, 48, 59
  in letters of administration, 105
  in marriage records, 30, 32, 43, 96
Marriage
  Lord Hardwicke's Act (1754) on, viii, 206–10

Marriage (*cont.*)
  place of, distance from residence, 85
Marriage records, 30, 95, 96, *illus.* 29.
  See also Vital records
  Church of England, 93, 94
  of Fleet chapel, 208, 209
  form for, 84
  in IGI, 195, 197
  licenses, 210
    in Latin, 172, 173
  under Lord Hardwicke's Act (1754),
    207
  nonconformist, 99
  Phillimore collection of, 90
  search for, on IGI, name linking in,
    202
  in War Office, 136
Married Women's Property Act (1882),
  105, 106
"Mayfair Marriages," 209
Medical care in poor relief records,
  152, 153
Merchant marine
  overseas deaths, 139
  records of, 144
Merchants, directories, 141
Methodist Church, 99
  clergy of, 140
Metropolitan Counties, *table* 18
Metropolitan District Councils, *table*
  18
Microfiche
  civil record indexes on, 34
  directories on, 69
  Family History Library Catalog on,
    184, *illus.* 191–93
  IGI on, 197
    techniques for efficient use of,
      92, 93
Microfilm
  census records on, 50, 51, 57
  civil record indexes on, 34
  directories on, 70

probate records and indexes on,
    107, 108, 122
Migration routes of emigrants, 178
Military records, 134–40
  Association Oath Rolls, 169, 170
  bibliography, 236–39
  early, 169, 170
  militia, 138, 139, 152, 169, 170
  vital, 38
Ministers
  directories, 140
  parish registers in custody of, 91
Minutes
  of borough courts, 152
  of probate courts, 122, 128
Missing records, 180
Monmouth Rebels, 170
Monumental inscriptions, 97
Municipal archives, 8
Muster rolls, 134, 138, 139, 169, 170
Names. *See also* Surnames
  of children, problems in, 43
  filtering of, in computerized
    searches of IGI, 92
*National Index of Documentary Sources in
  the United Kingdom*, 189
Naturalization records in Canada and
  United States, 177
Naval records, 135, 136
  death, 38
  merchant seamen in, 145
Networking, 5, 24
New Poor Law (1834). *See* Poor Law
  Amendment Act (1834)
Newspapers, 65, 75, 78, 79
  bibliography, 231
Nonconformist churches
  clergy of, 140
  history of, 97–99
  marriage in, 86
  records of, 99, 100
    at Family Records Centre, 27
    on IGI, 197

Nonconformists
  probate of estates of, 119
  on recusant rolls, 169
  will preambles of, 115
Note-taking, 4
Nuncupative wills, 115
Oaths of allegiance, 157, 168, 169
Occupations, 130, 133–47
  in apprenticeship records, 133
  bibliography, 236–39
  in census records, 48, 54, 58
  in death records, 30
  directories, 60, 68, *illus.* 143
    in Family History Library
      Catalog, 189
  of father, in baptismal and burial
    records, 86, 94
  in letters of administration, 105
  lists, addresses in, 60
  in marriage records, 30, 96
  of parents, on birth certificate, 32
  records, earliest, 165
Office for National Statistics, 26, 27
Officers
  in armed forces, records of, 134–37
  in merchant marine, records of,
    144
Old Style dates, 22
Open vestry, parish administration by,
  150
Order books of civil courts, 157
Organization of research, 2, 3
Orphans
  apprentices, as foster children, 34
  of merchant seamen, welfare records
    of, 145
Outdoor poor relief, 153
Overseas
  Army pensioners, 138
  births, registers of, for Army person-
    nel, 137
  civil records, 38
  deaths of military personnel, 139

property, probate jurisdiction in
  relation to, 114
transportation, as punishment, 157,
  158
Overseers of the poor, 150
  account books of, illegitimate chil-
    dren in, 154, 155
  as census enumerators, 58, 59
  electoral rolls compilation by, 71, 74
  rate books compilation by, 75
  removal of undesirables by, 154
  welfare records of, 152, 153
Oxford University, lists of students, 132
Palatinates, courts of, 157
Pallot's Marriage Index, 1780–1837, 90,
  96
Parents
  in apprenticeship records, 133
  association with children, in IGI on
    CD-ROM, 92, 202
  in baptismal and burial records, 86,
    94
  on birth certificate, 32
  on marriage certificate, 30
  in school records, 131
Parishes (Church of England)
  boundaries of
    changes in, 15, 17
    reference sources for, 88, 89
    finding aids for, in census research,
      62
  of groom in banns, 207
  historical changes in, 15, 85, 86
  IGI coverage of, weakness in, 203
  officials of, 148, 150–53
  probate jurisdictions of, 121
Parishes (civil). *See* Civil parishes
Parish records (Church of England)
  administrative, 149, 163
  apprenticeship, 133
  contents and organization of, 93, 94
  custody of, in Civil War (1642–49),
    83

Parish records (*cont.*)
  earliest, 165
  on IGI, 197
  in Latin, 172
  in locality section of Family History
    Library Catalog, 186
  Parish and Vital Records List for
    IGI, arranged by locality, 197
  research in, 87, 88
  settlement examinations in, 154
  tax on entries in, 84
Parliamentary papers, 142
Passenger lists in Canada and United
  States, 177
Passing Certificates of naval lieutenants, 135
Patrimony, guild membership obtained
  by, 133
Paupers, tax relief for entries for, in
  parish registers, 84
Pay records
  of armed forces, 134
  for laborers, 142
  naval records of sailors in, 136
PCC. *See* Prerogative Court of
  Canterbury (PCC)
Peculiars (extraparochial parishes), 83,
  87, 121
  marriages in, 209
  probate jurisdiction in, 114
Peerage, books on, 7
Pension records
  applications by widows of Army
    officers, in War Office, 136
  of armed forces, 134
  of Army, 138
  Association Oath Rolls in relation
    to, 169
Periodicals
  Annual Register, The, 139, 140
  Family History News and Digest, 142,
    163
  genealogical information in, 79–81

Periodical Source Index (PERSI), 80
PERSI. *See Periodical Source Index*
Phillimore transcripts of marriage registers, 90, 96, 97, 234
  on IGI, 197
Pitchfork Rebellion, 170
Place names, 21, 22. *See also* Gazetteers
  in manorial records, 172
Place of origin
  in England, determination of, 177
  of surname, IGI for tracing, 202
Poll books, 71, 74, *illus.* 76, 77
  addresses in, 60
Poll tax lists, 71, 166, 170
Poorhouses, 152, 153
Poor Law Amendment Act (1834),
  153, 155
  census in relation to, 59
  district boundaries under, 15
Poor Law Unions, 155
Poor relief records
  of Anglican parishes, 86
  kept by constables, 151
  for Protestants in Ireland, donor
    lists, 168, 170
  tax abatement, in parish registers, 84
  in vestry minutes, 151
  of widows and orphans of merchant
    seamen, 145
Poor relief taxes levied by parishes, 149
Population Act (1840), census in relation to, 58
Posse comitatus, 169
Preamble to will, religious affiliation in
  relation to, 112, 113, 115
Prerogative Court of Canterbury
  (PCC)
  overseas deaths of military person-
    nel in indexes of, 139
  probate in, 113–16, 119
  will indexes of, 118, 123–25
Prerogative Court of York, probate in,
  113

Presbyterian Church, 99, 100
Primary sources, examples of, 4
Principal Probate Registry, 105
Prison hulks (ships), 157
Probate, process of, *table* 128
Probate records. *See* Wills and probate
  records
Problem-solving, 178–82
Professional genealogists, 25, 35
  addresses, 211
  in will research, 108
Professions. *See* Occupations
Pronunciation, name spelling in rela-
  tion to, 22
Property. *See also* Land
  description of, in wills, 103, 104
  location of, probate jurisdiction in
    relation to, 113
  personal
    inheritance tax on, 117
    in wills, 128
  taxes on, settlement in parish in
    relation to payment of, 153
Protestants, poor relief for, in Ireland,
  lists of donors to, 168, 170
Protestation returns (loyalty oaths),
  168, 170
Provinces, of Church of England, *map*
  120, 121
Public Record Office (PRO), 27, 216,
  219
  apprenticeship records at, 133
  census records arrangement at,
    55
  Death Duty Registers at, 109
  Land Tax Assessments at, 158
  nonconformist church records at,
    99, 100
  research at, guides to, 142
  tax lists at, 166, 167
  wills at, 116
Quakers
  on Association Oath Rolls, 169

  marriages of, recognition of, viii, 84,
    209
  records of, 99
Quarter sessions court records, 156–58
  occupational licenses in, 141
  settlement examinations in, 154
Queries, 179
Railwaymen, service records of, 142,
  144
Rate books, 74, 75
  addresses in, 60
Raymond bibliography series, for local
  government and parish records, 163
Real estate. *See* Land
Record agents. *See* Professional geneal-
  ogists
Record group code for census records,
  55, 56, *table* 56
Record offices, 8, 9. *See also* Archives;
  County record offices; Public Record
  Office (PRO)
  addresses, 211–19
  bibliography, 225–8
Records
  developing familiarity with, 9, 12,
    67
  types of, in Family History Library
    Catalog, 186, 187
Record societies, serial publications of,
  160, 162
Recusant churches. *See*
  Nonconformist churches
Recusant rolls, 169
Redemption records of guilds, 133
Reference books, 25
Regimental Description and
  Succession Books, 137
  of Army, 138
Regimental histories, military officers
  in, 134
Regimental Registers of Birth, 38, 137
Registers of Seamen, in merchant
  marine, 144

Registrars of wills, indexing of wills by
name of, 124
Registration districts
civil record certificate ordering
from, 43, 44
codes, *table* 39, 40
Relatives
of Army officers, records of, in War
Office, 136
collateral, 67, 104, 110
in Death Duty Registers, 116
distribution of intestate estate to,
rules for, 105
records of, usefulness in research,
181
in sources of IGI records, 198
wills of, 119
Reliability
of census records, 47
of early civil records, 28, 30
of records, 183
Removal, illegitimate children in
records of, of undesirables from
parish, 154, 155
Repositories. *See* Archives
Research, elements of, 1–25
Research strategy, 3–5, 178–82
in Anglican church records, 87–97
in census research, 50, 51, 53,
56–59, 66
in church records, 102, 164
in civil record indexes, 38, 41–46
in civil records, 35
in directories, 69–71, 81
in early English research, 170, 171,
174–76
in electoral rolls, 81
in Family History Library Catalog,
190
in IGI, 91–93
in local government records, 159,
160, 162–64
in marriage records, 90

in military records, 139, 140
in newspapers, 79, 81
in occupational records, 147
in parish records, 102, 164
in periodicals, 81
in poll books, 81
in rate books, 81
in wills
before 1858, 118, 119, 121–23,
126, 127, 129
after 1858, 105–8, 110, 111
Residence
in baptismal and burial records, 86,
94
census index sorted by, 54
in directories, for census research,
68
in electoral rolls, 71
of executor, in Death Duty
Registers, 109
identification of, for census research,
59–62
in letters of administration, 105
in marriage records, 96
in rate books, 74
of relatives, in Death Duty
Registers, 116
in school records, 131
sources of, 60
in will extracts, 118
in wills, 104, 112
Residency requirement
for marriage, 94
for wills, 115
Roadblocks to research, 181, 182, *table*
180
Road repair
surveyor of highways responsible
for, 152
taxes for, levied by parishes, 149, 150
Roman Catholic Church
clergy of, 140
records of, 100

Roman Catholics, on recusant rolls, 169
Rose's Act (1813), baptismal and burial
  registers standardization by, 86
Royal Air Force, death records of, 38
Royal Commission on Historical
  Manuscripts, Manorial Documents
  Register at, 172
Royal Hospital Chelsea Soldiers
  Documents, 137
Royal Marines, records of officers in,
  135
Sailors
  in merchant marine, records of, 144
  naval records of, 135, 136
  poor relief records for traveling, 151
St. Catherine's House, civil records
  moved from, 27
School records, 131–33
  addresses in, 60
  bibliography, 236–39
Schools, types of, 131
Scotland, marriage in, Lord
  Hardwicke's Act in relation to, 209
Secondary sources, examples of, 4
Select vestry, parish administration by,
  150
Serial publications of local government
  and parish documents, 160, 162
Service Department, vital records of, 38
Service records of armed forces, 134,
  137
Session rolls of civil courts, 157
Settlement
  in parish
    documents for, 154
    requirements for, 153
  place of, in Canada and United
    States, records of, 178
Sheriffs, recusant rolls of, 169
Ship records
  of merchant marine, 144, 145
  musters, naval records of sailors in,
    136

Ships
  census enumeration on, 61
  death on, probate jurisdiction in
    relation to, 114
  lists of, 136
  prison hulks, 157
Shrouds, use for deceased recorded in
  parish registers, 84
Society of Genealogists (London), 6,
  217, 219
  directories at, 70
  investment records of Bank of
    England at, 117, 118
  parish registers at, 90
  school records at, 132
Sojourners
  in marriage registers, residency
    requirement in relation to, 94
  poor relief records for traveling sol-
    diers and sailors, 151
Soldiers
  poor relief records for traveling, 151
  records of, 137–39
Somerset House
  civil records moved from, 26
  wills at, 104, 105
Sources, vii, viii, 182
  citation of, 3, 183
  primary and secondary, examples of, 4
Spelling of names
  filtering of, in computerized
    searches of IGI, 92
  in IGI on CD-ROM, 202
  standardization of, in IGI, 198
  variations in, 19, 21
Stock records of Bank of England,
  117, 118
Street indexes in census research, 51
Subjects, Family History Library
  Catalog of, 185, 187
Subsidy rolls (tax rolls), 166, 170
Succession Duty Act (1853), 117
Succession tax, 109, 117

Surnames
  books of, 224, 225
  census index sorted by, 54
  distribution of uncommon, in
    England, 178
  Family History Library Catalog of,
    185, 187, 188
  in *Homes of Family Names of Great
    Britain* (Guppy), 61
  indexes of, 6
    at family history societies, 179
  origin of, 13, 14
  research organizations, 6
  spelling of, standardization of, in
    IGI, 198
  spelling variations in, 19, 21
  surveys for, IGI as tool for, 202, *map*
    204, 205
Surveyor of highways, 150, 152
Survey tools for surnames, IGI as, 202,
  map 204, 205
Taxes
  on entries in parish registers, 84
  inheritance, 109, 117
  by parishes, 149
  settlement in parish in relation to
    payment of, 153
Tax records, 71, 74, 75
  apprenticeship, 133
  in civil courts, 157
  early, 166, 167, 170
  in Family History Library Catalog,
    illus. 191
  Land Tax Assessments, 158
  for poor relief, 152
Temple records as source of IGI
  records, 199
Tenant records of manors, 171
Testamentary causes, location of
  records of, 115
Title, Family History Library Catalog
  of records by, 185, 187
Tombstone inscriptions, 97

Topographical dictionaries. *See*
  Gazetteers
Topographical maps, 88
Towns. *See* Cities; Local government;
  Parish records (Church of England)
Townships, parishes in relation to, 149
Trades. *See* Occupations
Translation of early English records,
  174
Transportation overseas as punishment,
  157, 158
Travelers, poor relief records for, 151
Trinity House Petitions by widows
  and orphans of merchant seamen,
  145
Twentieth-century research, wills in,
  110
Tyburn Ticket for exemption from
  parish offices, 150
University libraries, 8
University records, 131, 132
Vagabonds and vagrants
  in burial register, 94
  constables' records of, 151
Verbal wills, 115
Vertical files from newspapers, 79
Vestry
  minutes of meetings, 151
  parish administration by, 150
*Victoria History of the Counties of
  England, The*, 132, 160, 219, 229
Villages. *See* Local government; Parish
  records (Church of England)
Vital records, 26–46. *See also* Birth
  records; Death records; Marriage
  records
  addresses in, 60
  of army personnel, 137
  bibliography, 229, 230, 232–35
  in Family History Library Catalog,
    illus. 192
  occupation in, 141

Parish and Vital Records List for
IGI, arranged by locality, 197
in periodicals, 80
at schools, 131
Voter lists, 71, 74, *illus.* 76, 77
War Office, army records at, 136, 137
Web sites, 219. *See also* World Wide
Web
Periodical Source Index, 80
Welfare records. See Poor relief records
Wesleyan Methodist Church, 99
Whitaker's Almanac, 223
professional associations in, 140
rules for distribution of intestate
estate in, 105
school directory in, 132
Widows, 43
of Army officers, pension applications by, 136
of merchant seamen, welfare records
of, 145
William's Registry of births in nonconformist churches, 100
Wills and probate records, 103–29
bibliography, 235, 236
in early English research, 165, 176
at Family Records Centre, 27
in Latin, 172, 173
occupation in, 141
recording of information from, 4
at War Office, 136
Window tax, 167, 170
Witnesses to wills, 104, 110, 115
Women
on Association Oath Rolls, 169
widows, 43
of Army officers, pension applications by, 136
of merchant seamen, welfare
records of, 145
wills by, 106, 108, 110, 114, 119

Workhouses
census enumeration in, 61
records of, 153, 155
World Wide Web. *See also* Web sites
census finding aids on, 53
name lists on, 7
York
dioceses of Province of, *map* 120,
121
Prerogative Court of
probate in, 113
records of, 122
Yorke, Philip, Earl of Hardwicke, 206